BEFORE OUR TIME

A Theory of the Sixties

*From a Religious, Social and
Psychoanalytic Perspective*

Henry Idema, III

University Press of America, Inc.
Lanham • New York • London

Copyright © 1996 by
University Press of America,® Inc.
4720 Boston Way
Lanham, Maryland 20706

3 Henrietta Street
London, WC2E 8LU England

Library of Congress Cataloging-in-Publication Data

Idema, Henry.
Before our time : a theory of the sixties : from a religious, social, and
psychoanalytic perspective / Henry Idema III.
        p.   cm.
Includes bibliographical references and index.
1. United States--History 1961-1969. 2. Popular culture--United
States--History--20th century. 3. United States--Religion--1960- I.
Title.
E841.I34   1995   306'.0973'09046--dc20   95-39870 CIP

ISBN 0-7618-0145-6 (cloth: alk. ppr.)
ISBN 0-7618-0146-4 (pbk: alk. ppr.)

To the class of 1965 at East Grand Rapids High School

Contents

Charts

Acknowledgments

I would like to thank all those who made this book possible, Athelia Greer who typed it, John Jacobs who edited it, Aimee Polom who typeset it, Chandelle Roberts and her father who helped me on some computer problems, and David Shock who did the final proofreading. If there are any remaining errors, I will take full responsibility, although they all can share the blame because of the time they put in on this project. Lastly, I would like to thank my wife Karen and my two daughters, Jennifer and Meghan, who had patience with me as I relived the Sixties and listened incessantly to the music of the Doors. I should also mention the support of my congregation, St. John's Episcopal Church, who both support me in my writing and put up with sermons whose ideas later find a home in a book such as this one.

I would also like to thank the publishing firms which gave me permission to quote from these works:

1. From *The Sixties* by Todd Gitlin. Copyright © 1987 by Todd Gitlin. Used by permission of Bantam Books, a division of Bantam Doubleday Dell Publishing Group.
2. From *The Culture of Narcissism* by Christopher Lasch. Copyright © 1979 by W.W. Norton & Company, Inc. Used by permission of W.W. Norton & Company, Inc.

3. From *The Standard Edition of the Complete Psychological Works of Sigmund Freud*, translated and edited by James Strachey, 1959. Reprinted by permission of Harpercollins Publishers.

4. Scripture quotations are from the *Revised Standard Version of the Bible*, copyright © 1946, 1952, 1971 by the Division of Christian Education of the National Council of the Churches of Christ in the USA. Used by permission.

"Seek, and you will find; knock, and it will be opened to you."

— Jesus of Nazareth (Luke 11:9)

❧

"If I could find a white man who had the Negro sound and the Negro feel, I could make a million dollars."

— A statement that Sam Phillips, a white record producer at Sun Records, is reported to have made immediately preceding his discovery of Elvis Presley

❧

"The torch has been passed to a new generation."

— From John F. Kennedy's Inaugural Address

❧

"It's My Life (and I'll do what I want)."

— The title of an Eric Burdon and the Animals' song from the late Sixties

❧

"I'm glad I am not an alcoholic because I like to drink so much."

— An observation of a female friend to the author in 1967, following a University of Michigan fraternity party

"A conscientious objector is somebody who is conscious that he might die, and objects to it."

— A remark by an East Grand Rapids High School teacher in 1965.

❧

"The peace symbol is the track of the American chicken."

— A Marine veteran's criticism of the author's peace button in 1966.

Introduction

Jesus, Elvis, Freud and the Sixties Generation

This book is an interpretation of the Vietnam era, particularly the Sixties. All interpretations *must generalize* to some degree. I am here generalizing about America's recent spiritual and moral history. In that sense, this book is in large part *my views* about the feelings and thoughts of my generation, the Sixties Generation, and our search for meaning. And I base those views on my own experience, as well as that of others (gleaned from my friends, acquaintances and my reading).

I have written this book from several perspectives. My first is religion. It is my contention that the Sixties can not be fully understood without examining the role of religion, especially the role of religion among my generation. Even though I include other religions in the thrust of my arguments, Christianity is the dominant religious tradition in American culture. Jesus of Nazareth is thus a central figure in the story of the Sixties, not only because of the Church as an institution, but also through the wider cultural influence of his teaching, ministry, and destiny.

My second perspective is psychoanalytic. I will be constructing a theory of the Sixties based upon Freud's libido theory and some additional insights into narcissism from the work of Heinz

Kohut. My third perspective is popular culture, and Elvis Presley represents all that I will be driving at. He is likewise a key player in the story of the Sixties.

Lastly, I will be showing that the life—and especially the death—of President John F. Kennedy is crucially important for understanding what the Sixties were all about, both psychologically and socially.

The heart of my argument is that the loss of our moral and religious traditions—or at least their weakening—has deeply affected America, especially since the Sixties. Secularization gathered steam during the Vietnam era, and helped to unleash the narcissism that has so stamped our culture in recent years. We will see that the American psyche was forever changed by an avalanche of traumas, which we were unprepared to handle. My main thesis is that secularization left us highly vulnerable to the pain from these traumas. Those of us who were born soon after World War II were particularly affected.

During the course of this book, I sometimes use the term "Sixties Generation," at other times I simply refer to the "Baby Boomers." These two terms are really synonymous, and the variation is usually stylistic. Yet, there is a slight nuance of difference between the two terms. When I mention the "Sixties Generation" I have principally in mind those members of the Baby Boomers who brought about the vast social and cultural changes we have experienced. Some readers may argue that the Baby Boomers, en masse, fall into that camp. I would not take exception to that, although I do believe that some, more than others, had instrumental roles in cultural change, however small or large those contributions may have actually been.

"Baby Boomers" includes anyone born between 1946 and 1964, but I am concentrating on those who were born in the early years of that time span. 1964 was the year the "first wave" of Baby Boomers reached college. Freshman enrollments accelerated 37 percent that fall. Between 1964 and 1970, twenty million people turned eighteen. Those are the Baby Boomers I am most interested in.

In American history, no generation has been as visible as

mine—or as influential (thanks to the mass media). This book explains why (beyond the fact that there are roughly 76,000,000 Baby Boomers in all!). Lastly, let me emphasize that this book is also a Christian clergyman's view of the Sixties. I write it for members of my tradition and from the perspective of my tradition. More specifically, I write it with a concern for pastoral care. That is significant. Spiritual, psychological, and moral healing lie at the core of the minister's role in a church and in a community—indeed, in a culture. Even though I feature Christianity in this book, my concern throughout is the decline of religious and moral traditions in general, a decline that has had such devastating effects upon us all. This book is especially for the Church, but it is also for the wider society.

Before any tradition can speak to our cultural wounds (as I will be doing in Part II of this book), we must understand the nature of those wounds. We must understand the roots of our current spiritual malaise. I am here arguing that those roots lie, in large part anyway, in the Sixties. So we will be taking a long journey back in time.

Part I

A Theory of the Sixties

Chapter I

Religion and Culture

The Two Currents of the Libido

Any theory that attempts to tackle a decade as varied and colorful as the Sixties must treat both the psychological and cultural dynamics of the period. A weakness of academic psychology is its failure to consider the impact of culture—with all of its myriad changes and its variety of symbol systems and sources of meaning—upon people. Thus much academic psychology is as dry as a desert. It is divorced from culture and history. On the other hand, much sociology and most historical studies fail to consider the psychological contributions to social and cultural change. To fully grasp the Sixties, or any era for that matter, one must maintain a dual focus that includes both psychology and culture. This is especially important when we want to consider cultural change, something which certainly marked the Sixties.

The cornerstone of my theory about the Sixties might sound rather simple at first—and the psychological dynamic I am referring to isn't overly complicated—but it played itself out in many ways in American culture and contributed to the creation of some very complex psychopathology. Or, to put it another way, it produced deep-seated spiritual problems. I begin with a forgotten idea of Freud's from his theory of the libido. In fact, I am very surprised that Freud's many interpreters have not emphasized it. In one of his most important works, *Three Essays on the Theory of Sexuality*, Freud theorized that the libido has two currents, "the affectionate current and sensual current." Then he added:

> A normal sexual life is only assured by an exact convergence of the affectionate current and the sensual current both being directed towards the sexual object and sexual aim.[1]

The libido's affectionate current, of course, refers to our emotional life, our feelings, or what Freud often calls "affect." In his early writings on neurosis, he attributed neurosis' underlying cause to "strangulated affect "—an etiology he never abandoned but rather built upon as his theories became more complex. The sensual current, which is more biological, refers to our sexual drives or urges, lust included.

The *leitmotif* of my theory about the Sixties is simply this: for a variety of reasons, which I will be elaborating upon as we move along, these two currents of the libido split apart in many people. In others, they failed to converge in a healthy way. This split had all kinds of consequences, both social and psychological.

For the remainder of this chapter I will develop this leitmotif, building my argument step by step. I will begin with some pertinent background on Freud and his era.

The Libido and Repression

In Freud's thought, as it developed down through the years, both strangulated affect and a split between the two currents of the libido (a related but later idea) were caused by repression. Freud was first interested in the repression of emotions, then (later in his career) in the repression of drives, especially our sexual desires which so enrich and complicate our emotional life. One can't understand psychopathology from a psychoanalytic vantage without appreciating the centrality of repression in Freud's thinking on neurosis or emotional illness to put it in everyday language—an illness characterized by internal conflict. Repression, in essence, is a mental defense mechanism that repels from consciousness a painful feeling or desire. A desire may be painful or terrifying because it conflicts with one's conscience, what Freud called the "super-ego." And a feeling may be repressed simply because it is too intense to endure.

Freud's idea that the libido has two currents helped him envision something we all know to be true: that our biological urges have emotional counterparts; they are of whole cloth. Thus, the word "sexual" in Freud's thought has a rich emotional counterpart to its biological meaning, something most of his readers forget, including many Freudian practitioners and interpreters— perhaps because they remain entrapped by an outdated "mind-body" split, or by a false separation between psychology and biology. (Indeed, Freud's theories fought against this separation, even if his writings were not completely successful in maintaining a balance between the two.)

The theory of the libido was his attempt to build a permanent bridge between psychology and biology. He hoped in the future our advancing knowledge of body chemistry would provide more definitive links between psychology and our cognitive and affective processes, a mountain psychiatry is still climbing. We have to remember that Freud was a healer; after studying neurology at the university, he set up a general medical practice to support a family. And he turned to psychology—arguably, he invented modern psychiatry—when many problems he had to treat medically had no detectable physiological cause. Freud tried his best to provide us with helpful models of the mind, models he himself needed to treat his own patients through psychoanalysis. But he always expected these models to be expanded upon, or even, one day, supplanted by more accurate models. This has not yet happened; however, they have been enriched by thinkers such as Heinz Kohut, who was a professor of psychiatry at the University of Chicago until his death in 1981. My point here, however, is that Freud's ideas—in this case his theory of the libido— remain excellent tools with which to interpret culture. This should come as no surprise since culture was one of his own principal interests.

When the two currents of the libido split apart or fail to

converge effectively, such a split is characteristic of neurosis. Freud discovered that if feelings or sexual desires are repressed, the repressed libidinal energy is submerged, driven into the unconscious. *But what is repressed returns from the depths to haunt or plague a person; it returns to consciousness in the form of neurotic symptoms.* This dynamic, what Freud calls "the return of the repressed," lies at the heart of his theory of symptomatology. Neurosis, as he often said, means that the ego has failed in its task of integration. Sometimes he talked about neurosis as the ego's failure to integrate our thoughts with our feelings; at other times he referred to a split between the sensual and affectionate currents of the libido. But these are two variations on the same theme.

For Freud, a neurotic symptom not only indicated a failure of integration. The symptom itself was the ego's attempt at integration. He sometimes used the term "mnemic symbol" to refer to a symptom, thus emphasizing the symbolic nature of neurosis. Freud discovered that symptoms bind anxiety, anxiety being disruptive of consciousness, sometimes even causing its disintegration. *Thus, a symptom is a very costly way to unify consciousness because, instead of allowing us to struggle with anxiety or other painful feelings, we are forced to struggle with the symptoms themselves.* This not only short-circuits working through our feelings, but also maintains a disguise in consciousness for the real source of the feelings (this is why Freud called symptoms "symbols": they stand for something, or represent something, but in a disguised form). Reality is distorted. The integration of the psyche, or I should say, the lack of integration, will be a recurring theme in my analysis of the Sixties. Envisioning the libido as having two currents will enable us to see that repression may operate upon feelings or upon drives and desires —or upon all of these simultaneously.

The foregoing raises an interesting question and one highly pertinent to our discussion: What are the connections between culture and repression? This isn't easy to answer (but this book will be an attempt to do just that, at least in relation to the 1960s). Freud attributed repression not only to intrapsychic factors, such as the intensity of feelings or the ego's conflicts with the super-ego, but also to cultural factors, our chief interest. Families, of course, exist in a culture; the individual's inner world is shaped by that culture through socialization. In other words, our inner and outer worlds impinge upon each other.

Secularization was the single cultural factor that had particular significance in Freud's reflections upon culture, repression, and neurosis. He believed that the decline of religion in Western culture had left more and more people unable to manage anxiety and other powerful feelings arising from traumas and conflicts. Freud linked religious decline—and for him "religion" meant the institutional Church—with an increase in neurosis. This observation came, at least in part, from his clinical practice where he saw increasing numbers of people who, deprived of the aid of their religious traditions, were unable to withstand powerful emotions. And why couldn't people turn to their religion in a crisis, such as a death or a divorce? Because, Freud thought, faith was losing its psychological power, its emotional impact. He attributed this weakening of religion primarily to the rise of science, including psychology itself. In modernity, religion no longer could be believed (according to Freud). He called its promises "illusions."

As important as science is for understanding Twentieth Century secularization, there are other causes as well: industrialization, disillusionment resulting from wars, the burgeoning mass media, affluence, the use of drugs, urbanization, the increasing mobility of society, the breakdown of the extended family (and in recent times even the nuclear family), the revolt of the younger generations against their inherited religious traditions, scholarly criticism of the Bible, the breakdown of the community life in many parts of the country, and pluralization. This is not an exhaustive list, but points at those social forces especially relevant to the Sixties. Pluralization, the multiplication of world views, was especially endemic to the Sixties and was one of that era's lasting influences.

Secularization, in short, was the broad sociological framework within which Freud viewed the kinds of neurotic material he was encountering in his patients.[2] Secularization will also be the social context in which I will be locating the psychological problems that emerged in the Sixties. One of the chief arguments of this book is that the configuration of neurosis in the Sixties was different, in the main, from that of Freud's era; moreover, it was the peculiar nature of American culture in the Sixties that accounts for this difference. I elaborate upon this now because it will be a recurring theme.

I will begin with an observation crucial to my interpretation of the Sixties. Institutional religion—and here I am thinking particularly of the mainline churches (e.g., the Episcopal, Presbyterian, Lutheran, Methodist, Roman Catholic, and the various Reformed denominations, as well as much of Judaism)—has continued to erode since Freud's era, centered upon the Twenties. By the time the Sixties arrived, the social process of secularization —the encroachment of "the world" upon the soul and society— had become even more pronounced. In fact, secularization accelerated rapidly throughout the decade, tightening its grip on American culture and leaving many legacies for the Seventies, Eighties, and the Nineties.

Secularization in the Sixties will be treated below. Here I want to explain the chief difference between psychological problems in the time of Freud and those that emerged in the 1960s. In many respects these two eras were very similar. There was a war which embittered many people. People experimented with drugs and sex. The younger generations abandoned or revolted against their parents' moral and religious standards. Alcohol was abused. People suffered noticeably from mental illnesses of various kinds. Wild parties, music, and easy money characterized each period. Music by blacks was especially prominent. In the Twenties Fletcher Henderson and Louis Armstrong were changing the shape of music by popularizing jazz. Later on, in the Sixties, Motown would be doing the same thing by putting "soul music" into the mainstream of the music world through such artists as Smokey Robinson and the Miracles, Mary Wells, Marvin Gaye, the Temptations, the Supremes, and the Four Tops. And here, because of their influence upon other artists, we should not forget the Atlantic recording label artists such as Wilson Pickett, the Drifters, and Aretha Franklin, or those at Stax such as Otis Redding. The motion picture industry also thrived in both eras, and took risks—think of the Charlie Chaplin movies and the advent of "talkies," or such movies from the Sixties as *The Graduate*, *The Collector*, or *Bonnie and Clyde*. New dances associated with each era also came into vogue; the Charleston symbolized the Roaring Twenties, and the Twist caught the optimistic mood of the early Sixties. Most importantly, young people self-consciously found themselves searching for meaning in life. But many abandoned the search, dissatisfied.

The Great Depression of the Thirties and the World War of the Forties, along with the readjustments and the prosperity of the Fifties, may have slowed down secularization a bit between the Twenties and the Sixties. Or, the overwhelming presence of organized religion in the public arena during the intervening period may have made the erosion of our moral and religious values less visible or less destructive for the psyche. After all, the Fifties were the heyday of the mainline denominations. Young postwar families, stuffed into their Ford Ranch Wagons, flocked to their local churches, probably located in suburbs. But even back then, in a period some of you may now associate with the television shows, "Leave It to Beaver" or "The Adventures of Ozzie and Harriet"—and with the tranquility and warmth of the neighborhoods portrayed in such shows—there was discontent. Underneath the surface of American society there were embers slowly smoldering, which would later touch off the firestorms of revolt in the Sixties. The frustrations of black people over oppression and poverty come immediately to mind, or the frustrations of women with their traditional roles of mother and housewife. In such songs as "Heartbreak Hotel," "Jailhouse Rock," and "Hound Dog," Elvis Presley tapped energies of defiance that would re-emerge in the rebellion of a generation that grew up with his music. Also, Marlon Brando in the movie *The Wild One*, and James Dean in *Rebel Without a Cause*, portrayed, and then symbolized, an alienation from society that became one of the Sixties' principal themes. I question *how deep* the spiritual currents ran during the so-called "religious revival" of the Fifties.

Be that as it may, the Twenties and the Sixties are more closely related than any other two decades I can think of separated by intervening years, the number of which in this case makes the similarity even more striking. Secularization is the key for interpreting the culture of each era. The devastating effects of religious and moral decline spiritually link these two eras more than any other single factor—especially when we look at the experience of young people, both psychological and moral.[3] In the Sixties, however, something new was emerging. While the transference neuroses were particularly prominent in Freud's day (hysteria and obsessional neurosis), in the Sixties narcissism and narcissistic disorders were coming to the fore. It is not that narcissism did not exist in Freud's era, or any other era for that matter. It did. Freud saw it and theorized about it—employing his libido theory, the same interpretive tool he used to dissect the transference neuroses. Still, narcissistic disorders show up rather infrequently in his case studies. Why? Here is a probable and rather simple explanation. Narcissism was not emphasized in Freud's writings as much as hysteria and obsessional neurosis because, in his practice, he saw far more of the latter.

Hysteria and Obsessional Neurosis

George Rosen in his book, *Madness in Society*, argues that "as cultures change in history, new styles of mental illness arise; and in the same culture psychopathologies differ at different periods."[4] Granting this—and I refer the reader to his book for documentation—we should be able to see reasons why hysteria and obsessional neurosis were so prevalent in Freud's day. The explanation lies in the nature of the culture. Further, we can link narcissism and narcissistic disorders to the culture of the Sixties. But to begin, let's examine several characteristics of Western society during the first thirty years or so of this century (Freud died in 1939).

What kind of society existed then, in the era of the Baby Boomers' parents or grandparents, or even great-grandparents? First of all, there was a double standard for men and women in the realm of sexuality. Women had much less freedom to express themselves sexually than did men, something which changed dramatically in the Sixties. This double standard contributed to the predominance of hysteria among women; dammed up feelings and repressed desires are particularly significant in its etiology. Freud was very aware of this connection between the social order and mental illness, as were his followers. Here I will just mention one, Sandor Ferenczi, who in 1908 observed:

> That psycho-neurosis is more frequent among women is comprehensible when we consider the difference in degree of the cultural pressure that weighs upon the two sexes. Much is permitted to men in youth that is denied to women not only in reality but also in fantasy. Marriage, too, knows two moralities, of which one applies to the husband and the other to the wife. Society punishes sexual lapses much more strictly in women than in men. The periodic pulsations in feminine sexuality (puberty, the menses, pregnancies and parturitions, the climacterium) require a more powerful repression on the woman's part than is necessary for the man.[5]

Let me emphasize once again that it was this "much more powerful repression on the woman's part than is necessary for the man" which was the chief culprit behind the hysteria then so common among women (although Freud discovered that men could be hysterics, too).

If women had to put up with double standards, was there anything peculiar to men in their own psychological struggles? Freud found that they, too, had their own set of difficulties. Industrialization and urbanization were literally reshaping the landscape of Western society. The family farm was beginning to rapidly disappear, a trend that has continued to this day. Increasing numbers of men were leaving home for long hours in industry, often walking out the door at the crack of dawn and not returning home until long after the kids were in bed. With the rise of industrialization the pressures in the work place became immense. The stress, the pressure to succeed and to attain a decent living for one's family, the noise, the insensitivity of bosses, the poor communication on all levels in large organizations, the time away from home, and the competition—all contributed to make obsessional neurosis very common among men. Indeed, it still afflicts both Wall Street and Main Street. And with more and more women in the work force since the Sixties, one of that decade's most significant legacies, women undoubtedly have been afflicted with more of this kind of neurosis, too. But back in Ferenczi's and Freud's day, gender roles had not yet changed enough to alter the patterns of neurosis. With the social conditions of his own time in mind, Ferenczi concludes his observations on the incidence of the psychoneuroses by pointing out that "women are in overwhelmingly the greater number, especially among the hysterics, while men take refuge in obsessional neuroses."[6]

Freud knew the pressures of the work place, although the contribution of work to obsessional neurosis is only mentioned in passing in his writings. Nor did it play much of a role in the thought of his followers. The pioneers of psychoanalysis concentrated more on diseased relationships, traumas, and intrapsychic conflicts. How work affects a person—emotionally, mentally, and physically, and, thus, spiritually—is something too often overlooked by modern psychology in general and psychoanalysis in particular, but not necessarily by psychoanalytically oriented sociologists. They are more sensitive to social factors in mental illness. Karl Marx, who wrote of the spiritual horrors he saw in British factories, has been highly influential here.[7] Weinstein and Platt, for instance, said this about the sons of the Industrial Revolution:

> Sons. . . were exhorted by their fathers to develop self-control and self-discipline, to be self-observant, and to fear the loss of control stemming from emotional response. They were told that emotional expression, sentimentality, and sensuality were harmful (feminine) and that if they did not exercise self-control they would never become men. *At home and at school the sons were urged to be industrious, calculating, and self-contained.* The sons observed the controlled behavior of the parents, they identified with the active, competitive father, and they accepted the necessary restraints. It was thus possible for males to view personal feelings, even within the family, as obstacles to the achievement of the most important social goals (my italics).[8]

In sum, Freud and his followers found that women often bottled up their sexual feelings and then suffered from physical symptoms. Freud called such symptom formation "conversion," and it was considered to be the classic characteristic of hysteria. Men in contrast tended to be obsessional neurotics. They sublimated their libido into their work. Think of the stereotypic businessman of the first half of the Twentieth Century, "the man in the gray flannel suit." He is rational, driven, unemotional, superficial, preoccupied with money ("anal retentive" in Freudian terms), and always in a hurry. He often neglects his wife and children, and finds it hard to communicate intimacy (no wonder she is hysterical!). As we have just seen, this stereotype has a historical base. With the rise of industrialization, the demands of the work place drew upon a person's cognitive capacities at the expense of his emotions. Emotions, after all, might interfere with job performance or the success of the company! The novels of the Twenties and Thirties are filled with obsessional men and hysterical women. F. Scott Fitzgerald's *The Great Gatsby* and *Tender is the Night*, along with Sherwood Anderson's *Winesburg, Ohio* and *Dark Laughter* are examples. Or consider the plays of Eugene O'Neill, who was heavily influenced by Freud but no doubt could see for himself what was happening around him. Much of the literature of the first half of this century substantiates what Ferenczi was observing in 1908 about the connection between gender and types of neurosis.

The disintegration of the psyche emerged as a central theme in psychoanalysis because it was emerging in the social world of the first analysts. And now the split between thought and feelings—and especially the split of the sensual current of the libido from the affectionate current—has become a distinctively Twentieth Century theme. In part this is because of the influence of Freud. But, more importantly, this theme is connected to the nature of Western industrial society. Indeed, let me close this part of our discussion with a comment on Western culture made by Michel Foucault in 1954 (note that he, too, related the disintegration of the psyche to the nature of our industrialized society):

A great deal has been said about contemporary madness and its connection with the world of the machine and the disappearance of direct affective relations between men. This connection is, no doubt, a true one, and it is no accident that today the morbid world takes on the appearance of a world in which mechanistic rationality excludes the continuous spontaneity of the affective life.[9]

Now, remembering that Foucault observed this when the Sixties lay right around the corner, let's turn to narcissism, our chief theme concerning the era.

The Emergence of Narcissism

"You are not in touch with your feelings!" was a common accusation thrown around during my college years (1965–69), an accusation often made in the heat of battle between intimate partners. Ironically, alongside this accusation there was the explosive emotionality so characteristic of the Sixties. The emotional upheaval of the times, however, was not in service of intimacy, nor was it in service of cognition, or the social order.

No doubt much of the emotionality of the Sixties was indeed a reaction to the sort of "mechanistic rationality" Foucault so accurately described in 1954, a rationality very prevalent in higher education when the Vietnam War started ripping American society apart. Students reacted to this rationality—symbolized by course grades—with rage. The war acted as a catalyst for this rage but, even before the war, much of America felt resentment toward the competitiveness not only in education, but in the professions and industry as well. The Sixties' narcissism can first be clearly seen as a component of this rage.

I believe—although it will not be my task to prove—that narcissism was a greater psychological, sociological, and moral problem in the Sixties than in previous periods of American history. Some would argue that narcissism was only *noticed* more during the Sixties and their aftermath. Whatever the case may be, this much is clear: the Sixties cannot be understood historically without bringing narcissism into the picture. Christopher Lasch, offers the following analysis in his book *The Culture of Narcissism:*

Every age develops its own peculiar forms of pathology, which express in exaggerated form its underlying character structure. In Freud's time, hysteria and obsessional neurosis carried to extreme the personality traits associated with the capitalist order at an earlier stage in its development—acquisitiveness, fanatical devotion to work, and a fierce repression of sexuality. In our time the preschizophrenic, borderline, or personality disorders have attracted increasing attention, along with schizophrenia itself. This "change in the form of neuroses has been observed and described since World War II by an ever-increasingly number of psychiatrists." According to Peter L. Giovacchini, "Clinicians are constantly faced with the seemingly increasing number of patients who do not fit current diagnostic categories" who suffer not from "definite symptoms" but from "vague, ill-defined complaints." "When I refer to 'this type of patient,'" he writes, "practically everyone knows to whom I am referring." The growing prominence of "character disorders" seems to signify *an underlying change in the organization of personality, from what has been called inner-direction to narcissism* (my italics).

To reinforce his point, Lasch goes on to quote several other clinicians:

Allen Wheelis argued in 1958 that the change in "the pattern of neuroses" fell "within the personal experience of older psychoanalysts," while younger ones "became aware of it from the discrepancy between the older descriptions of neuroses and the problems presented by the patients who came daily to their offices. The change is from symptom neuroses to character disorders." Heinz Lichtenstein, who questioned the additional assertion that it reflected a change in personality structure, nevertheless wrote in 1963 that the "change in neurotic patterns," already constituted a "well known fact." In the seventies, such reports have become increasingly common. "It is no accident," Herbert Hendin notes, "that at the present time the dominant events in psychoanalysis are the rediscovery of narcissism and the new emphasis on the psychological significance of death." *"What hysteria and the obsessional neuroses were to Freud and his early colleagues. . . at the beginning of this century,"* writes Michael Beldoch, *"the narcissistic disorders are to the workaday analyst in these last few decades before the millennium"* (my italics).[10]

Heinz Kohut is the theorist most associated with this new emphasis on narcissism in psychoanalysis. In his important book, *The Analysis of the Self* (1971), Kohut argues—in agreement with what Lasch would later observe—that identity (who am I as a person, a self?) and related narcissistic issues such as mirroring, idealism, psychic wounding, emptiness, depression, not feeling real, narcissistic rage, and sexual dysfunction have become increasingly common in clinical practice, while hysteria and obsessional neurosis have become less so.[11] With these findings, Kohut attempted (not without controversy) to loosen up classic psychoanalytic thought to accommodate the new phenomena or, at least, the increasing awareness of the phenomena.

Kohut's interpretations cannot be fully understood apart from their sociological context, the Sixties—more broadly, the acceleration of secularization from Freud's day to his own. Both Lasch and Kohut (as well as other thinkers working in the new school of "the psychology of the self") were interpreting the spiritual problems then emerging, and which subsequently carried over into the Seventies and well beyond. The things Kohut and others were seeing were simply not as noticeable in Freud's time, things such as the fragmentation of the self, or better, the self that no longer feels whole, or cohesive, the self that no longer knows who he or she is, or what to do or be in life, the self who can't love. This self can have physical sex, to be sure, but not sex with love.

Now let me insert the role of tradition into the equation. Freud assigned a strong role to tradition in his interpretation of the causes of the transference neuroses:

> We have learnt that libidinal instinctual impulses undergo the vicissitude of pathogenic repression if they come into conflict with the subject's cultural and ethical ideas. By this *we never mean that the individual in question has a merely intellectual knowledge of the existence of such ideas; we always mean that he recognizes them as a standard for himself and submits to the claim they make on him* (my italics).[12]

The people Freud treated knew their traditions. They not only had an intellectual knowledge of moral standards, but *felt* their power. Freud found that many of his patients rebelled against their standards—and then experienced anxiety and guilt as a result. This often led to repression and neurosis.[13] On the other hand, Freud also analyzed people who never even approached their desires; they didn't dare, they were too frightened of their conscience (super-ego). They didn't dare cross swords with their internalized tradition. The ensuing anxiety would be too threatening, too painful. As Freud said of such a person, he "submits to the claim they [the standards of tradition] make on him." Instead of rebelling against tradition, such people repressed their desires because of the power of that tradition. In this scenario of neurosis, repressed desire is the accomplice of tradition.

There is yet a third scenario of neurosis in Freud's work, one that I mentioned earlier. Freud also discovered that many people became ill because secularization had deprived them of the resources of tradition. Such people fell ill when traumas struck. They could not deal with them.

This is the important point for our purposes: tradition played a powerful role in all three scenarios of neurosis, either by its overwhelming presence or by its devastating absence. The standards of tradition were known—and internalized—even if they were later lost through neglect, rejection, and abandonment, or even if they were later weakened by secularization. But *tradition characterized and shaped the culture*—that is the important thing to remember when we turn to the Sixties in America.

Now let's contrast the relation between neurosis and tradition in Freud's time with that of the Sixties. To give us a clear picture of the psychopathology then emerging I will turn to Kohut. In the following description he is clarifying the central difference between the transference neuroses and the narcissistic disorders he was seeing so often:

In uncomplicated cases of transference neurosis the psychopathology does not primarily reside either in the self or in the archaic narcissistic self-objects. The central psychopathology concerns structural conflicts over (incestuous) libidinal and

aggressive strivings *which emanate from a well-delimited,
cohesive self...*
*... In the narcissistic personality disturbances, on the other
hand, the ego's anxiety relates primarily to its awareness of
the vulnerability of the mature self* (my italics).[14]

The role of tradition in Western culture is crucial for fully appreciating the contrast Kohut is offering.

The cultural context of the narcissistic disorders Kohut described is religious and moral decline—the continuing erosion of those very traditions so noteworthy in Freud's own analysis of neurosis. Even though Freud saw and commented upon the effects of secularization, tradition was still very much of a force to be reckoned with. It still had plenty of power to cause guilt, anxiety, and repression (as well as providing such benefits as guidance and security). Indeed, tradition *was* weakening, and Freud stood at the precipice between the tradition-oriented culture behind him and the chasm of secularism yawning before him. But even though tradition was weakening, like a wounded bear it still could cause a lot of damage.

By the time the Sixties arrived, the revolt against moral standards and inherited traditions did not have nearly the same psychological repercussions as it did in Freud's era (e.g., guilt, anxiety, physical symptoms). Most important—and this is what Kohut was seeing so often—*tradition no longer contributed, to nearly the same degree, to the wholeness and cohesion of the self.* For many, tradition neither created nor affirmed a "well-delimited, cohesive self," to use Kohut's words. In contrast Freud worked primarily with people whose identities and sense of self were solidified by tradition.

The Baby Boomers in particular did not know their traditions (and later on I will examine the social and psychological consequences of that). They certainly did not know them as well as the people walking in and out of Freud's office. I am not referring to abstract, intellectual knowledge, but emotional loyalty to a tradition, and "submission" to its standards as Freud put it. Such loyalty and submission were lacking in the Sixties. Thus a spiritual vacuum was created.

It is true that in the Sixties fewer people, especially young people, experienced conflicts between desire and an internalized standard that said to that desire, "thou shall not!" And since the Sixties, internalized brakes on fantasies and immoral or anti-social behavior have weakened or disappeared. Moreover, people are less and less frightened of their own feelings; they are less fearful of their intensities, and they have become more open to fully experiencing them, especially in the area of sexuality. People today are more apt to cave in to their desires. All of that was another legacy of the Sixties, and perhaps a positive one at times if we consider the damage to the soul inflicted by the repression of Freud's time. *However, without the strength and guidance of tradition, for many people the libido was not channelled in constructive directions.* This failure has become one of the major social problems of our time, and characterizes our present spiritual dilemma. So my chief argument from here on out is that tradition failed to curb narcissism.

In his work on narcissism Kohut gave a great deal of attention to the preoedipal period of development. The preoedipal period occupies approximately the first five years of life. During that time the chief fears of the infant are fears of separation, abandonment, and loss, especially loss of love. The relationship with the mother is thus predominant. The chief developmental hurdle facing the child during this period is establishing a differentiation between the self and the mother. To accomplish that, some of the child's narcissism is transfigured into object-love. The libidinal currents begin to disengage from the self, in other words.

Even though Kohut put more of an emphasis on the preoedipal years than Freud, the latter also appreciated their psychological influence upon adult emotional life. Indeed, Freud discovered that connection, and often commented about the uniqueness of a child's relationship with his mother. Like Kohut, and Freud before him, I will also be considering the preoedipal years. My angle will be the Baby Boomers' childhoods following World War II. But I will be interpreting narcissism from a somewhat different perspective than Kohut. My perspective will be the libido theory. Kohut, of course, also began his investigations with the libido theory.[15] But unlike Kohut and his followers, I am singling out one dynamic of that theory—the split or lack of convergence between the libidinal currents—an idea that has not found any emphasis in self-psychology. Moreover, I am highlighting the role of culture in narcissistic disorders more than did Kohut or his followers at psychoanalytic institutes. I am emphasizing only one aspect of the libido theory because it supplies, I think, the simplest —yet the most comprehensive—answer to the question so many Baby Boomers have asked about the Sixties: "What happened to us, what went wrong and why?" The libido theory is "Occam's razor." It cuts through the superfluous to the core issue of the Sixties—the disintegration of the psyche.

I have intimated that there was something unique about the Sixties in that so much narcissism was unleashed. Moreover, narcissism was what my generation bequeathed to those decades which followed. The materialism, selfishness, and corruption of the Seventies, Eighties, and Nineties are merely the outward signs of it. Three descriptions of the Sixties quickly showcase the significance of narcissism for understanding the period: "the decade of the sexual revolution," "the ME decade" (or the "ME generation"), and lastly, "the drug culture." Or remember the cliches: "If it feels right, do it," "do your own thing," "my bag is ___ ," and "anything goes" (borrowed from Cole Porter and the 1920s)? Some would also attach such labels and catch phrases to the Seventies and Eighties. I would not quarrel with that, but the social and psychological origin of those descriptions—the focus on the self (both the body and inner processes)—can be traced back to the Sixties. And Freud's libido theory gives us the most direct route to do that.

I will now turn to the nature and function of narcissism in Freud's libido theory. But as I open this segment of my discussion, we should remember one thing: the word "narcissism" in psychoanalytic thought does not have the same moral tone the word has in popular culture. Narcissism in psychoanalysis simply means "self-cathexis," or emotional self-investment. Of course, the degree of this cathexis is the criterion people use when they make moral judgments on narcissism. When I examine the effects of narcissism, I will be doing this myself.

Narcissism and the Libido Theory

Freud discusses his libido theory and narcissism in many of his works, but what he says about the subject in two will suffice to bring to the table, so to speak, what I need here. In *Group Psychology and the Analysis of the Ego* he offers this succinct definition of the libido:

Libido is an expression taken from the theory of the emotions. We call by that name the energy, regarded as a quantitative magnitude (though not at present actually measurable), of those instincts which have to do with all that may be comprised under the word 'love.'[16]

It is very important to remember that unlike Carl Jung, who thought of the libido as more of a "life force" or psychic energy in general, Freud always maintained that the origin of the libido is sexual. But we must simultaneously recall that for Freud the word "sexual" has a rich emotional dimension which our American use of the word fails to convey. The libido is experienced in consciousness as both emotion and desire, corresponding to the affectionate *and* sensual currents of the libido. The psyche, however, may utilize defense mechanisms, such as repression, to defend itself against extremely powerful emotions or threatening desires. The libido may be at war with both the ego and the super-ego.

We may also think of the libido as the underlying energy giving rise to what we experience in our relationships. In this sense, libido also underlies what we feel about ourselves. Freud often uses the terms "ego-libido" and "object-libido" to talk about the direction of the libidinal energy (ego-libido is equivalent to narcissism). Let me quote him, drawing upon *Three Essays on the Theory of Sexuality*:

When it [ego-libido] is withdrawn from objects, it is held in suspense in peculiar conditions of tension and is finally drawn back into the ego, so that it becomes ego-libido once again. In contrast to object-libido, we also describe ego-libido as "narcissistic" libido. From the vantage point of psycho-analysis we can look across a frontier, which we may not pass, at the activities of narcissistic libido, and may form some idea of the relation between it and object-libido. Narcissistic or ego-libido seems to be the great reservoir from which the object-cathexes are sent out and into which they are withdrawn once more; the narcissistic libidinal cathexis of the ego is the original state of things, realized in earliest childhood, and is merely covered by later extrusions of libido, but in essentials persists behind them.[17]

Freud discovered (and then Kohut emphasized) that narcissism predominates during the preoedipal period of development; as he says, "narcissistic or ego-libido seems to be the great reservoir from which object-cathexes are sent out." For an infant, especially during the early months of its life, the world revolves around his or her needs. There is little or no differentiation between the self and the parents. During the course of development, however, the libido begins to disengage from the self and make attachments to the outer world, as alluded to earlier. The differentiation between the self and others then begins. The mother is no longer experienced simply as an extension of the self. Emotional bonds are also created with other members of the family, with relatives and friends, as the preoedipal period comes to a close.

Freud theorized that the libido is also the energy that creates loyalties to the various symbols within a culture, such as religion, or the trappings of a college or a political party. I knew the Michigan fight song, "The Victors," before "Brahms' Lullaby," and in my photographs from infancy I am constantly wearing University of Michigan garb. So perhaps, as with so much else that happens to us in life because of the first five years of development, I was "determined" to attend Michigan. In other words, more than our early relationships shape our adult emotional and intellectual life. The symbols and myths of culture, associated initially with our parents, come into play very early in our childhoods.

This is equally true of music. For instance, as far back as I can remember, I have loved the music of the Big Bands of the Swing Era, bands such as Benny Goodman, Artie Shaw, Glenn Miller, Jimmy and Tommy Dorsey, Charlie Barnet, and Gene

Krupa. One time I went to our local record store (when there were such things, I was ten at the time) and I purchased a Duke Ellington album, prompting the owner—I can still remember the store's name, Sinfonia Records—to ask me, "Are you buying this album for yourself or for you parents?" I looked at him haughtily, "For myself, of course!" He sheepishly replied, "Then I compliment you on your musical taste." (He didn't know that I also loved Elvis.) I have often wondered whether or not my passion for the great dance bands of the 1930s didn't originate from the fact my parents played this music on old 78s when I was a baby. In any case, my point—and this is highly important for my theory of the Sixties—is that *culture influences us very early in our development, and its initial impact remains with us throughout our lives.* Culture has such a great effect upon us because symbols and myths draw upon the libido for much of their power, especially narcissistic libido.

Though I will eventually expand that claim, for now I want to stay focused on the role of the libido in our attachments to people rather than to culture. Why? Because this discussion of the dynamics of our relationships will be essential background for my later interpretations of the ways secularization adversely affected so many people in the Sixties—not only in their relationships to others, but also in their feelings about themselves.

In a healthy adult sexual relationship, there is a balance between sensuality and affection, a "convergence" between the two currents of the libido, to use Freud's term. And not only that, there is a balance between narcissism and object-libido (below I will show that institutional religion, when it functions effectively, helps people achieve these balances). In all of our relationships, however, the libido moves back and forth between an object and the self. In many relationships, the libido also moves back and forth between sensuality and affection. As a rule, the younger we are, the more narcissistic we are—the more narcissistic libido predominates. (This will also be important in my analysis of the Sixties because I will be arguing that many young people regressed to this narcissistic stage when confronted with traumas, a regression that is best understood in light of weakening religious traditions.) But as we grow up, our relationships with family, friends, and authority figures *combine with culture, especially religion, to draw more and more of our libido away from the self.* This shift from narcissistic libido to object-libido strengthens not only our relationships, but also our attachments to the institutions of society. That particular function of religion broke down in the Sixties, as we shall see.

In relationships with siblings and friends, as a general rule the affectionate current of the libido is more in evidence, although the sensual current may dominate some of these early relationships. Playing "dirty doctor" with a sibling or a childhood friend is only one obvious manifestation of this. Taboos, however, usually channel or checkmate the sensual current of the libido within a culture, e.g., against incest. The sensual current, of course, later electrifies eroticism between lovers. In the eyes of the Church, marriage is the "green light" for the full expression of sensuality. After the first few years, however, keeping this current of the libido flowing is a married couple's greatest challenge, as any veteran of that venerable institution knows. The failure to do so is a major cause of divorce, something else that became much more common—and acceptable—in the Sixties.

If we are unable to make social attachments to others, or if our attachments are very weak, because we were raised in a family full of conflict or lacking in love, there is a real danger of psychosis or schizophrenia. In both, the libido remains directed inward. Inner processes predominate in the lives of such individuals. Life is like a nocturnal dream in which the person is awake. Artists, in particular, draw upon narcissistic libido in their work, but most artists can make social attachments and function in the world while maintaining a rich fantasy life.

Freud's theory that the libido has two currents, and his additional idea that the libido moves back and forth (between the self and others, and between the self and culture) gives us the framework we need to begin our specific interpretations of the Sixties. We will begin with an observation about sexuality, one which will illustrate narcissism and the dynamics of the libido theory. *What was so evident in the Sixties was a sexuality with all or most of the emotional components stripped away—pure sensuality without affection.* All too often a sexual partner became merely an object, an object for personal pleasure, which was then popularly called "using" a person. This was a neurotic, highly narcissistic sexuality. It was promiscuity. The focus was on the self—its needs, its pleasure and sexual release—not the feelings and hopes of the other. This kind of sexuality was not only unfulfilling emotionally and spiritually, but it lacked any kind of moral context.[18] Moreover, it lacked security, a void which caused severe psychological damage, not only because of easy and quick betrayals, but also because of unfulfilled longings for commitment. When the birth control pill became widespread, this scenario became even more common. The pill was looked upon as a godsend by those men and women who only wanted a one night stand or a short affair. Yet for those men who wanted to make a commitment (but who found themselves involved with a woman who, in turn, did not want that same commitment) the pill became a threat. The pill made it possible for women, for the first time in history, to have multiple sexual partners with a greatly reduced danger of pregnancy (the illusion of "safe sex" was born during the Sixties). Of course, many men were only feeling the sort of insecurity women have experienced for centuries because of the double standards we examined earlier.

One can't overestimate the significance of the pill for understanding what happened psychologically and socially within the culture. To conclude this section on narcissism, I will offer one illustration of the kind of sexuality I have been alluding to— and now for the first time in this book I am making a moral judgment on something specific. Not all narcissism is bad, by any means. If it were, we would have no art and little meaningful religion! In this case, however, it was bad—and highly destructive.

In my fraternity at the University of Michigan, Alpha Delta Phi, several of my brothers constructed a "screwing room" in the basement of our house on State Street, right next door to the Michigan Union (a student center and a hotel for alumni). They christened it "the grinder." They outfitted it with a large bed. They wired in a speaker from the juke box in our basement party room. Thus the "lovers" were able to listen to the same songs we were so feverishly dancing to in the next room, songs such as

"Good Lovin'" by the Young Rascals, Sam and Dave's "Hold On! I'm a Comin'" and "Gimme Some Lovin'" by the Spencer Davis Group. My brothers proceeded to install a black light in "the grinder" and tacked up psychodelic posters on the walls, such as garish portraits of Jimi Hendrix and Jim Morrison, lead singer of the Doors. To top it off, they provided plenty of toilet paper, and then charged couples $2.00 during fraternity parties for an hour in "the grinder." Even in our immaturity, I think the entire fraternity knew there was something degrading and disgusting about this whole business. Cockroaches eventually took over "the grinder," thus concluding a sick chapter in the history of my fraternity. Yet sick as it was, "the grinder" reflected the culture of the times and, today, reveals the weakness of our internalized moral values. Moreover, it symbolizes, dramatically, all that I am trying to describe when I use the somewhat abstract language of psychology to discuss the split between the two libidinal currents.

Now that we have explored narcissism and the libido theory, we are prepared to examine a matter we have anticipated for sometime: religion's role in transforming narcissism. Later on, we will then be able to interpret, very specifically, the way that institutional religion failed so many in the Sixties, and the way so many failed their institutional religion.[19]

Narcissism and Religion

In American culture, one of the traditional functions of religion, and here I am thinking particularly of the institutional Church or "organized religion," has been to help people deal with their narcissism. More specifically—and in language worshippers are more likely to use—the Church helps us curb our "self-love," our emotional investment in ourselves, in short, our self-preoccupations. The Church does this in several ways (and I include here synagogues and mosques). First of all, through its ethic of loving others the Church helps put a limit on narcissism. As Ferenczi says, "We are able to love (recognize) objects only by a sacrifice of our narcissism, which is after all but a fresh illustration of the well-known psychoanalytic fact that all object-love takes place (at) the expense of narcissism."[20] Much of Jesus' teaching, for example, is a variation on the theme of loving and serving both God and our neighbor. The Parable of the Good Samaritan is probably the best known example, but nowhere is Jesus' social ethic put forth with more power than in the Parable of the Sheep and the Goats in Matthew 25:31–46:

When the Son of man comes in his glory, and all the angels with him, then he will sit on his glorious throne. Before him will be gathered all the nations, and he will separate them one from another as a shepherd separates the sheep from the goats, and he will place the sheep at his right hand, but the goats at the left. Then the King will say to those at his right hand, "Come, O blessed of my Father, inherit the kingdom prepared for you from the foundation of the world; for I was hungry and you gave me food, I was thirsty and you gave me drink, I was a stranger and you welcomed me, I was naked and you clothed me, I was sick and you visited me, I was in prison and you came to me." Then the righteous will answer him, "Lord, when did we see thee hungry and feed thee, or thirsty and give thee drink? And when did we see thee a stranger and welcome thee, or naked and clothe thee? And when did we see thee sick or in prison and visit thee?" And the King will answer them, "Truly, I say to you, as you did it to one of the least of these my brethren, you did it to me." Then he will say to those at his left hand, "Depart from me, you cursed, into the eternal fire prepared for the devil and his angels; for I was hungry and you gave me no food, I was thirsty and you gave me no drink, I was a stranger and you did not welcome me, naked and you did not clothe me, sick and in prison and you did not visit me." Then they also will answer, "Lord, when did we see thee hungry or thirsty or a stranger or naked or sick or in prison, and did not minister to thee?" Then he will answer them, "Truly, I say to you, as you did it not to one of the least of these, you did it not to me." And they will go away into eternal punishment, but the righteous into eternal life.

As a corollary of his social ethic, Jesus is critical of anxieties or "worries" about the self which today we would call neurotic in many instances. Matthew 6:24–34 is a good example:

> No one can serve two masters; for either he will hate the one and love the other, or he will be devoted to the one and despise the other. You cannot serve God and mammon. Therefore I tell you, do not be anxious about your life, what you shall eat or what you shall drink, nor about your body, what you shall put on. Is not life more than food, and the body more than clothing? Look at the birds of the air: they neither sow nor reap nor gather into barns, and yet your heavenly Father feeds them. Are you not of more value than they? And which of you by being anxious can add one cubit to his span of life? And why are you anxious about clothing? Consider the lilies of the field, how they grow; they neither toil nor spin; yet I tell you even Solomon in all his glory was not arrayed like one of these. But if God so clothes the grass of the field, which today is alive and tomorrow is thrown into the oven, will he not much more clothe you, O men of little faith? Therefore do not be anxious, saying, "What shall we eat?" or "What shall we wear?" For the Gentiles seek all these things; and your heavenly Father knows that you need them all. But seek first his kingdom and his righteousness, and all these things shall be yours as well.
>
> Therefore do not be anxious about tomorrow, for tomorrow will be anxious for itself. Let the day's own trouble be sufficient for the day.

Note that Jesus' harsh criticisms of self-preoccupations border on being moral criticisms. Indeed, for him what we are preoccupied with psychologically does have a moral dimension, something we too are evaluating in relation to narcissism. For Jesus there is even a moral dimension to our fantasies ("You have heard that it was said, 'You shall not commit adultery.' But I say to you that every one who looks at a woman lustfully has already committed adultery with her in his heart," Matthew 5:27–28). Jesus talked about money almost more than any other subject. Following Jesus, the Church teaches that faith in God's providence and service to others work together to diminish both anxieties and feelings of insecurity, which now seem to be so much part of modernity ("the Age of Anxiety," according to W. H. Auden).

The Church helps us limit our narcissism not only through its ethical teachings about love and service, but also *through the emotional ties established within the religious community itself* (if, in fact, there is true community in one's church, something else we are evaluating in relation to the Sixties). Freud talks about this function of the Church and similar groups in *Group Psychology and the Analysis of the Ego*: "A limitation of narcissism can, according to our theoretical views, only be produced by one factor, a libidinal tie with other people. Love for oneself knows one barrier—love for others, love for objects"[21] (e.g., religious symbols).

A chief function of worship is the creation of these emotional ties. And if a church has a strong ministry into the wider community, emotional bonds with others are also established through a variety of channels (such as visiting people in nursing homes, working for affordable housing in the community through organizations such as Habitat for Humanity, feeding people in soup lines, or venturing on outreach trips of various kinds).

While serving as the senior associate minister in the Church of the Holy Spirit in Lake Forest, Illinois, an extremely affluent and gracious community on the North Shore of Chicago (where narcissism is a serious moral and psychological problem for many), I led outreach trips to the Wind River Indian Reservation in Wyoming. About fifty of us, of all ages, went out there for three consecutive summers under my leadership (now in the capable hands of other leaders, the Church of the Holy Spirit continues to send a large contingent each summer). We did work projects and ran a vacation Bible school at St. Michael's Mission, a ministry of the Episcopal Church located in Ethete (where they have a beautiful log church with a picture window in back of the altar that offers a panoramic view of the Rocky Mountains). We mainly worked with the Arapaho, who share this reservation with the Shoshones, although Indians from many other tribes also live there. These trips were wonderful ways for people, some of them seriously troubled, to "get outside of themselves." The metaphorical power of this cliche returned. A caring community, highly charged emotionally, was built among ourselves, and lasting friendships were established with the Indians. Prejudices on both sides were overcome, as well as mutual fears. Reaching out to others through such a ministry proved to be a form of liberation from the self, its pride and petty concerns. As Freud writes, expressing a psychological insight that could pertain to any effective ministry, "in the development of mankind as a whole, just as in individuals, love alone acts as the civilizing factor in the sense that it brings a change from egoism to altruism."[22]

The psychology of religion illuminates other ways the Church curbs narcissism. If a church is truly effective in its ministry, it not only helps a person maintain a healthy balance between narcissistic libido and object-libido ("love your neighbor as yourself"), but also a healthy balance between the affectionate and sensual currents of the libido. Take the institution of marriage. This is what Freud said about it: "A man shall leave his father and his mother—according to the biblical command— and shall cleave unto his wife; affection and sensuality are then united."[23] In other words, *religion helps check the narcissism that may divide the two currents of the libido or prevent them from converging.* Let's examine this power of religion in greater detail.

Primary socialization (early socialization within the family) is where the internalization of culture begins. Secondary social- ization within the school, the Church, and the wider community reinforces that process. In a religious household, a child is usually exposed to some of the teaching of his or her particular religious tradition — teachings about loving others, for instance, or warn- ings about selfishness. A child learns to share and be kind to others, especially siblings. A child is taught to respect parental authority ("Honor your father and your mother," as the Old Testa- ment commands in Exodus 20:12). In a religious family, a child is also taught that he or she is not the center of the universe, that God loves others, too.

During both primary and secondary socialization, the religious symbols of one's church, such as God the Father, Mother Church, providence, the Eucharist, Jesus, Moses, or St. Paul, become as- sociated psychologically with the strength and love of the par- ents. Such symbols draw upon parental power and authority (more on this in a moment). In his work, the psychoanalyst Erik

Erikson has shown that it is very difficult to experience religious faith as an adult if trust was not experienced earlier within the family of one's upbringing. If it was difficult to trust one's own father, for instance, it will be very difficult to trust God the Father. In *Childhood and Society* Erikson has a rich passage about religious trust and its foundations within the family:

> The parental faith which supports the trust emerging in the newborn, has throughout history sought its institutional safeguard (and, on occasion, found its greatest enemy) in organized religion. Trust born of care is, in fact, the touchstone of the *actuality* of a given religion. All religions have in common the periodical childlike surrender to a Provider or providers who dispense earthly fortune as well as spiritual health; some demonstration of man's smallness by way of reduced posture and humble gesture; the admission in prayer and song of misdeeds, or misthoughts, and of evil intentions; fervent appeal for inner unification by divine guidance; and finally, the insight that individual trust must become a common faith, individual mistrust a commonly formulated evil.[24]

If religion plays a strong role in primary socialization, by creating trust in God for instance, libido will be drawn away from the self towards religious symbols and social attachments, such as those within a church.

Religious symbols may also have a rich psychological life of their own, divorced from any kind of institutional support. Because of this almost autonomous life in our inner world, symbols also have an important intrapsychic function in curbing narcissism. Like containers or vessels, they become filled up with our narcissistic energies during our psychological development. To shift metaphors a bit, religious symbols are like storage bins, into which we pour our narcissistic libido. This is one reason why religion is very narcissistic. Here I am referring to a "healthy narcissism." It is very comforting, and healing, to believe that God loves you, the believer; that your hairs are numbered (Matthew 10:30); that God has a will for you, and that history, including your own life, has purpose and meaning; that your well-being is in God's hands; that he is concerned about your problems, and answers your prayers; that "your bodies are members of Christ" and "a temple of the Holy Spirit within you" (I Corinthians 6:15,19). The Church teaches that all of the foregoing is integral to our relationship with God. What could be more comforting to the sinner than the Christian belief that Jesus is a savior? What could be more comforting to the person who fears death than the hope of eternal life because of Jesus' victory over death on a cross? All of those religious ideas and beliefs are empowered, in large part anyway, by narcissistic libido.

To use one final metaphor, religious symbols and the theological ideas which surround them, are like icebergs. What we see in a religious symbol, and experience consciously, is the tip of the iceberg. Underneath the "manifest" symbol (to borrow an idea from Freud's theory of dreams), there is a vast subterranean "latent" reality extending deep into the unconscious, a reality we dimly intimate but rarely see. Just as icebergs are moved by powerful ocean currents, religious symbols are similarly dependent upon the currents of the libido. Symbols "ride" those currents, metaphorically speaking. The power and dynamism of religion are what I am driving at. Let me explain this in another way.

Freud has a helpful concept for interpreting the psychology of religion, namely "displacement." What Freud means by displacement is that the libido may shift (often as a defense) from one object to another, or from the self to objects, or from objects to the self. In other words, the libido—and the emotions arising from it—move around. The libido is not static, it is mobile, which gives great volatility and passion to our emotional life, including our feelings about religion. Now here is where the idea of displacement comes into play in the psychology of religion: not only are libidinal energies, which were originally directed at the parents (object-libido), displaced onto religious symbols during socialization, but narcissistic libido as well. Consequently, just as religious symbols may be a healthy vehicle for regression to feelings once associated with our parents directly (feelings such as love and security), symbols may likewise be vehicles of regression to feelings rooted in narcissistic libido (grandiosity, feelings of self-esteem and self-confidence, or a healthy sense of pride in one's accomplishments). Thus the symbol of God the

Father, for instance, takes over much of a young child's grandiosity, and then mirrors that back to him or her along with parental love and security. And symbols such as the Cross are infused with a great deal of idealism and other aspirations associated with narcissistic libido. The libido theory helps us understand the process psychodynamically; it helps us to appreciate the power of symbols in our lives.

To sum up, through religion the believer may regress to strong feelings of love and security, without the oedipal guilt that might be aroused by regression to the parental images themselves, and to all the feelings associated with the parental complex. Likewise, the believer may use religion to regress to feelings of grandiosity and healthy self-esteem without damaging fixations, and without "narcissism" or "egoism" in the popular sense of those words.

Narcissistic libido has another important function in the psychology of religion. Narcissistic libido enables the believer to feel that he or she is "in union" with God or "in touch" with religious feelings. The libido theory enables us to envision how a person might feel, at times, that he or she is "one with God," and thus believe in the possibility of mystical union. By "riding" the currents of the libido (and we should remember that the sensual and affectionate currents of the libido are components, in varying degrees, of both object-libido and narcissism), the believer is "transported" by religious symbols deep into his or her inner world. In *Civilization and It's Discontents* Freud described such experiences as "oceanic." He thought that mystics were somehow able to return psychologically to that period in childhood development when there was no differentiation between the child and the mother, that this was the experience that was then interpreted as "mystical." Romain Rolland gives us a picture of such an experience in his book, *The Life of Ramakrishna*, where he writes this about the Hindu saint:

Very few go back to the source. The little peasant of Bengal by listening to the message of his heart found his way to the inner Sea. And there he was wedded to it, thus bearing out the words of the Upanishads: "I am more ancient than the radiant Gods. I am the first born of the Being. I am the artery of Immortality."[25]

The libido theory is not only instructive for interpreting "normal" religious experience, but the extraordinary as well. *The important point is that religion helps us master, utilize, and curb our narcissism.* Feelings originating from narcissistic libido, like all feelings, have no sense of time, they are literally "timeless." A wound to our self-esteem during childhood, for instance, may feel like it just occurred. Thus powerful narcissistic feelings are always present in the psyche, ready to be tapped, and various religions and cults offer ways of doing this. Potentially, therefore, religion is very beneficial—and dangerous. If we fail to appreciate the power of narcissism—and the role of religion in curbing it—something highly significant about psychology will be overlooked, especially the psychology of religion within the Sixties Generation.

Kohut's Theory of Self-objects

There is a close parallel between the psychology of religious symbols that I just developed and Kohut's theory of self-objects. I want to clarify this parallel because it offers yet another psychoanalytic angle from which to view narcissism and the psychology of religion. Self-objects are external objects which are internalized and then experienced as part of the self. After they are internalized, they are invested with large amounts of narcissistic libido. Internalizations of parental images become our first self-objects in development. Self-objects help us regulate both anxiety and narcissism. What is particularly significant for us is that religious figures become self-objects. Once religious figures are internalized during primary socialization, they function similarly to those inherited from the family. (To my knowledge, Kohut never drew this parallel, but it is a natural deduction from his work.)
Psychologically, self-objects operate independently of the actual people involved, to a large degree anyway. For instance, the people who were originally internalized may have died. But

in a real sense, none of us ever dies. Once a person is internalized, he or she is "immortal." He or she is "alive in the head," so
to speak. The people who have been close to us emotionally have
lingering influences upon us throughout the life cycle, often very
powerful influences. As self-objects, they become part of the
symbolic structure of the mind. Indeed, they shape it. If it is true
that none of us ever completely dies as long as there is someone
left to remember us, think how true that is for the great religious
figures of history such as Jesus, Moses, the Buddha, Krishna, and
Mohammed!

There is an important caveat in Kohut's theory, however. As
Freud discovered and Kohut later explained more fully, what we
internalize about a person is a mixture of fact and fantasy. The
super-ego (the repository of tradition) does have a historical base.
We do internalize images of real people (of course, we also internalize images of fictional people, too; once they become self-
objects, they may influence us just as much as real people). But
we also make interpretations of these people in the process of
internalization. What you think about and feel when I mention
such people as Mick Jagger, John F. Kennedy, and Humphrey
Bogart, or someone from literature such as Scarlet O'Hara or Jay
Gatsby, will be different from the things that I see and feel. Obviously, there will be some similarities, too, especially if we share
a common culture. What I have just said about differences in
interpretation applies equally to such symbols as the Cross, the
swastika, or the American flag.

When we make interpretations of real people, who may then
become powerful self-objects, these interpretations may or may
not be congruent with the characteristics of the actual people
involved. Almost inevitably, our interpretations are a mixture of
fact and fantasy. But why is this so? Our interpretations are usually laced with distortions because we bring to those interpretations our personal experiences, our particular age and thus our
place in the life cycle, our own personalities, our family background, our needs, race, and gender, the nature of the culture in
which we find ourselves, our own internal conflicts, and lastly,
our hopes, dreams, and ideals. And not only that! We also bring
to bear on what we interpret the power of our imaginations. Our

capacity for fantasy both enhances and distorts what we interpret. Moreover, when we interpret something we receive from the mass media, we are already confronted with their own interpretations. Distortion may compound distortion. Thus when we interpret religious figures such as Jesus or Krishna, for example, what we are actually interpreting is not the "reality" of those individuals, their factual life histories as if we had been there to see and know them in person. What we are interpreting are the interpretations others have already made of those life histories. Some of those interpretations may be based on eyewitness accounts, their own or someone else's, but this, too, calls for an interpretation!

Let me offer an illustration from the field of Biblical criticism. When we interpret Jesus, what we are actually interpreting are the New Testament writers' own interpretations. What in the New Testament conveys historical data about Jesus and what only expresses the needs and concerns of the early Church, or the writers' own interests, requires an additional interpretation. Consequently, we see Jesus "through the eyes" of the New Testament writers—and the communities in which they lived—before we see him through ours.

Once we internalize people (however accurately or distorted), then as self-objects (i.e., symbols) they influence subsequent interpretations we make of our world. Moreover, self-objects inspire and shape our fantasies. In other words, what we internalize (especially images of people because they stimulate the most emotion) affects all that enters into the mind through the senses. And, in turn, self-objects affect what we project back into that outer world. The symbolic structure of the mind is a "filter" through which we view our world, or "a set of lenses" to use another metaphor.

Now I will summarize the important points I wanted to establish about the psychology of religion in the last two sections: (1) narcissistic libido is the "glue" which cements symbols into our psyches (2) symbols, especially religious symbols, have a great psychological role to play in the cohesion of the self (3) symbols help us balance the two currents of the libido by curbing narcissism; to use Kohut's terms, "self-objects" help us attain "narcissistic homeostasis," and lastly (4) by "borrowing" much of their energy from other self-objects (displacement), religious symbols, such as God the Father, may radiate love, security, and empathy (or perhaps wrath and other frightful feelings in some cases).

Symbols and Society

Let's now pause for a moment and catch our breath. I have been discussing some very complicated psychological dynamics. Before forging ahead and touching upon their social correlates, I will first review the most important of those dynamics. Symbols reduce the amount of libidinal energy we direct towards the self. Religious symbols, in particular, do this not only by nurturing the bonds within communities unified by such symbols (e.g., a church), but also through the process of internalization. During that process, both people and cultural symbols become part of the self (self-objects). As a result, narcissistic libido is less directly attached to the self. The self is less obviously its object, in other words. Symbols then enable us "to store up" narcissistic libido. They become receptacles. We then can draw upon these energies through regression when the need arises. Narcissistically invested symbols thereby give direction and structure to our lives. They "make us feel good," by making us feel loved and secure. Such symbols may radiate a "glow" in the psyche, but let me also add here that some symbols may haunt us, too, and fill us with dread and conflict (consider the Nazis' use of symbolism).

Thus far I have been discussing symbolism primarily from the standpoint of individual psychology. Now I will briefly sketch a parallel process in the social sphere. A theory of symbolism is a constructive way to wed psychology and sociology.

We all can remember the people or cultural symbols which have had great importance for us individually, but we can also do the same thing for "the collective psyche," which is only a heuristic metaphor for the sum total of the individual psyches in a society. Reflect for a moment about such people as Martin Luther King, Franklin Roosevelt, Greta Garbo, Richard Nixon, Marilyn

Monroe, or Gary Cooper (when we deal with movie stars we not only have to consider "the reality" of who these people were as persons, but also all their starring roles, which more than anything else determine how we see such people; this is also true of politicians vis-à-vis the way the media have presented them to us). Such people may or may not have importance for us as individuals, but they most certainly have had great significance for American society. Once our collective psyche internalizes such people—and here add in the great religious figures of history—they take on a life of their own beyond the bare facts of their lives (facts which may or may not be recoverable). Famous people become "larger than life," as we often put it, and we—collectively—make them that way. In modern culture, the media have further amplified this process. Ronald Reagan did the best acting of his career when he turned to politics and cultivated his cultural image through the media. He had a shrewd sense of social psychology. He calculated—accurately, as it turned out—that the American public would react positively to that image (e.g., identifying with him as a "warm grandfather," an identification facilitated by Americans' experiences with their actual grandfathers).

Just as an individual may distort an image in making an interpretation, so, too, may the culture. I have already pointed out that individuals bring their own psychological dynamics to bear on their interpretations. This is equally true of society. It, too, brings its own peculiar nature to its collective interpretations of people and symbols. Thus certain symbols and people unify a society—or divide it (think of the peace symbol in the Sixties, or Gene McCarthy). Moreover, symbols may curb a society's narcissism (e.g., religious figures) or foster it (e.g., patriotic symbols, as politicians know only too well).

We have now discussed symbolism in relation to narcissism and religion on both the psychological and the social levels. At this point I will turn to an additional function of symbols. They not only help us to master narcissism, but also help us to establish an identity. I will here argue that *identity channels libido*. Then later on in the book I will show that *the upheavals of the Sixties dramatically changed our identities*.

Identity and the Libido

"Identity," like the "collective psyche," is another heuristic term, one we use to account for the coalescence in development of a variety of tendencies, both pushed and pulled by the libido. Identity is a "balancing act" that we find difficult to talk about in any other way. It is one of those concepts like "personality," which is helpful in our thinking even if it is somewhat vague, or mushy. Erikson is probably the psychological thinker most associated with the concept. In his "eight stages of man" presented in his book, *Childhood and Society*, "identity vs. role confusion" is the fifth stage. For the reader unfamiliar with Erikson's work, I will list all eight: basic trust vs. basic mistrust; autonomy vs. shame and doubt; initiative vs. guilt; industry vs. inferiority; identity vs. role confusion; intimacy vs. isolation; generativity vs. stagnation; ego integrity vs. despair. My particular interest in the concept of identity is that it provides yet another excellent model for understanding how the libidinal currents get channelled, and thus balanced, during the course of the life cycle. Here is what Erikson says about the subject in a discussion of the advent of puberty:

> The integration now taking place in the form of ego identity is, as pointed out, more than the sum of the childhood identifications. It is the accrued experience of the ego's ability to integrate all identifications with the vicissitudes of the libido, with the aptitudes developed out of endowment, and with the opportunities offered in social roles. The sense of ego identity, then, is the accrued confidence that the inner sameness and continuity prepared in the past are matched by the sameness and continuity of one's meaning for others, as evidenced in the tangible promise of a "career."[26]

Up to the Sixties Generation—and even including it, although this was one of the things that was rejected by many—young people were expected to prepare for a traditional career of some sort, or for the life of a "homemaker." And during the "in between period," while being trained and/or spouse hunting at a college or university, fraternities and sororities and school affiliations became highly important identifications, especially at large universities where alienation was such a problem in the Sixties (and no doubt remains so). The search for identity is one of the reasons intercollegiate athletics have become such an obsession in American society since the 1960s, particularly for those late adolescents in the lonely interim between leaving home for good and beginning a career or a marriage. However, we probably all know people who, even as they approach senility, still find their chief identification in life through their school, or their fraternity or sorority. They parade around their community decked out in maize and blue or green and white or scarlet and gray as if they were still undergraduates, and they perhaps bring as deep a psychological hunger to those symbols as if they were still cruising through their undergraduate library rather than the supermarket. (It is such people who pressure their schools to prostitute themselves by admitting athletes who are far below their normal admission standards.)

At the University of Michigan, our undergraduate library was called "the ugli," and it was just that, ugly. Each fraternity and sorority, like apes, would have their own territory staked out on each floor, where all the members sat, thereby attracting or repelling members of the opposite sex. Much pride was attached to those Greek letters written across the chest of their sweatshirts, or etched for immorality on the walls of bathroom stalls, or even lyricized there in what we called "toilet poetry." For many people in the Sixties, school and Greek identifications answered the cry for community, a lingering cry in our culture.

As I headed off for college in the fall of 1965, most of my female contemporaries, even if they dreamed of a career of some kind, had in the forefront of their minds that one day they would marry, settle down and raise a family. The males were expected to train for a career, preferably in one of the professions. In 1965 this aspect of identity formation was fairly clear. Socialization and opportunity (or for women, I should say the lack thereof) were then operative in decision making. Women, of course, could be stewardesses, teachers, and secretaries, but they were encouraged to do little else. This widely shared "life map" was not yet openly challenged in the relatively stable culture that still

existed, but out of the later social upheavals emerged the women's movement, plus broader options for men. According to
Erikson's theory of identity, successful socialization channels
libido into a career or motherhood for example, thereby providing
a feeling of integration, a secure place in the world, and the
knowledge that life has purpose and meaning.
   Just as an individual establishes an identity, a culture does,
too. Erikson also discusses this in *Childhood and Society*, and
then concludes, "the study of identity, then, becomes as strategic
in our time as the study of sexuality was in Freud's time."[27] His
observation is particularly apt for the Sixties. So, I will, for now,
contract the scope of our discussion and focus on religious
identity—religion's role in the creation of our identities.
   As Freud discovered, and Erikson showed us even more
thoroughly, our first sense of identity emerges from the identifications we make with our parents. Freud, of course, stressed
the importance of the "oedipal crisis" in all of this. He theorized
that we identify with the parent of the same sex as we move into
adulthood, realizing that we can't "have" our real mothers and
fathers; thus we identify with our "rival" in the hope of one day
marrying someone like the desired parent.[28] But there is much
more to it than that. As we identify with our parents, we also
incorporate their roles in society; we internalize their traditions,
identifications, and values. We may follow their footsteps into a
particular career or role, and we may aspire to have the same life
style. Or, we may rebel against all of that, finding that traditional
gender roles, for instance, are straight jackets, or that parental
authority, backed by religion, is overly repressive. Such rebellion,
of course, characterized the Sixties. It was a rebellion very
similar to that of the Twenties, when the Baby Boomers' grandparents revolted against their own religious and moral traditions
in the midst of their own war disillusionment.[29]
   If we are a Christian, Jew, Muslim, or Hindu, or an Episcopalian, Roman Catholic, Methodist, Unitarian, or Orthodox Jew,
we are likely to have this particular identity because we were
socialized into such a tradition within our family. We probably
also grew up in a culture characterized by the same traditions.
For most people, their religious identity is inherited from their

parents and the surrounding culture. Often the parental religious tradition will be the focus of a rebellion or rejection at some point, most likely during late adolescence; but after a hiatus, chances are that the rebellious youth will return to the fold, perhaps when they begin a family of their own. Such a rebellion is more normal than not, although some people never return to their childhood traditions; indeed, such an "exodus" has particularly marked the mainline traditions since the Sixties.

The influence of our parents' religious tradition upon our own adult religious identification is now almost common sense, which shows how influenced we are by the ideas arising from the social sciences. Most of us know, for instance, that children closely follow their parents' political voting patterns. The obviousness of those observations, however, should not lead us to underestimate them. As I have been emphasizing, libido—especially narcissistic libido—is the "glue" that cements symbols into the structure of the mind, even deep into the unconscious. In most instances, we first encounter these symbols through our parents, who bring the culture into the home. From that point on, we associate many of those symbols with our parents. These identifications have deep emotional and intellectual ramifications throughout the life cycle.

Once we identify with our parents, and once we internalize the cultural symbols associated with them, it is very difficult to eradicate, abandon, or completely reject those symbols. In my pastoral experience, I have discovered that Roman Catholics, to cite but one example, find it especially troublesome to leave their inherited traditions behind, even if they violently disagree with their church's teachings and moral positions, and very much wish to join another denomination. St. Ignatius said something to the effect, "Give me a child until he is five, and I will have him for life." The discoveries of Freud have proven the truth of that. Many Roman Catholics have been leaving their childhood traditions in recent years, in large part due to secularization, but they often experience guilt in doing so, and have many subsequent reservations.

The theory of identity formation also contributes a helpful perspective for interpreting social and psychological stability. The role of tradition in creating social stability needs little further comment. Any student of history knows the importance of religion for providing continuity in a culture. This has been true for both the East and the West. But before turning to cultural change, let me offer one illustration of the psychological stability religious identity provides, one that I see constantly in my pastoral work. This illustration also shows us the strong connection between psychological and social stability.

I have discovered time and time again that when parishioners of mine experience horrible tragedies, such as the death of a loved one or affliction with cancer or some other deadly disease, most of the time they somehow accommodate such tragedies into their personal theology. They will affirm God's providence in spite of what has happened to them. They will say to me that a death or a disease was God's will, or they will confess that "it is a mystery," but they continue to uphold their faith in a God who cares for them and can intervene in their lives miraculously. Many find comfort in the Cross of Jesus Christ; they feel that the Cross represents God's participation in suffering in order to overcome it, or they find hope of victory over death in the Resurrection. Some people will quote the Book of Job (1:21):

> Naked I came from my mother's womb, and naked shall I return; the Lord gave, and the Lord has taken away; blessed be the name of the Lord.

In my experience in the Church, I have found that most of the people who have been effectively socialized into a religious tradition remain loyal to that tradition in spite of whatever tragedies they personally encounter, or those they see in the larger world. If they were raised a Christian, they remain a Christian. If they were raised an Episcopalian, they remain an Episcopalian. One reason for this loyalty— and probably its best explanation— is the strong emotional identifications people have made with the central figures in each of the great world religions, Jesus for Christianity, Mohammed for Islam, Krishna for Hinduism, the Buddha for Buddhism, and Moses for Judaism, as well as other religious figures of slightly less stature, such as St. Francis or St. Paul for Christians, or Jeremiah and Elijah for Jews. Many other figures could be named, nor should we overlook our identifications with the clergy who represent those figures and proclaim them in preaching and teaching. Religious figures—once they have been internalized, and have helped us to establish an identity —create the staying power of a tradition in spite of what happens to the believer, or what happens to society, or even the world. To be theological about the relation between identity formation and the central figures in the major world religions, one could argue that God revealed himself in world history through men and women in the various religious traditions precisely to create emotional loyalties to a tradition, loyalties which then build psychic structure. And it is this structure which fends off threats to the self. Religious identity would then be an aspect of God's grace. Moreover, one could argue that God revealed himself through human beings precisely because religious identity is difficult to establish with abstractions; there is no human warmth in an abstraction. Thus John writes in his Gospel, "No one has ever seen God; the only Son, who is in the bosom of the Father, he has made him known" (John 1:18). Regardless of whether one would take that theological step, to interpret the psychology of anyone's religious identity at least three things must be examined: (1) the believer's libidinal attachments to the central figures in his or her religious tradition; one's emotional investments, in other words (2) the importance of religious identity for a person's sense of self (3) the role of religion in establishing goals and ideals.

In sum, both the symbolic structure of the mind and the libido theory enable us to appreciate the strength of religious identifications when confronted by "reality," a reality that so often challenges religious beliefs and loyalties. Even if a churchgoer has not yet suffered personal tragedies, he or she still reads the morning papers or watches the evening news on the television, or encounters "the world" in some other way. Thus all religious people—unless they are completely insensitive or blind—must incorporate tragedies into their world view, even if these tragedies seem far removed from the self. The fear of death, as well as other anxieties and needs, certainly plays a strong role in creating our religious identifications. Here I am emphasizing, however, our emotional identifications with the prominent figures in the history of religions. (This dynamic in the psychology and sociology of religion is too often overlooked by scholars.) In my pastoral work I also see people who leave their inherited traditions in anger during a crisis, but then that, too, shows the power of one's religious identity, because in most cases their religion continues to haunt them, even if it no longer provides comfort or evokes much allegiance. Once our libido attaches to religious symbols and the ideas surrounding those symbols, and once a tradition becomes part of the symbolic structure of the mind, thereby creating our religious identity, it is almost inevitable that we will continue to see our world through the lens of that tradition—or in reaction to it. Thus our internalized traditions—even if neglected—will usually continue to arouse in us the feeling that God exists, and is even pressing down upon us.

I have also discovered in my pastoral work that even many nominal churchgoers feel, for example, that God appoints "their time to die"; they believe this in the face of others dying in plane crashes or children dying in wars or from diseases, seemingly in contradiction to their personal view of providence. Perhaps this is where we see most clearly how narcissistic religion truly is. I am not arguing, however, that narcissistic religious feelings and our religious identities created by those feelings are spurious or false. I am merely pointing out their strength, or better, the psychological source of that strength. (The libido is indeed the fountainhead of religion.) Nor am I arguing that religious loyalty is misguided. On the contrary! *But I am pointing out the degree to which religion is psychological, an aspect of religion which does not make it false but rather explains its power.* Religion thus offers stability to both the individual and society. And one of the themes of this book, of course, is that secularization has been eroding that function of religion in American culture.

Let me make one final observation in this section on identity. Neither cultural determinism (à la Marx) nor psychology (à la Freud) can explain all there is to religion, but they do explain a great deal. Religion is inescapably psychological because everything "religious"—including theological writings and what is perceived as revelation (either in scriptures or in experience)—is first filtered through the psyche before it registers in consciousness. *Then* an interpretation is made. In other words, psychology comes before hermeneutics. Indeed, psychology is part of hermeneutics.

Symbolism and Cultural Change

Our consideration of the power of symbols and their importance in the establishment of an identity, has brought us to the point where we can now consider cultural change. In this section I will offer a theoretical model. Here I am particularly indebted to Max Weber, the great German sociologist who, in opposition to Marx, argued that the power of ideas can change the structures of society and revolutionize its symbol systems. Marx appreciated the conservative nature of society, a conservatism he attributed to both a rigid class system and a small elite's control of the means of production. Marx argued that the ruling and wealthy classes produced ideas, such as religious ideas (or at least used those ideas), to perpetuate their own power and position. That is, the powerful used religion to maintain their own privileges and the status quo of society. For Marx, religion was an ideology, an ideology tailor-made to keep a small handful of people in power while at the same time preventing others from sharing that power.

Marx's arguments about religion contain profound truth. Religion may very well be an opiate, quelling rage and dampening demands for both justice and the fair distribution of power and wealth in a society. His philosophy, however, does not remain open enough to the possibility of the great individual who bursts into history like a comet with a whole constellation of new ideas, ideas which eventually are crystallized as symbols. These symbols, in turn, change history, including the structures of society. That is the Weberian argument. For Weber, religious symbols and creative ideas are more than the superstructure of society (which they were for Marx). They are more than the frosting on the cake, intended to give a nice appearance to an underlying reality which may be deeply unjust. Weber, like Marx, knew that symbols may distort reality, but more than Marx he knew that symbols can change reality, too. For Weber, religious symbols are like the switchmen who change the direction of the railroad tracks at a junction, thus moving the train—history—into this direction or that.

Weber, unlike Marx, however, was interested in the charismatic individual. "Charisma" is one of his ideas that has now become part of the mainstream of Western ideas. The ultimate source for this idea was, of course, the Bible itself. Weber was interested in men such as Jesus of Nazareth and Martin Luther, men who were religious geniuses and changed the course of history through their ideas and the symbols which conveyed the emotional and intellectual power of those ideas. Weber's thesis about the charismatic individual who changes a society can also be applied to such figures as Franklin Roosevelt or Winston Churchill, or even figures in popular culture such as Elvis Presley, Paul McCartney, and John Lennon.

Weber's work also opens up the door to a theological interpretation of how the creator God of the Old and New Testaments works through history, although Weber himself would not take this step. One could suggest or claim or assert that God calls forth charismatic individuals in history, such as the Biblical prophets, and inspires these men and women (artists and musicians, for example) with new ideas and new creations. These ideas and creations then in turn change the course of history and the patterns of meaning within a culture when sufficient numbers of people become influenced, even transformed. Or, stating this in terms of my model for cultural change: once an entire generation internalizes new ideas and new creations offered by charismatic individuals (all of these, even the individuals themselves are condensed over time into symbols and rituals), history then changes, including the culture and the structures of society. In other words, once the same symbols, the same ideas, and the same rituals and artistic creations—indeed, the same people—shape the minds, hearts, and identities of large numbers of people in similar ways, great changes take place in both history and culture. These changes, in turn, influence the psyche in such a way that the libido may be channelled into new directions. Or perhaps the psyches of great numbers of people are stabilized by these changes after a period of time, and then society becomes fairly stable. Whether the libido is channelled into new directions or stabilized by symbols and rituals (such as the Cross, the Eucharist, or Baptism) may account for the "pendulum" effect that some people call the ebb and flow of history.

Weber said something else about ideas and symbols that is highly important. He observed—and history here was his laboratory—that once new ideas and new creations become accepted and established in a society, and once some time has passed, then these ideas and creations often lose their punch. They become stale, and they no longer seem new and fresh, as they once did. They may be thought of by most people as "old-fashioned." In Weber's terminology, they become "routinized." They come to be taken for granted. Then what was new and creative becomes so accepted and "old hat" that no one takes notice anymore. People may become bored with these symbols and ideas, even with the creative, charismatic individuals who originally gave them to us—and they all may eventually die out. Think how rapidly people in the music business or the film industry fade away. Whatever happened to Thomas Wayne? He went to the same high school as Elvis Presley, Humes High in Memphis, and he scored a hit with his recording of the song "Tragedy" in 1959, a haunting song many in my generation danced to, cheek to cheek (a song made more eerie by the deaths in a plane crash in Iowa of Buddy Holly, the Big Bopper, and Ritchie Valens soon after the song's release). Or, whatever happened to the Fleetwoods? They had numerous hits such as their own early-Sixties version of "Tragedy," and other silky smooth recordings such as "Mr. Blue," "Come Softly to Me," "The Great Imposter," "Lovers by Day, Strangers by Night," "Runaround," and "Outside My Window"—all classic "makeout songs" during the Sixties Generation's youth. Most popular songs and most of their creators drift in an out of consciousness like wind-swept clouds on the fading sky of an autumn afternoon.

In the case of a religious culture undergoing secularization, Weber uses the graphic term "disenchanted" for its spiritual decline. What he means is that something is lost in a secular culture; there is then a sense of mourning, even depression, that seeps into a society in reaction to the erosion of tradition. Most likely there is also a lot of nostalgia for the way things once were, or were believed to have been. In other words, secularization may usher into a culture a feeling of sadness, a longing for some lost "golden age," which may be reinforced by the nostalgia people commonly feel for their own childhood and adolescence. Disenchantment in this Weberian sense has, for example, been the experience of many Native Americans. I saw it myself among the Arapaho during my church work on the Wind River Indian Reservation in Wyoming.

Now let's join my model of cultural change to the idea of revolt, since it is particularly pertinent to the Sixties. The ideas and creations of charismatic individuals are often energized, both in the creator and in those they influence, by revolt against or judgment upon previous conditions, attitudes, and traditions. Moreover, the emotion of anger often provides much of the power or "fuel" for the "new message," or the new way of looking at things, including the new symbols and creations which convey it. Some of this anger may be oedipally driven. The innovative rock group the Doors (featuring their inimitable lead singer, Jim Morrison) exemplifies this. Listen to their song, "The End," with its oedipal rage and fantasies of incest. (Beginning with their 1967 hit, "Light My Fire," one of the anthems of my generation, the Doors had a tremendous influence on the music of the Sixties and well beyond.) Or the anger may originate from deeper psychological roots in the preoedipal period of development, when fears of loss, separation, and abandonment dominate. These fears are powerful themes in Woody Allen's movies, for example, although the anger in his movies—and the fears—often have a thick veneer of humor, which then appears to act as a defense against powerful feelings, such as longings for security and intimacy. Allen's preoedipal themes are most visible in his portrayals of the feelings of men towards women. These men are usually insecure in their relationships; they are fearful of loss, and become traumatized when it occurs. But Allen also pokes fun at the Oedipus complex, with all of its confusion, rage, and turmoil. He does this especially well when he films relationships between fathers and sons. Allen obviously knows his Freud, whose name and ideas often pop up in his movies. And he obviously knows the subtle Jewish nuances in psychoanalysis, many of which he must have experienced in his own Jewish upbringing.

Whatever may be the psychological origin of the emotion and high level of creativity in the great originator of new ideas and new artistic forms, their revolutionary message changes history when they tap the feelings (a similar rage and longing, for instance, or even a similar current of creativity when an artist or musician is the originator of a movement) of an entire generation—and they, in turn, also revolt. This revolt, of course, may be constructive or destructive, creative or stultifying, lasting or ephemeral. The Sixties were a mixture of all of these. Here once again we could make a theological interpretation: God works through history using the rage and creativity of individuals to change the course of history. The responses of the Biblical prophets to social injustice and idolatry provide ample illustrations.

Something else often happens in this scenario of revolt. The emotions fueling the revolt may eventually die out, or the ideas which marked the revolt may become socially accepted. They become "routinized," to use Weber's term once again. These ideas are then buried in history, encrusted with layer upon layer of cultural stagnation. But then something happens. Ideas long given up as dead and buried suddenly find new life; they are resurrected by a St. Paul, a Martin Luther, a John Wesley, or the genius of a Jesus, a Buddha or Mohammed, or that of a Lennon and McCartney in the realm of popular culture. Ideas are revived—whether we are considering religious ideas, musical or artistic ideas, or philosophical and political ideas—and they are then given a fresh interpretation by another creative individual, perhaps living in a different age. As a result, another powerful movement begins in a society.

To illustrate my theory of cultural change, in the next chapter I will take a charismatic figure from the field of popular music, one who had a tremendous influence not only upon American society in general, but especially upon the Baby Boomers. We will turn from religion to popular culture and examine Elvis Presley. I am not pointing to him to illustrate the theological aspects of my theory, although I believe God works through creative people in popular culture. Anyone who believes that God works through history (arguably the Bible's central tenet) must be open to that possibility. Here, however, I want to concentrate on the social and psychological ideas I have presented. With Elvis we will see that symbols, especially symbols working in conjunction with a charismatic figure who exuded revolt and sexuality, reveal one place where psychology and sociology meet and coalesce—explosively.

Notes

1. Sigmund Freud, *Three Essays on the Theory of Sexuality*, in *The Standard Edition of the Complete Psychological Works of Sigmund Freud*, edited by James Strachey (London: The Hogarth Press, 1953), 7:207. See also 11:179–190 for his most complete discussion of the topic.

2. See my book, *Freud, Religion, and the Roaring Twenties* (A Psychoanalytic Theory of Secularization in Three Novelists: Sherwood Anderson, Ernest Hemingway, and F. Scott Fitzgerald), (Savage, Maryland: Rowman & Littlefield Publishers, Inc., 1990).

3. Ibid., pp. 223–231.

4. George Rosen, *Madness in Society* (Chicago and London: The University of Chicago Press, 1968), p. 261.

5. Sandor Ferenczi, *Further Contributions to the Theory and Technique of Psycho-analysis* (New York: Brunner/Mazel, Publishers, 1926), p. 25.

6. Ibid.

7. Marx wrote: "Religious suffering is at the same time an expression of real suffering and a protest against real suffering. Religion is the sigh of the oppressed creature, the heart of a heartless world, and the soul of soulless conditions." "Contribution to the Critique of Hegel's Philosophy of Right, Introduction," *Karl Marx: Early Writings*, trans. T. B. Bottomore, (New York: McGraw-Hill, 1964), pp. 43–44.

8. Fred Weinstein and Gerald M. Platt, *The Wish to be Free* (Berkeley: University of California Press, 1969), p. 179.

9. Michel Foucault, *Mental Illness and Psychology* (New York: Harper & Row, Publishers, 1954), p. 84.

10. Christopher Lasch, *The Culture of Narcissism* (New York: Warner Books, Inc., 1979), pp. 87–89.

11. Heinz Kohut, *The Analysis of the Self* (New York: International Universities Press, Inc., 1971), pp. 1–34.

12. Freud, "On Narcissism: An Introduction," in *The Standard Edition*, 14:93.

13. Idema, *Freud, Religion, and the Roaring Twenties*, pp. 83–86.

14. Kohut, *The Analysis of the Self*, pp. 19–20. Kohut defines "self- objects" as "objects which are themselves experienced as part of the self " (p. xiv).

15. In the preface to *The Analysis of the Self*, Kohut writes, "This study concentrates almost exclusively on the role of the libidinal forces in the analysis of narcissistic personalities," p. xv.

16. Freud, *Group Psychology and the Analysis of the Ego*, in *The Standard Edition*, 18:90.

17. Freud, *Three Essays on the Theory of Sexuality*, ibid., 7:217–218.

18. One definition of "spiritual" that is helpful here is the union of power and meaning. The power comes from our emotions, and the meaning comes from our religious and moral values.

19. See Idema, *Freud, Religion, and the Roaring Twenties*, pp. 13-35, for a fully developed psychoanalytic theory of religion.

20. Ferenczi, *Further Contributions to the Theory and Technique of Psycho-Analysis*, p. 377.

21. Freud, *Group Psychology and the Analysis of the Ego*, in *The Standard Edition*, 18:102.

22. Ibid., p. 103.

23. Freud, "On the Universal Tendency to Debasement in the Sphere of Love," ibid., 11:181.

24. Erik Erikson, *Childhood and Society* (New York: W.W. Norton & Company, Inc., 1963), p. 250.

25. Romain Rolland, *The Life of Ramakrishna* (Calcutta, India: Adaita Ashrama, 1984), pp. 13–14.

26. Erikson, *Childhood and Society*, pp. 261–262.

27. Ibid., p. 282.

28. See Idema, *Freud, Religion, and the Roaring Twenties*, pp. 27–29.

29. Ibid., pp. 7–68.

Chapter II

Elvis Presley and Popular Culture

Elvis and the Music of the 1950s

When Elvis Presley first burst into American culture in 1955 and 1956, his music and aura were revolutionary, needless to say—at least to anyone then under thirty! His purple shirts and pink Cadillacs, his songs such as "Reddy Teddy," "Long Tall Sally" and "Trying to Get to You," with their driving beat and energy, his rolled-up sleeves, turned-up collar, sideburns, and ducktail outraged, and then threatened, the older generations. When Elvis made his final appearance on "The Ed Sullivan Show," the cameraman would not even show him below the waist because of his gyrations, something else the older generations didn't like. Our parents had fears of our libido running amuck, with perhaps some justification! The libido of the younger generations was indeed stirred to a fever pitch by his music—in spite of the best efforts of the older generations to suppress Elvis and Rock and Roll or to dismiss them as ephemeral. As old film clips of his early live appearances show, he brought crowds to a frenzy. Elvis' persona —compounded of crooked smile and leering lip, open rebellion, alienation from society, vulnerability, loneliness, and a seductive sexuality—captured the imaginations and touched the hearts of the postwar generations like no one else. Our parents had Frank

Sinatra, we had Elvis. Music and testosterone were a powerful combination with Elvis, and, indeed, with his audience (where a heavy dose of estrogen was added to the fire). Elvis' musical roots were early Rock and Roll (e.g., Bill Hayley and the Comets), Gospel, Country and Western (e.g., Hank Williams), Rhythm & Blues, Blue Grass (e.g., Bill Monroe), and the early Fifties Pop music of such singers as Dean Martin and Nat King Cole. Elvis' discoverer, Sam Phillips of Sun Records in Memphis, said that in the early 1950s he was looking for a white man who could sing like a black man, and Elvis fortuitously turned out to be that white man. Elvis brought to his music a voice that could reach the high notes with a falsetto which became a trade mark (listen to "Blue Moon" or "It's Now or Never"). Yet he had an operatic lower range heard in such songs as "Peace in the Valley," "Don't," and "Surrender." I don't know of any other popular singer, then or now, who had the range Elvis had. And, of course, he had that unique phrasing and sound.

At the time Elvis released his first single, "That's All Right," a Southern regional hit in 1954, most radio stations in the country, which were owned by whites, had succumbed to the pressures of a prejudiced society; in their air time they avoided most of the music sung by black Rhythm & Blues artists. White singers would "cover" these black artists' songs, and these were the records that, for the most part, were played on the radio stations. For example, the saccharine Pat Boone covered Fats Domino's "Ain't That a Shame,"and the insipid Crew-Cuts covered the Penguins' "Earth Angel," although to the credit of the teen audience of the Fifties, the Penguins' version sold almost as many 45s as the bland white version without anything like the same amount of radio play. The Crew-Cuts also covered "Sh-Boom" by the Chords in the summer of 1954.

This practice of white singers covering black artists was obviously a social and financial injustice, as well as an artistic and moral one. Little Richard has said that to this day he has not been justly compensated for all the white renditions of his songs, including those by Elvis. Even though, apparently, RCA never gave Little Richard what he considered fair compensation for Elvis' use of his compositions, Elvis did help to rectify this situation by popularizing Rock and Roll—in part through his own cover versions of such songs as Little Richard's "Reddy Teddy," "Long Tall Sally," and "Rip It Up." Elvis popularized Rock and Roll to such an extent that the Baby Boomers developed an intense interest in its musical roots—and those roots were, of course, the very artists then being discriminated against or unjustly compensated (Fats Domino, Chuck Berry, Little Richard, etc.). These singers and composers became the musical heroes of the white kids in the suburbs as well as the black kids in the ghetto.

The burgeoning popularity of Rock and Roll in the Fifties made it virtually impossible to keep on discriminating against such highly talented blacks. The younger generation simply would not stand for it. They wanted to hear the black singers themselves, not just their covers. However insignificant its role may appear to us today, this demand by the youth was one of the ways racial discrimination began to break down in American society. I am hardly claiming that the white youth of the Fifties were not prejudiced; they were, if only because American society was then so segregated. Music, however, along with sports, was one of the "places" blacks and whites began to communicate better with one another.

Elvis affected American society in many ways. Most important, he popularized Rock and Roll. He also ignited the revolt against authority that was already noticeable in the midst of so much conformity. He stirred sexual feeling. He mobilized more and more protests against the still relatively intact "thou shall nots," to the point that Elvis himself became the chief symbol of that protest. This, I think was the true beginning of the "sexual revolution" we now so closely associate with the Sixties. After Elvis, some Americans were freer, more uninhibited in their dress or hair style. Those were some of the ways Elvis affected American life, particularly its Baby Boomer contingent. We did not forget what we had learned from him—especially how to rebel. We also did not forget how we felt when we first heard his music, nor did we ever forget how much we had been changed by him. Elvis symbolized our youth, and perhaps he always will.

Elvis and the Youth of the Sixties Generation

I was nine years old when I first heard Elvis' music in the summer of 1956. I can still remember, almost with the initial excitement, the emotional energy I felt that summer when I originally heard the ground breaking "Heartbreak Hotel," or the romantic ballads, "I Was the One," and "I Want You, I Need You, I Love You." His music sounded so fresh, it felt so vibrant, so alive. The other songs I listened to that summer on the radio were numbers such as Pat Boone's "I Almost Lost My Mind" (another cover, but the best song he ever recorded; except for his later hit, "Moody River," it was the only time the singer, seemingly always smiling, ever touched the dark underbelly of life), Doris Day's "Whatever Will Be, Will Be," Gogi Grant's "The Wayward Wind," and Cathy Carr's "Ivory Tower." These were all good songs, typical of the Pop music of the day, and they are still occasionally heard on the radio. But compared to such ballads, Elvis' music was so different—so erotic, so rebellious. There was something damp and mysterious about his music, something raucous, with a tinge of vulnerability, even violence, which is probably why the "hoods"—who were always hanging around the soda bars in my home town, Grand Rapids, Michigan —identified personally with his music.

As I now look back on that summer of 1956, I can truthfully say that the Weberian word "charisma," which my professors at the University of Chicago so often used in relation to the great religious figures of history, was really invented for Elvis. I don't think too many of my generation would take issue with that, at least for his early years. I spent that summer with my family in a cottage we rented at Ottawa Beach on the sandy shores of Lake Michigan. Ottawa Beach (near Holland, Michigan) is an old resort, with several rows of wonderful gingerbread Victorian cottages that face the lake. In 1956 they were being encroached upon by the nearby state park, nestled up alongside the Holland pier which juts far out into the lake.

In a Michigan summer the soft breezes come off the lake and kiss you gently on the cheek like a lover, unless you are facing one of those sudden Lake Michigan gales, in which case they act like a banshee. 1956 was a summer when I was still caught up in the Davy Crockett fad begun the previous year, and, yes, I had all of his bubble gum cards, a coon skin cap, and I paraded around the cottage with my plastic flintlocks (now probably worth a fortune). It was a summer of spying on "lovers" necking up in the sand dunes, especially Mt. Pisgah that hovers over Lake Macatawa to the south and Lake Michigan to the west. My childhood friends and I, Dan Aument, Dick Alt, and many others I can't remember now, would heave "sand bombs" (sand stuffed into paper bags poked full of holes) over their heads; the sand would drift down upon them from the trails of our projectiles like freshly falling snow. We would then high-tail-it into the grapevine forest to escape our victims' wrath.

In the woods where we played you could still see the tall, stately white pines the Ottawa Indians had trimmed so many years ago (except for the tops) to create excellent watchtowers from which to sight an approaching enemy. These ridged the crests of many of the sand dunes. The summer of 1956 was a summer of Eisenhower tranquility, a summer of walking through the shimmering beach grass and feeling the sand between your toes. It was a summer of watching royal purple and red sunsets splashed like freshly stirred paint onto the sky dome enclosing Lake Michigan. It was a summer of our innocent youth.

Elvis Presley stirred something in my nine-year-old soul that summer. Even then I felt something was in the air, an intimation of change. I knew that something was coming; I knew that at nine, and I think we all knew it, if not quite then, then soon after. Almost literally, Elvis symbolized what was coming, even if we didn't know exactly what it was. But we knew it would be exciting, and we looked forward to it with anticipation. The Baby Boomers wanted to be part of what was whispering to us in the wind and we were—some ten years later when the world changed.

Elvis himself was not one of the Baby Boomers, but he belonged to us. We took him over for ourselves, and we bought the majority of his records, many even before we were officially classified as "teenagers." During that summer of 1956, my friends and I would spend many an afternoon "hanging out" at the local soda bar on Lake Macatawa, playing pool and drinking chocolate sodas or root beer floats, and chewing wads of grape bubble gum. As we did all of that, we would put our nickels in the juke box and listen to Elvis. And the "real" teenagers would then dance on a pock-marked wood floor in this long forgotten soda bar, near where the old Ottawa Beach Hotel once stood before it burned to the ground early in the century.

That soda bar is gone now, too, torn down many years ago, leaving only ghosts of summers past. All that is left are the memories, and the echoes of plaintive music drifting over the lake amidst the laughter of youth and the tinkling of glasses and the thud of Cokes rolling out of pop machines. I can still picture those teenagers dancing to Elvis—glorying in their white pants and white bucks and pink shirts, with their collars turned up in back, their cigarettes rolled up in their shirt sleeves, and their greasy hair slicked back into a ducktail with the help of Wild Root. The girls had breathtakingly tight plaid skirts and sweaters, and their ponytails swung sensuously as they danced. When the later afternoon summer sun turned the lake to silver and gold, those kids would pile into their 1956 Chevys, Corvettes, and Fords and blast off with their radios blaring some haunting melody of that summer . . . "hold me close, hold me tight, make me thrill with delight" . . . we stood there looking down the road, wishing we were older. Waiting for our time to come.

Music and Identity

To sum up, in 1955 and 1956 and well beyond, Elvis challenged not only musical conventions in America, but cultural ones as well. After Elvis, we all expressed our rebellious feelings a bit more, and many of us were less "uptight." Elvis' ostentatious Cadillacs and Lincolns challenged conservative tastes. Sexuality was more openly paraded. Elvis symbolized the revolt against authority—a revolt which would have such far-reaching consequences in the Sixties. It was his music, however, which had the most lasting influence on popular culture, an influence that still remains strong.

Both Elvis and his music were given an almost religious blessing by Ed Sullivan, one of American culture's "father figures" in the 1950s (or, if he was not that, he was at least a high priest of making or breaking the careers of show business talent). Although Sullivan played on his image of being a "square," he was in reality a very shrewd judge of talent. Most important, he was a daring television executive. Sullivan showcased Elvis before he was mainstreamed, and he did the same thing later on with the Beatles. When Elvis appeared on television before millions on "The Ed Sullivan Show," the host said that Elvis was "a real decent fine boy," and that he had been a delight to work with. He implied that Elvis did not have a "big ego," like some other big name stars; that he was humble and polite, an aspect of Elvis' image carefully cultivated by Colonel Tom Parker, his manager.

By that time, the younger generations were already identifying with Elvis, but Sullivan's "blessing" gave Elvis, if not a religious sanctity, at least a legitimacy within American culture he hadn't had before, evidenced by many a snowy Christmas morning with Elvis albums lying under the tree. Moreover, Sullivan made it a whole lot easier to openly identify with Elvis in suburban households, although I went too far in testing that acceptance when one school morning I arrived at the breakfast table with my hair slicked back into a ducktail. My father promptly ordered me back to the upstairs bathroom for another, more traditional hair style (for a year he had urged me to get a "Princeton" at the barber shop). But that didn't stop me from trying again. I waited until I got to school, and in the secrecy of the bathroom, I proceeded to comb my hair once more in the style of my youthful hero—except that I used Vicks VapoRub for the grease supply. When I entered my classroom at Wealthy Street Elementary School in East Grand Rapids, my classmates began to sniff the air. And then, to my horror, they started yelling, "Who smells? Who smells?" I wanted to crawl under my desk, but that humiliation didn't dampen my identification with Elvis and the rebellion he embodied.

If the music of our adolescence remains our favorite music through the life cycle—which I think is true—then maybe this explains why Elvis continues to symbolize something the Sixties Generation once felt, feels no longer, but longs to feel again. Maybe it is a hayride on a winter day, along with the hot dogs, hot chocolate, and dancing afterwards that an old Elvis song recalls for us, or the spring dance when we had our first date. Music is so important to us when we are growing up because we are trying to establish an identity for life, and we temporarily identify with music—its rhythms, its musicians, composers, and singers, and its message and melodies. *Music was how we marked and measured time.* Here is a "Top 40" chart (May 24, 1958) put out by a Grand Rapids radio station, WMAX. What memories are stirred up for you? (Notice the mixture of music in the 1950s— Pop and Rock, and slop!)

Chart I — WMAX Top 40 — May 24, 1958*

No.	Title	Artist
1	All I Have to do is Dream	Everly Bros.
2	Return to Me	Dean Martin
3	Twilight Time	Platters
4	He's Got the Whole World in His Hands	Laurie London
5	Witchdoctor	David Seville
6	Chason D'Amour	Art & Dotty Todd
7	Big Man	Four Preps
8	Secretly	Jimmie Rogers
9	Book of Love	Monotones
10	Looking Back	Nat King Cole
11	Let the Bells Keep Ringing	Paul Anka
12	Oh Lonesome Me	Don Gibson
13	Sugar Moon	Pat Boone
14	Kewpie Doll	Perry Como

No.	Title	Artist
15	March fron the River Kwai	Mitch Miller
16	Rave On	Buddy Holly
17	Zorro	Cordettes
18	Jennie Lee	Jan & Arnie
19	Johnny B. Goode	Chuck Berry
20	Flip, Flop and Bop	Floyd Cramer
21	Wear My Ring Around Your Neck	Elvis Presley
22	Endless Sleep	Gene Ross
23	Stairway of Love	Marty Robbins
24	Billy	Kathy Lindin
25	Lollipop	Cordettes
26	Walkin' the Low Road	Randy Sparks
27	Little Train	Vassel & Storz
28	Purple People Eater	Sheb Wooley
29	Believe What You Say	Ricky Nelson
30	El Rancho Rock	The Champs
31	Teacher Teacher	Johnny Mathis
32	Rumble	Link Wray
33	Yakety Yak	The Coasters
34	What am I Living For?	Chuck Willis
35	Cha-Hua-Hua	The Pets
36	Little Pig	Dale Hawkins
37	For Your Precious Love	Jerry Butler
38	Road Runner	Gus Jenkins
39	You'd Be Surprised	Kathy Lindin
40	Torero	Andrew Sisters

*All charts are reproduced as originally published.

At the same time the adolescent is trying to establish an identity, the body is rapidly maturing. Hormones are flowing through the blood, making it hot, and affecting the emotions. Sexual desires are about as intense as they will ever be. A girl's breasts are blossoming, and boys start to prowl around the hallways of school like young tom cats. Romance begins to be highly important, a romance inspired by the sublimation of libido.

During the Sixties Generation's adolescent years, sexual feelings were not permitted much range of expression, certainly not beyond the kissing stage, what we then called "first base." Some of us tried to steal "second," but the prohibitions against "third" and "fourth" base—real sex—were still very much in force when we were "maturing" in the early Sixties. These prohibitions were reinforced by the Church, reinforced by society, and reinforced by our parents. Sexual feelings were further complicated by the fear of pregnancy, which readers who only know life *after* the pill must strive to appreciate if they want to understand us. The terror we felt was very real, adding to our frustrations, and it was those very fears and frustrations which made the pill so revolutionary later on. (Sexuality in recent times, of course, has been further complicated by the advent of the disease AIDS.)

Not too long ago I held a discussion about sexuality in my present church, where one of my parishioners, a member of the Tommy Dorsey generation, commented to me: "Today's generation has sex without guilt, your generation had sex with guilt, and my generation had guilt without the sex!" There is an important kernel of truth in that observation, although I think many of my generation also fell into the third camp. Whatever the case, the role of religion and morality in sexuality will get fuller attention later. But here I want to develop the following hypothesis: music, as much as anything else, shaped the emotional identity of the Sixties Generation during an adolescence which sexuality made so confusing, and yet so exhilarating. I am now going to be looking back on what it felt like to grow up in the late Fifties and early Sixties. As we do that, let us remember that "identity" channels the libido.

I will begin by mentioning a phenomenon that has just about disappeared, the Hit Parade, or the "Top 40," or the "Top 100," or whatever the format was in your home town for playing the popular music of the day on the radio.[1] Many AM radio stations in the '50s and '60s kept track of which 45s were selling best in the local record stores.[2] The Sixties Generation went through high school spending many an evening "cruising"[3] around town at night while listening to this popular music on the radio. The boys, who were piled into one car, would fantasize about the girls, who in turn were driving around in another car, thinking about the boys. And all of those cars were listening to the same songs on the same radio stations as they cruised through town. The music we listened to was intensified, emotionally, by all of that pent-up sexual desire we then were feeling but could not satisfy. This "dammed up" desire, to use Freud's word, created a highly romantic mood during those magical nights, such as after a football game with the smell of burning leaves in the air, and the trees which lined the roads looking ghostly in the smoke.

All of this pent-up sexual desire also created an appetite for greasy hamburgers and french fries. So the local drive-in was the ultimate destination for all our cruising. The lights from the Dog 'n' Suds, the Big Boy, or McDonald's would reflect off the shiny cars pulling in and out, or passing by. Songs such as the Dell-Vikings' "Come Go With Me," Sonny James' "Young Love," "Born Too Late" by the Ponytails, or "Misery" by the Dynamics mingled in the night air with orders for malts, burgers, and fries blaring on the loud speakers near your car. When you pulled into one of those places, you could immediately hear the grease sizzling and smell the burgers frying. In Grand Rapids, it was a little joint called the Glass Hut on the corner of Michigan and Fuller where we all ended up on a Saturday night for 15 cent "greaseburgers." There I witnessed many a fight between "warriors" from my high school, East Grand Rapids, and those from Catholic Central. Fights at the drive-in were as much part of the early Sixties as worries about "zits" and cars with glasspacks.

One of my best high school friends, Dave Hardy, used to borrow his father's 1964 Grand Prix for our Saturday night cruising. It was one of the classiest cars around town, with a 421 (a 421 cubic inch engine) and three two-barrels (carburetors), delivering 370 horsepower. It was navy blue with wire wheels, and it had one of those reverb radios (no tape decks back then). When he would floor it, the engine would whine, and then that accelerating Pontiac would jerk our heads back into the seats as if we had been shot with a gun. We would all hold on for dear life as it howled down the street. We could outrun just about everybody in high school—including the police, as we found out one harrowing night. This car, and the hopeful passengers, drew girls like flies to honey.[4]

Cars, cruising, McDonald's, greasy diners with greasy french fries covered with mounds of catsup, as well as blaring radios playing melodic songs—these were some of the things the Sixties Generation grew up with. They affected us emotionally, and unless you lived through that romantic and relatively innocent era—when cars could still be recognized for their year and make (everybody knew what a '57 Chevy looked like, for instance, or a '62 Pontiac), and everybody (including our parents) listened to the same songs, and hamburgers were still 15 cents at McDonald's, or 35 cents at a diner—you might not know what I am talking about. As the Sixties Generation now looks back, it is the music that reminds us of that old girlfriend or boyfriend, a summer dance, or an all night beach party at Lake Michigan on Labor Day weekend.

To make my point in somewhat different fashion let me ask, what do you remember when you gaze over the "Top Ten" from these old hit parade charts compiled by WGRD and WLAV in Grand Rapids?

Chart II — WGRD's Fabulous "50" — March 30, 1962

No.	Title	Artist
1	Good Luck Charm	Elvis Presley
2	Nutrocker	B. Bumble
3	Johnny Angel	Shelley Fabares
4	I Can't Say Goodbye	Bobby Vee
5	Come Back Silly Girl	Lettermen
6	Twistin' The Night Away	Sam Cooke
7	Charlie's Shoes	Billy Walker
8	Dream Baby	Roy Orbison
9	Love Letters	Ketty Lester
10	Ballad Of Thunder Road	Robert Mitchum

Chart III — WGRD's Fabulous "50" — February 15, 1963

No.	Title	Artist
1	Ruby Baby	Dion
2	Hey Paula	Paul & Paula
3	Walk Like A Man	Four Seasons
4	Rhythm Of The Rain	Cascades
5	Little Town Flirt	Del Shannon
6	From A Jack To A King	Ned Miller
7	It's Up To You	Ricky Nelson
8	I Saw Linda Yesterday	Dickie Lee
9	Up On The Roof	Drifters
10	Java	Floyd Cramer

Chart IV — WGRD's Fabulous "50" — December 13, 1963

No.	Title	Artist
1	Popcicles and Icicles	Murmaids
2	Louie Louie	The Kingsmen
3	Dominique	Singing Nun
4	Be True To Your School/ In My Room	Beachboys
5	There I've Said It Again	Bobby Vinton
6	Drip Drop	Dion
7	She's A Fool	Leslie Gore
8	Hey Little Cobra	Ripchords
9	Talk Back Trembling Lips	Johnny Tillotson
10	Hey Little Girl	Major Lance

Chart V — WGRD's Fabulous "50" — January 31, 1964

No.	Title	Artist
1	She Loves You	The Beatles
2	I Want To Hold Your Hand	The Beatles
3	You Don't Own Me	Lesley Gore
4	UM-6	Major Lance
5	Anyone Who Had A Heart	Dionne Warwick
6	Out Of Limits	The Markets
7	For You	Rick Nelson
8	There I've Said It Again	Bobby Vinton
9	The Nitty Gritty	Shirley Ellis
10	A Fool Never Learns	Andy Williams

Chart VI — WLAV FAVORITE 40 — June 24, 1965

No.	Title	Artist
1	Mr. Tambourine Man	The Byrds
2	I Can't Help Myself	The 4 Tops
3	Crying In The Chapel	Elvis Presley
4	New Orleans	Eddie Hodges
5	Seventh Son	Johnny Rivers
6	I Can't Get No Satisfaction	Rolling Stones
7	What The World Needs Now Is Love	Jackie De Shannon
8	You Turn Me On	Ian Whitcomb
9	Darling Take Me Back I'm Sorry	Lenny Welch
10	Wonderful World	Herman's Hermits

Our course, I can't know what thoughts and emotions these names and titles evoke (if they evoke anything) for each individual reader. In a sense, the richer the associations, the better—the more we have to work with. It is time to bring the libido theory once again into the discussion. The emotions and biological drives of the Sixties Generation were creating havoc. Nature put us into a double bind: we all felt deep sexual longings, but our society and our religion and our parents all combined to say, resoundingly, "NO!" All those feelings, urges, hopes, and fantasies, created by the demands of the libido, were "dammed up." The ensuing emotional pressures led us to ask of society, religion, and our parents, "What about our feelings, what about our desires, what about our dreams, what are we supposed to do with them?" Society answered with a profound silence, religion answered with a profound silence, and our parents . . . well, we wish *they* had answered with a profound silence! In short, the *sensual current* of the libido was blocked, but the *affectionate current* was given free rein. We were permitted to feel, and feel deeply, we just were not permitted to act on those feelings (to any great extent anyway). My generation—with all of that sublimated libido—became intensely romantic. We remain so at heart, and it is that romanticism which now fuels our nostalgia.

One of my high school friends had an evening ritual. He would listen to songs, such as the Lettermen's "When I Fall in Love," Lenny Welch's "Since I Fell For You," or Dick and Deedee's "Tell Me," late at night in his bedroom. And he would sit there and thumb through his yearbook, dreaming of this girl or that. He finally wore that yearbook out. His emotional "stock market" was up or down depending on his plans for Saturday night. That is almost a parable of the era. Those of my generation who did act on their sexual desires and "went all the way," as we used to put it (usually in the locker room), felt so much guilt and fear they didn't enjoy it anyway. At least that is what they told us. Biology is cruel and the conscience is harsh!

Music was our outlet. It was the music of the era which expressed our longings and frustrations, songs such as Roy Orbison's "Only the Lonely," "Blue Angel," "Running Scared," "In Dreams," and "Crying." Music captured the moral and psychological dilemmas we felt trapped in, songs such as Gene Pitney's "Town Without Pity," "It Hurts to be in Love," or "True Love Never Runs Smooth." Music caught our fears, fears about betrayal, fears about the way we looked or whether we were popular in school. Music expressed our guilt, and fueled romantic fantasies about this particular boy or girl. Remember Paul Anka's "You Are My Destiny," or "Lonely Boy"? They were overblown, to be sure, but they spoke to us at the time. Music expressed what we were feeling about our parents, our boyfriends or girlfriends, or what we were feeling about our school, or our society. Music was our guru and psychiatrist and religious counselor wrapped up into one. So we latched onto the advice and psychological truisms offered by songs, such as Ral Donner's "You Don't Know What You've Got Until You Lose It." Music was pop psychology before there was pop psychology. Music made our dates memorable, or marked a season in a particular year. Nor should we ever forget (how could we?) that music eroticized "making out"... "You've gone from me, oh tragedy."

Perhaps more than anything else, music conveys the passing of the years, and it transports us, psychologically, far back in time. Bobby Vee's "Take Good Care of My Baby," Troy Shondell's "This Time," and Dick and Deedee's "The Mountain's High" are recordings that will forever evoke for me the summer of 1961; back then I was at YMCA camp in upper Michigan, Camp Hayowent-ha on Torch Lake, a lake colored in ten shades of blue on a bright sunny day. And the Rolling Stones' "Satisfaction" will always remind me of the summer of 1965, and of the dances called "Beach Bashes" at the Grand Haven Roller Rink; there hundreds of beautifully tanned teenagers would migrate off the beaches of Lake Michigan on a Saturday night, and then stare at each other in huge rotating circles while mustering up the courage to ask someone to dance. Jimmy Ruffin's "What Becomes of the Brokenhearted" still takes me back to the fall of 1966 when I was going through Hell Week in my fraternity, and the Four Tops' "Reach Out, I'll be There" does the same thing. Similarly, the Mamas and the Papas' "California Dreamin'" and "Got a Feelin'" still resurrect the winter of 1966, when we were required as fraternity pledges to clean up after the Friday night beer parties in the house basement (called "TGs"—"Thank goodness its Friday"). That was our regular Saturday morning chore that bleak winter, and the smell of all that stale beer nearly made all of us sick, especially if we had indulged ourselves the night before. If an active member felt surly that particular morning—read "hungover"—he would roll empty beer kegs at us while we mopped the floors or scrubbed out the overflowing urinals, and we would scatter in all directions like cockroaches when those kegs came rumbling down upon us. I am sure you can supply similar examples from your own storehouse of memories, at least if you were born sometime during the '40s or '50s. Certain songs will forever remind the Sixties Generation of a memorable dance or party in the fall or winter, perhaps a time when the snow was blowing violently in your face, or a time when the leaves were falling gently from trees of myriad colors and you were with a very special person. Often the events we remember through music stir up pain or regret, sadness or longing. A song might remind us of a time we received flowers, or were kissed passionately for the first time, standing on the doorsteps of your house while the rest of the family was asleep. Songs remind us of friends we have lost trace of, or friends who have died—in Vietnam perhaps. One such friend of mine was Alan Groom, a fraternity brother who was drafted out of the University of Minnesota Law School and was then killed in Vietnam . . . "The sun ain't gonna shine anymore . . . ." Music is indeed a powerful force among the Sixties Generation.

One can't even begin to interpret the Sixties without considering the psychological and social effects of all that pent-up emotion, longing, and suppressed sexual desire which, before Vietnam became a true war in 1966, created an era and a genre of popular music that truly can only be described as romantic. My generation continues to long for that era and the romantic feelings which Vietnam (and all that happened in the culture along with it) took from us. Our nostalgia and regret—indeed our rage at Vietnam and perhaps at the Sixties in general—are intertwined in our collective psyche with one basic feeling: *we were deprived of something important before we were ready to give it up.*

Perhaps it was our innocence we most regretted losing, although we did have to grow up, I guess, and God knows, we needed a swift kick in the pants. All of that pent-up emotion from the early Sixties, and then our longing in the late Sixties for the romance and innocence of an earlier era, are important dynamics in the decade's explosion. It was when Vietnam heated up that all of the pent-up emotion and suppressed sexual desire burst like a bomb, because it was a bomb, a psychological bomb, waiting to go off. And it did—when we were threatened. But that jumps us ahead in our story. So for now I want to simply point to two songs which graphically illustrate better than a thousand words the transition from one era to another, from the innocence and romance of the pre-Vietnam years to the cultural revolution that soon followed. In 1964 the Beatles' recording of "I Want to Hold Your Hand" became a #1 hit. Then not too much later the Rolling Stones recorded a song called "Let's Spend the Night Together" (which they had to change to "Let's Spend Some Time Together" when they appeared on "The Ed Sullivan Show"). These two songs—and the short time which passed between their releases—show quite clearly the rapidity of the changes that were occurring in American society. We went from an age of innocence to an age that was anything but that, let's call it an age of tumult or turmoil. Certainly without those dramatic changes, that song by the Rolling Stones, or others such as the Doors' "Light My Fire," would not have been possible. They would have been censored in an earlier era, even if they had been conceived. We gained some things when America changed—but we also lost other things, a great deal in fact.

There exists today a lingering sense of regret among the Sixties Generation, a sense that "I would have done some things differently." There is also the nostalgic, "I wish I could go back." We miss the emotional intensity of the late Sixties, but we also miss the romance and innocence of the early Sixties.

In sum, when we were growing up we sang to the songs on the radio; when David Ruffin and the Temptations sang "My Girl" or "Ain't Too Proud to Beg," we sang along with them. We sang along with them in our cars, and we sang along with them in our showers before our dates (teenagers today tell me that they don't date, they go out in groups; if that is true, I wonder what songs they sing before going out with a group). We especially sang along with the Temptations and the Four Tops when we were dancing; we would pretend that we, too, held a mike in our hands while we imitated their syncopated dancing. As we grew up, we unconsciously identified each stage of our development with the popular songs of the day, and then the popular albums when that format became the rage among the Sixties Generation, albums such as *Rubber Soul* by the Beatles. That album is still connected in my mind with the Christmas of 1966, a time when my friends and I made a snowy drive home from Ann Arbor for a vacation filled with rounds of parties. The Beatles were never better than they were on that album. We also identified with the singers who gave us the songs that marked and measured the time of our lives, Elvis first of all, and then those who followed him.

No doubt the role of music in identity formation has always been important. No doubt every generation searches for and then discovers its own music that "tells the story" of what it is going through, music that sets it apart from its parents' generation. No doubt each generation mixes its hormones and works out its own Oedipus complex with the help of the popular songs of the day. Every generation searches for meaning through its own music.

My parents had Glenn Miller's "Don't Sit Under the Apple Tree," and we had Elvis' "Don't Be Cruel." It is not necessarily true that songs from one era are better than songs from another, although parents always think their music is better than that of their children, including this writer (and parent). It is just that Elvis' songs were our songs, at least until Motown and the Beatles and the Rolling Stones came along (themselves heavily indebted to Elvis). When we were young, however, Elvis was ours.

But something happened to Elvis along the way, something which illustrates the other half of my theory of cultural change. He was domesticated. His music was imitated by Ral Donner, Terry Stafford, and a host of others. The revolutionary things Elvis had symbolized became an accepted part of American culture. Elvis was "mainstreamed." Today many truck drivers have sideburns and sometimes have ducktails or shoulder length hair, and nobody notices or cares. Even business executives had sideburns in the early Seventies. Elvis was emulated by the mass culture, a mass culture he was instrumental in shaping. Then Elvis got fat, he used pills, he had affairs, he was mismanaged, and he starred in all those horrible movies with all of those horrible songs, few of which are memorable. By 1964, when the Beatles and the other English groups invaded American soil in force, Elvis was maybe not dead and buried, but close to it. He had become "routinized." He had become a parody of himself, even in his comeback in the late Sixties, and especially during the early Seventies when he performed in Las Vegas in those awful jump suits which never fit him quite right.

In sum, by the late Sixties Elvis had been domesticated, and assimilated. He had lost his power as a symbol—at least for most Americans. There were always all of those fat women who never quite gave up on him or forgot him—but almost everyone else did, especially the Baby Boomers. What Elvis had represented—cultural revolt, palpable sexuality, Rock and Roll, rebellion, garish fashion and outlandish hair styles—simply entered into the mainstream of American mass culture. America seemed to pass him by. Elvis from 1964 on seemed out of touch. And then the Beatles, the Doors, and the groups from Motown, along with countless others, entered into the American youth consciousness. By that point, Elvis seemed more and more out of touch. (Some readers may even be surprised at the cultural significance I have given him.) The Sixties Generation entered their late adolescence with a whole new set of heroes. The ducktail and sideburns had lost the sense of rebellion they once expressed. Stockbrokers and businessmen sporting long hair and sideburns illustrate in the simplest possible terms what I mean by "routinization." Elvis' records after 1962 or 1963 never had the spark or the explosive power of his first few albums, especially *Elvis*, his second album and his first recorded solely at RCA; it had that wonderful profile of Elvis on the cover, with his stripped purple shirt and slicked back hair and sideburns. And the music was wonderful. Listen to that album—and such songs as "Love Me" and "So Glad You're Mine"—if you want to hear the real Elvis.

I think most of my generation wished he had stayed as he was in those first few years of his career. He didn't; but, then, neither did we. He was never better, and we were going to get a whole lot worse. To that I now turn.

Notes

1. MTV put the final nail in the coffin of the "hit parade" as a widely played format on AM radio; but well before its advent Rock and Roll had become exhausted, having run out of talent and original ideas. In the Fifties and Sixties even my parents knew what the popular songs of the day were. In the Eighties and Nineties, Rock and Roll has been fragmented into competing styles, such as "heavy metal." Most of the Sixties Generation now neglect popular music, preferring "oldies," jazz, and classical music.

2. Now even 45s are disappearing, along with the local shops that sold them. The CD and cassette have replaced the 45, and that small record with the doughnut hole in the middle, which the Baby Boomers grew up with, is going the way of our parents' 78s.

3. Probably cruising was more of a phenomenon in small and mid-size towns than in cities like Chicago. The movie *American Graffiti* captured the flavor and excitement of this weekend pastime.

4. If you want a simple explanation for the demise of the American auto industry, compare the design of a 1964 Grand Prix with a new one. American cars have lost the flair for styling. Makes and production years have also seem to have lost their distinctiveness.

Chapter III

The Revolt Against Tradition

Religion and the Sixties Generation: an Hypothesis

We are now prepared to examine the heart of my theory of the Sixties. We will be considering the role of tradition, particularly institutional religion, for the Sixties Generation. I will be focusing upon our religious upbringing, paying special attention to some of the reasons religion failed so many during the Vietnam years. Conversely, I will also be asking why so many members of the Sixties Generation failed their traditions. My broad hypothesis is this: *organized religion in American society failed to curb the narcissism of the Sixties Generation.* (I am especially concerned with mainline Christianity and the Episcopal Church in particular, because that is what I know best, but I do not exclude other traditions from my argument.)

Of course, a certain amount of narcissism is part of the "normal" psychological constitution of every human being in every era, but the Vietnam War and other traumas—working in conjunction with serious institutional weaknesses of the Church—played crucial roles in accentuating, or unleashing, more narcissism than was healthy for either individuals or society. In other words, *a healthy balance between self-love and object-love— traditionally achieved with the help of religion—was lacking for many.* Consequently, narcissism became a serious moral, psychological, and social problem in American culture, a problem that still has us reeling. I am not arguing that the experience of the Sixties Generation was necessarily unique—other generations have also been threatened by traumas—*what was unique* was the fact that the largest generation in American history went through the same traumas at the same time, and reacted to them in similar ways. It was the sheer size of my generation, and the nature of its shared experience, which had such far-reaching consequences for American culture.

For the remainder of Part I of this book I will be offering a series of theoretical positions about the role of tradition in my generation. I am not trying to verify these positions "scientifically." On the other hand, I am supplying a range of data to fill out my arguments, and I am drawing upon my own personal experience as well.

I travelled through those turbulent years with a large circle of friends. Even back then we reflected upon the meaning of our experience. In a way, we were like the ancient Jews, always wanting to know the meaning of our history. For the Jews, it was their myths, rituals, symbols, and stories—i.e., their traditions—which supplied that meaning. My generation lacked this strong religious identity. We lacked a tradition through which to view, and then interpret, our experience (although we found some substitutes). But, we did tell our stories to each other, stories of what we were going through, in the effort to make some sense of life. During the Sixties, many a late night "bull session" over pizza and beer was devoted to precisely that. My friends and I knew, even then, that what we were experiencing was an important era for American history—for good and for evil—and one that will be debated for centuries. Thus my many observations about American culture in this book, such as the role of religion in my generation, do have a solid historical basis. My chief concern, however, is not documentation. My chief concern is "telling the story," as did the ancient Jews, and then interpreting it. I want to explain *why* things happened to my generation the way they did. The "what" most of us know; chronologies of the Sixties are readily available. Most books on the Sixties, however, are weak on the "why"; they are weak on both theory and emotional content. The bare facts are important, but even more important— and interesting—is the meaning of those facts. I hope that the upcoming theoretical positions will shed some new light on the Sixties. I hope they disclose some things not noticed before. A good theory reveals, or uncovers, and then offers fresh interpretations. The proof of the pudding, however, is how you, the reader, react to my arguments when you bring your own experiences to bear on the following chapters. For some of you, there will be a "fit"; for others, perhaps there won't be, and the most likely reason will be that my experiences were different from yours. But at least I hope I am providing a thought-provoking interpretation of the Sixties.

In a sense I am now going to play the role of a juggler. I am going to "throw" a number of balls up into the air, each ball being a different theoretical position about the role of tradition in American culture, especially within the Sixties Generation. My overall theory keeps all of the balls in motion. Some of these balls may collide, i.e., may contradict each other at certain points. But how could it be otherwise when interpreting something as complex, varied and, yes, crazy as the Sixties? In this chapter I will treat the revolt against tradition. My overarching theme is the loss of tradition. At the conclusion of this book I will then discuss possibilities for the retrieval, recovery and reformation of tradition.

Repressive Religious Traditions

The first ball I am casting into the air is this: some members of the Sixties Generation grew up in a repressive religious atmosphere, one that most likely degraded sexual feeling, one that may have fostered the belief that men and women are "totally depraved," which means a person is completely incapable of doing good without the help, or grace, of God. Such a view of human nature obviously creates much pessimism about history, the human body, and any possibility of social improvement. The doctrine of sin is emphasized in these traditions at the expense of the doctrines of creation and redemption. This type of religious tradition is usually full of "thou shall nots," whether we are talking about playing cards, dancing, going to the movies, or even watching television. Drinking and smoking are strictly forbidden, as well as working on Sundays. Even kissing is frowned upon (or especially kissing, I should say, not to speak of what might follow). In the small corner of America where I was raised, Western Michigan, the various Calvinist traditions would, in most instances, be illustrations of this kind of very restrictive religion, especially during the 1950s and 1960s. Other conservative traditions, however, such as Baptists, Assemblies of God, independent Bible churches, and even much of the Roman Catholic Church, would also fall into the same camp. Members of the Sixties Generation revolted against this kind of religion. They revolted against the authoritarianism, which was so often associated with their parents. They revolted against the repression of feeling—especially sexual feeling—that these traditions so often seemed to be ramming down their throats. Part of the revolt in the Sixties was out and out rebellion against what was perceived to be, or experienced as, an overly restrictive, moralistic religion, one where all the feeling had been sucked dry, like the shell of a dead bug in a spider web. Dogmatism and rules were all that remained of tradition.

Some of the churches I'm thinking of were fundamentalist, some weren't, but they were all very conservative. They often inculcated bigotry against those outside the tradition. These kinds of churches were—and remain—prejudiced against other Christian denominations (e.g., Roman Catholics being intolerant of Protestants, and Protestants in turn perceiving Roman Catholics as "unsaved" or "in error"). Moreover, these kinds of churches were—and remain—intolerant of other world religions. Television evangelism, for instance, has been filled with this sort of intolerance. It exudes anger and prejudice. Arguably, religious prejudice is the only "socially accepted" form of bigotry left, since so few people today dare to show their racial prejudices in public; but it is "OK" to "bash" Muslims or Hindus, or even Roman Catholics or Episcopalians, and sometimes Jews. (The Holocaust has made Judaism a touchy subject, however; thus conservatives usually give it a wide berth, at least in public, even if they privately look down upon Jews as "unsaved.") In my pastoral experience, many "born again" Christians quickly become "born again" bigots. Conservative religious traditions fit hand and glove with Freud's now classic theory of group formation (see *Group Psychology and the Analysis of the Ego*). He theorized that a group is held together by a common ideal and a shared hostility for out-groups. Let me illustrate. A Christian Reformed man said to me in 1969, during a conversation we were having about religion and "salvation," that all the Chinese on mainland China—all those millions upon millions of people, whom he contemptuously dismissed as "commies"—were going to Hell, all except for the few who were Christian. More specifically, he was certain of the fate of all except for the few "who had accepted Jesus Christ as their *personal* Lord and Savior" ("personal" is a "code word" among religious conservatives, and for me is sometimes a subtle signal of religious bigotry). That way of thinking has been all too typical among many conservative Protestants and Roman Catholics.

The Sixties Generation bristled at such ideas. They found the moralism to be a straight-jacket and suffocating. Many left their traditions altogether. This exodus contributed to the creation of the Sixties' particular form of pluralism, a pluralism which still stamps mainstream American culture. Some from the Sixties Generation violently rebelled against their inherited traditions while others quietly left their traditions behind. At the same time, there were people who remained loyal to their churches. But they sometimes experienced nagging sexual conflicts created by the rules of their traditions coming into conflict with an onslaught of sexual stimuli, not to speak of new freedoms. After all, the "gospel" of the sexual revolution was being spread fast and furiously by the mass media and the youth. These sexual conflicts would show up in various ways. Teenage pregnancies have been a serious problem for conservative traditions. The birth rate of children out of wedlock has been extremely high for years in the conservative Dutch areas of Western Michigan, for example. Not surprisingly sexual behavior is frequently a form of revolt against the repressiveness of tradition.[1] I witnessed a similar sort of rebellion in Ann Arbor during the Sixties. Incredible drinking binges and sexual excesses were part and parcel of some conservative Christians being away from home—and from their churches—for the first time. (Being away from "home" often meant escaping a stifling small town environment, as well.)

In these conservative religious traditions, the place for sexual behavior was very clear—no grey areas here. The only permitted place for any expression of sexual feelings was in marriage, *even if a person waited until fairly late in life to marry*. But the convention of early marriage was prominent among the "assumptions" that were challenged by the rebellion of the Sixties, when life styles became so much more varied, and so many people rejected traditional paths to careers and families.

In the Fifties and early Sixties, however, the goals set by conservative Christians were fairly clear, and here I am thinking particularly of Protestants. Work and self-sacrifice were undertaken for the glory of God. Christians in conservative traditions were socialized to seek God's will in all that they did, especially in moral decisions or those concerning a vocation or a spouse. And this search for God's will, nurtured by a thorough knowledge of the Bible, has been the chief source of strength for such traditions.

Most conservative Christians I knew in my fraternity at the University of Michigan had a strong sense of vocation, a strong sense of a "calling" in Luther's sense. Usually they were enrolled at great sacrifice to their parents. Most of these students also had to work their way through school. They studied extremely hard; they knew exactly what they wanted to do in life.[2] On Sunday mornings, when the rest of us were struggling to get out of bed (many being severely hung over) and then take those first few steps down to the community breakfast table, these conservative Christians were getting ready for church. When the rest of us had heads splitting like ripe melons under a machete thrust, headaches exacerbated by the smells of sex and stale beer throughout the house (and the smell of vomit in the bathroom), they hovered together downstairs in the foyer of the Alpha Delt house. They were all dressed neatly in coats and ties, their short hair slicked down and their shoes polished. Everything was in place to begin their walk to church for a Sunday morning of praise and prayer. It was not the case that we mainliners in my "WASP" fraternity rejected church with the same vehemence shown by some of my conservative friends—and, as is evident from my narrative, some did not reject their traditions at all. Yet for others, as for myself, *it never occurred to us to go to church* on a Sunday morning after a wild party the night before. Perhaps it might have occurred to us during the Christmas holidays, when we could go with our girlfriends to our home town church and listen to the music of the season. But after a late Saturday night party in Ann Arbor? "You've got to be kidding," as we used to say. Besides, we would have missed all those tall tales at the fraternity breakfast table, celebrations of the wild bacchanalian excesses of the night before, and we would have missed seeing each others' girlfriends sitting there eating bagels and cream cheese in their nighties.

There was something else I learned about my conservative Protestant friends. They knew their Bibles much better than I—much, much better. In fact, I had never read the Bible before, even though I had been raised in the Episcopal Church. This was a weakness shared by most mainliners in the Sixties, being the offspring of rather "liberal" traditions which did not emphasize the Bible too much within their educational programs and sermons. On the other hand, in the Sixties my conservative friends experienced far more religious conflict than we mainliners did. Some of these conservatives had a true intellectual crisis when they were exposed to courses on the sciences (many of them were pre-med) or scholarly approaches to the Bible, which then made a literalist interpretation of the sacred text extremely difficult to uphold. (The "mainline" weakness in Biblical knowledge will be extremely important to my analysis of the Sixties later on.)

Conservative religious traditions were more securely within the mainstream of American culture during the Fifties and early Sixties than they are today. The change is a source of consternation for these traditions. Recently, therefore, they have sought—through politics and television for instance—to recapture the center, or I should say, capture it for the first time since I don't think they ever *completely* had it. However, back in the Fifties and early Sixties conservative religion did have a great deal to do (at least indirectly) with what we saw and heard in the popular culture. Religion was a watchdog, one with teeth. And it used those teeth. Let me illustrate. In the late Fifties, Elvis Presley recorded a song called "One Night." It began in the original version, "one night of sin," but this was not deemed "acceptable" to the American public. RCA thus changed that opening line to "one night with you" when the record was released. RCA did not dare to challenge the conservative nature of American society at that time. (But, of course, after 1966 or so, such fear evaporated like mist in the hot summer sun.)

I now want to spend some time discussing the interactions between popular culture and conservative religion (focusing predictably on the Fifties and *early* Sixties). My purpose is to show a startling contrast to what followed in the *late* Sixties—the accelerating pace of secularization. In my view, the Sixties contributed greatly to the marginalization of fundamentalism and other conservative religious traditions in American society— particularly as that society has been depicted by the mass media ever since. The values (or the lack thereof!) presented by the majority of today's television shows, popular music, movies, and best selling books clearly demonstrate how wide the gulf is between our mass culture and conservative religion. This gulf is something that all religious traditions understand very well, and have been trying to rectify—thus far without much success. Conservative religious traditions, in particular, have been struggling to remain America's moral watchdog, but now that watchdog's teeth have been filed down by secularization. So religious conservatives attempt to "gum" what they are against—but money and the American public's insatiable demands for explicit sex and violence are social forces which, to this point, have been far too strong for any form of institutional religion to overcome. I will begin by looking once again at popular music.

Conservative Religion and Rock and Roll

One reason Elvis Presley was so popular in the Fifties—and so accepted—was his function as a bridge, or compromise, between the black singers who founded Rock and Roll on the one hand (with all the steaming sexuality their Rhythm & Blues music so often exuded), and the more reserved, even inhibited, mostly white masses on the other. Elvis' music fed the fantasies of the youth culture. But to many adults, even Elvis was too much of a symbol of sex and rebellion—too potent (and I use the word deliberately) to be palatable on the family hi-fi in the living room. Songs such as "Baby Let's Play House," "Money, Honey," and "Lawdy, Miss Clawdy" were too energetic and raucous for them to bear—or understand. Thus soon after Elvis' initial impact upon American culture, a whole array of white crooners started to become extremely popular, *some* of whom could sing— performers such as Bobby Vee[3] (e.g., "Run to Him," "Devil or Angel," and "The Night Has a Thousand Eyes"), Bobby Darin (e.g., "Mack the Knife," "Dream Lover," and "Treat My Baby Good"), Ricky Nelson (e.g., "Poor Little Fool" and "Lonesome Town"), and Paul Anka (e.g., "Diana," "Puppy Love" and "Put Your Head on My Shoulder"). Even though others like Fabian could barely hold a tune. Some like Terry Stafford (e.g., "I'll Touch a Star" and "Suspicion") and Ral Donner ("Girl of My Best Friend" and "She's Everything") began as Elvis imitators, but without conveying the same rebellion. The common denominator among most of these singers was simple. They were good looking, "cute" as the girls I knew put it (to my consternation). Moreover, they posed much less of a threat than Elvis to mainstream (i.e., white) Protestant culture, and far less of a threat than the black singers then having such a difficult time getting equal air play and equal financial compensation.

What the white crooners sang certainly was not Rock and Roll, but more of a revival of Tin Pan Alley. True, the music appealed to emotion, but not to the raw sex drive. As I said above, this sort of music expressed the trials and tribulations of sublimated "young love," or simply being young. And much of it is undeniably memorable, and wonderfully melodic. Recordings such as Curtis Lee's "Pretty Little Angel Eyes," Cathy Jean's "Please Love Me Forever," Johnny Tillotson's "Poetry in Motion," or Frankie Avalon's "Venus" are excellent representatives of this genre, and they still dominate the air time of the "oldies" radio stations (a relatively new but highly popular format that appeals to Baby Boomers).

I should point out that groups also sang this romantic, melodic music. There were white groups such as the Fleetwoods, Dion and the Belmonts ("I Wonder Why" and "Where or When"), the Safaris ("Four Steps to Love" and "Image of a Girl") Randy and the Rainbows ("Denise"), and the Skyliners from Philadelphia, whose 1959 recording of "Since I Don't Have You" perhaps represents best that whole era's melodic music. Then, too, there were black groups such as the Platters, with such songs as "Twilight Time" and "Smoke Gets in Your Eyes"—and racially mixed groups, such as the Dell-Vikings (perhaps the first such group), with their equally representative "Come Go With Me," the quintessential Fifties record. Rich harmonies and the heavy use of falsetto mark this music. (I would argue that the Beach Boys were its heir, e.g., "In My Room," "All Summer Long," and "Wendy.")

Some of this music is popularly called "doo-wop." The Marcells' 1961 recording of "Blue Moon" and their follow-up "Heartaches" not only parody "doo-wop" but are excellent examples themselves of the genre. The white Canadian group, the Diamonds, did the same kind of parody with their records "Little Darlin'" and "She Say Oom Dobby Doom." "Doo-wop" had a great following among the youth culture in the late Fifties and early Sixties.

Social factors explain why we witnessed this blossoming of romantic music (sung mostly but not exclusively by whites) which dominated the air waves soon after Elvis, and continued to populate the hit parade charts until the coming of the Beatles, whose own beautiful melodies have roots in this genre. Arguably the Rolling Stones' lineage goes back to the black roots of Rock and Roll in Rhythm & Blues; in the middle and late Sixties, they revived that part of our musical heritage. The Beatles, on the other hand, combined those roots—after all, they loved Elvis, Bo Diddley, and Chuck Berry, too—with romantic music. The Beatles were also influenced by early Motown, which was itself a hybrid, combining Gospel, Rhythm & Blues, and commercial (mostly white) pop music. But what are the social factors I mentioned in opening this paragraph? First of all, Elvis went into the army; Buddy Holly was killed in that Iowa plane crash; Jerry Lee Lewis' popularity sank dramatically when he married his teenage cousin; Chuck Berry was arrested in St. Louis and charged with violating the Mann Act (transporting a minor across state lines for immoral purposes); lastly, Little Richard joined the ministry after "Sputnik." So the first social factor giving rise to this genre of melodic music was the exit from the musical scene of the chief architects of Rock and Roll. A void was thereby created, and the revival of Tin Pan Alley filled that void.

Secondly, there was money to be made, lots of it, and even more would be made if Rock and Roll were homogenized—made more mainstream—and thus made more palatable to those good suburban church-going parents with large broods of children. Your parents might not let you play Elvis Presley or Chuck Berry on the family record player, and certainly not Little Richard (whose "Keep a Knockin'," "Jenny, Jenny," and "Good Golly Miss Molly" emptied the house). But within ear shot of your parents you were permitted (even encouraged!) to listen to Pat Boone, Bobby Rydell, or Frankie Avalon (their albums under the Christmas tree disappointed me on more than one occasion). Back then, could you see your mother, or better, your grandmother, walking into the local record store and asking, "Could I please have the latest Elvis Presley album, and that hot new release by Fats Domino?" But to ask for a Bobby Darin or a Ricky Nelson record did not feel so odd. Hence the sprinkling of such artists in the typical teen's album collection. Another social factor accounting for the popularity of this romantic music was all of the sublimated libido crammed, as sardines are crammed, into all of those hot cars cruising around town on a Saturday night. As I pointed out earlier, the role of religion in creating this sublimation was pretty substantial. And in conservative religious circles, the fear of sexuality—a fear bordering on being phobic at times —is highly significant for interpreting the flavor or moral tone of American culture in the '50s and early '60s. This was an era when Protestantism in particular still had much influence on the shape of American popular culture. Religious conservatism was decaying, but it remained formidable, and helped to dictate what was "acceptable" and what was not acceptable in so much of the music, literature, art, and cinema of the period. Remember this was the era of Senator Joseph McCarthy and the "Red Scare," this was the era of Hollywood blacklisting and accepted segregation. American culture was simply more conservative and "uptight" than what we are used to today. Of course, the Sixties had a lot to do with the changes. When the Baby Boomers were growing up, however, *it was religion* which colored the culture (to a great extent, anyway)—and colored it white.

My hypothesis about the role of conservative Protestantism and Roman Catholicism in American culture, before the Sixties' revolution, is born out by the speed at which this romantic music disappeared. It died out as rapidly as the dinosaurs—along with the crooners who gave it to us. But why? *Because sensuality became so much more explicit in the culture during the later Sixties, or "less sublimated" to use Freudian terms.* Indeed the "crooners" now symbolize that whole innocent era they helped to create.

Secularization is the strongest social dynamic here. Changes in the religious climate of American culture brought about changes in sexual mores. Those changes, in turn, doomed a genre of music dependent upon fantasies and *sublimated libido.* The so-called "sexual revolution" killed this music. When young people abandoned, rejected, or neglected their inherited traditions, they also left behind a form of music that seemed passé during the upheavals of the Sixties. This music didn't quite fit the Vietnam era. I mean Connie Francis' "Where the Boys Are" or Neil Sedaka's "Breaking Up is Hard to Do" didn't groove with our mood when blood was being spilt in Vietnam and in our inner cities, and when our politicians and civil rights leaders were being assassinated. Some of us then missed that earlier era when we held our partners while dancing, but, by the late Sixties, "Strange Days" by the Doors was more appropriate to the "feel" of our world. Such songs stirred up an escapist frenzy during parties when, as automatons, my fraternity brothers and their dates spun around the Alpha Delt dance floor like whirling dervishes.

In sum, the Age of Innocence (the era of Brian Hyland's "Sealed with a Kiss," Del Shannon's "Runaway," Gene Chandler's "Duke of Earl," etc.) came to an end when the sublimation upon which it was based, the sublimation its music drew upon, disappeared. Or almost disappeared. When that happened—at the latest, by 1967—most of the authentic crooners (mainly white, occasionally black) faded from the public scene, along with the groups singing similar ballads. They didn't literally disappear, of course. Their music waited for its time to come again, which is exactly what happened when the Baby Boomers began to age and then started wallowing in nostalgia ("like maggots in garbage," a teenager in my church recently said to me, his voice unmistakably accusatory and contemptuous). This nostalgia has inspired many of those singers to dig out their electric guitars from the attic and buy a hair piece. Now they have emerged once again within our world—albeit older, greyer, or balder, and with faltering voices which can no longer hit the high notes.

There is one good thing about being in "Rock and Roll heaven," the one the Righteous Brothers sang about in 1974 after a remarkable toll of deaths, beginning with Buddy Holly's (who, arguably, was one of the five white singers who can stand beside Elvis as "giants" of Rock and Roll before the Beatles—the other four being Roy Orbison, Jerry Lee Lewis, and Don and Phil Everly). The dead singer is saved from being paraded around in front of aging Baby Boomers at "oldies" concerts. *We are very intolerant of the physical changes we see in the crooners from our adolescence, because we are intolerant of our own aging— another aspect of our narcissism.* Thus all of these singers who have died—Elvis, Buddy Holly, Ritchie Valens, John Lennon, Roy Orbison, Bobby Darin, Ricky Nelson, Sam Cooke, Jim Morrison, Marvin Gaye, Janis Joplin, Jimi Hendrix, Eddie Kendricks, David Ruffin—will forever remain young in our imaginations. They won't remind us of how old we are getting, and for that most of the Baby Boomers will be eternally grateful. In fact, those people—who, obviously, can't get any older—will always remind us of how young we once were, and perhaps wish to be again (Glenn Miller, who died in a plane crash in the English Channel in 1944, stirs up the same sort of memories and longings in my parents' generation).

In our discussion of this pre-Beatles genre of romantic music, we have seen once again the significance of my generation's population size in the creation of social trends, such as musical tastes. The Baby Boomers were—and are—the numerical bulge in the nation's population. Even in the Fifties, with such fads as Davy Crockett and the hula-hoop, we started to flex our economic muscles and began to significantly affect the culture (a continuing theme of this book). Let me offer here a contemporary example. More and more radio and television stations are now targeting the Baby Boomers in their programing and advertising. Corporations have been increasingly "pushing" products which appeal to aging hippies and the rest of the Baby Boomers, products such as hair loss treatments or hair coloring, laxatives, and diet aids (the same teenager who was so critical of Baby Boomer nostalgia warned me not too long ago, "Pretty soon they will be advertising coffins on TV for your generation!"). This economic factor, more than anything else, doomed the "hit parade" on AM radio stations, many of which, including the station that I listened to while growing up, WLS in Chicago, have in recent years abandoned Rock and Roll, often for an "around the clock" news format or talk-radio. "The news" is, apparently, what my generation now wants to listen to if they turn on AM radio at all—if they want to hear music they will either turn on their tape players or tune into one of the FM "oldies" stations which can now be found in almost any town. The Baby Boomers have lost interest in contemporary Rock. Radio stations thus had to respond to a dwindling audience for current popular music, especially since the present younger generation is so much smaller than we Baby Boomers. We think the music died when Motown moved out of Detroit for the West coast.

Let me now wrap up this section on conservative religion and popular music before we turn to the westerns of the Fifties and early Sixties. The birth of Rock and Roll was only possible in an urban, industrialized society, where the pace of the music paralleled the pace of modern life. The beat of the music, in other words, echoed the rhythm of our mass culture and changing society. The electric guitar symbolizes the transition from Swing to Pop, and then from Pop to Rhythm & Blues, and then the emergence of a completely new genre of music: Rock and Roll. This new genre had deep roots in all those earlier forms of music, as well as in Gospel, and Country and Western. Elvis combined all these elements and initiated a new trend (as he once said in an interview, "I've been very lucky. I happened to come along at a time in the music business when there was no trend. I was lucky. The people were looking for something different, and I was lucky. I came along just in time"). Rock and Roll has always drawn upon the libido for its power, as much as upon the electricity and modern technology which it requires.

But its libidinal nature threatened America's conservative culture, particularly the white culture of the suburbs. Thus the romantic music of the crooners emerged, drawing upon sublimated libido for its appeal. Of all the social factors making that short era of romantic, melodic music possible, the role of religion was the most significant. Religion, more than anything else, created the moral climate that then existed. And it was this moral climate that brought about so much libidinal sublimation, thus making homogenized Rock and Roll inevitable and acceptable, as well as popular. However, if you don't think this music of the early Sixties is appealing (some people feel it represents "the dark ages" of popular music), listen to the Everly Brothers' "Walk Right Back" or "Crying in the Rain," certainly two of the best songs of that pre-Beatles era, and representative of the best music that period had to offer. But as in any period, there was a lot of junk, too, as the following chart reminds us.

Chart VII — WGRD'S Fabulous "50" — June 22, 1962

No.	Title	Artist
1	Roses Are Red	Bobby Vinton
2	Shame On Me	Bobby Bare
3	Loco-Motion	Little Eva

No.	Title	Artist
4	Sealed With A Kiss	Bryan Hyland
5	The Stripper	David rose
6	Follow That Dream	Elvis Presley
7	I Can't Stop Loving You	Ray Charles
8	Swinging Gently	Earl Grant
9	Dr. Kildare Theme	Richard Chamberlain
10	That's Old Fashioned	Everly Brothers
11	Snap Your Fingers	Joe Henderson
12	West Of The Wall	Toni Fisher
13	Till Death Do Us Part	Bob Braun
14	Lipstick Traces	Benny Spellman
15	Speedy Gonzales	Pat Boone
16	Cindy's Birthday	Johnny Crawford
17	Violetta	Ray Adams
18	Palisades Park	Freddy Cannon
19	Sharing You	Bobby Vee
20	Hollywood City	Carl Perkins

The moral climate which made that melodic, romantic music possible was soon going to disappear—a phenomenon that perhaps began with President Kennedy's assassination, and its attendant disillusionment and bitterness. The transformation of the Beatles from their first American album, *Meet the Beatles*, to *Sgt. Pepper's Lonely Hearts Club Band*—a shift not only in the music and its message, but also in personal appearance and life style—illustrates the sweeping cultural changes between 1963 and 1967. As I said earlier, the libido was no longer as sublimated as the Sixties progressed. It was more openly expressed, sexually and culturally. Sexuality became blatant (I remember only too well how I felt the first time I saw a woman without a bra in public; I was in my undergraduate library, and had planned to concentrate on my zoology exam). Sexuality was certainly much more blatant than, lets's say, in 1962 when "Johnny Angel" by television's Shelly Fabares ("The Donna Reed Show") topped the record charts, or even in 1963 and early 1964 when the Beatles' first

American records were released (take "She Loves You," a song which captured the vitality and innocence of our youth). To really prove my point, compare two record charts from the early Sixties to the one I have included from 1968:

Chart VIII — WGRD's Fabulous "50" — July 13, 1962

No.	Title	Artist
1	Ahab The Arab	Ray Stevens
2	The Stripper	David Rose
3	Breaking Up Is Hard To Do	Neil Sedaka
4	Roses Are Red	Bobby Vinton
5	Sheila	Tommy Roe
6	Sealed With A Kiss	Brian Hyland
7	Surfin' Safari	Beach Boys
8	Have A Good Time	Sue Thompson
9	Loco Motion	Little Eva
10	Shame On Me	Bobby Bare
11	Speedy Gonzales	Pat Boone
12	Theme From Dr. Kildare	Richard Chamberlain
13	Little Red Rented Rowboat	Joe Dowell
14	Route 66	Nelson Riddle
15	Johnny Get Angry	Joannie Sommers
16	Al Di La	Emilio Pericoli
17	Air Travel	Bob & Ray
18	Theme From A Summer Place	Dick Roman
19	Fortune Teller	Bobby Curtola
20	Till Death Do Us Part	Bob Braun
21	West Of The Wall	Toni Fisher
22	Silver Threads & Golden Needles	Springfields

No.	Title	Artist
23	Loveless Life	Ral Donner
24	Born To Lose	Ray Charles
25	Girls Are Made To Love	Eddie Hodges
26	Wah Watusi	Orlons
27	I Misunderstood	Wanda Jackson
28	Baby Sitting Boogie	Ralf Bendix
29	I'll Never Dance Again	Bobby Rydell
30	Follow That Dream	Elvis Presley
31	Little Diane	Dion
32	Violetta	Ray Adams
33	Boys Kept Hanging Around	Dorsey Burnette
34	When I'm Alone	Dick Noel
35	Keep Your Hands In Your Pocket	Playmates
36	So Wrong	Patsy Cline
37	Dancin' Party	Chubby Checker
38	It Started All Over Again	Brenda Lee
39	Too Late To Worry	Glenn Campbell
40	Party Lights	Claudine Clark
41	Ain't That Funny	Jimmy Justice
42	Goodnight Irene	Jerry Reed
43	Wanderin' Eyes	Jimmie Rogers
44	Beach Party	King Curtis
45	Call Me Mr. Between	Burl Ives
46	Alley Cat	Brent Fabric
47	Lt. Col Boogey Parade	Steve Douglas
48	But Not For Me	Ketty Lester
49	Dance With Mr. Domino	Fats Domino
50	Ballad Of Palladin	Duane Eddy

Chart IX — WGRD's Fabulous "50" — August 16, 1963

No.	Title	Artist
1	My Boyfriend's Back	Angels
2	I'm Afraid To Go Home	Brian Hyland
3	Judy's Turn To Cry	Lesle Gore
4	Gone	Ripchords
5	Hello Mudder, Hello Fadder	Allen Sherman
6	Candy Girl	Four Seasons
7	Green, Green	New Christy Minstrels
8	When A Boy Falls In Love	Mel Carter
9	Six Days On The Road	Dave Dudley
10	I Want To Stay Here	Steve & Eydie
11	Surfer Girl	Beachboys
12	Kind Of Boy You Can't Forget	Raindrops
13	Fingertips	Little Stevie Wonder
14	Painted, Tainted Rose	Al Martino
15	Everybody Monkey	Freddie Cannon
16	You Can Never Stop Me Loving You	Johnny Tillotson
17	Devil In Disguise	Elvis Presley
18	If I Had A Hammer	Trini Lopez
19	Wipeout	Surfaris
20	Abilene	George Hamilton IV
21	How Many Teardrops	Lou Christie
22	True Love Never Runs Smooth	Gene Pitney
23	Wait Til' My Bobby Comes Home	Darlene Love
24	Danke Shoen	Wayne Newton
25	Faded Love	Patsy Cline
26	Frankie and Johnnie	Sam Cooke
27	The Minute You're Gone	Sonny James
28	Martian Hop	Ran-Dells
29	Still #2	Ben Colder
30	Wham!	Lonnie Mack
31	Please Don't Talk To The Lifeguard	Diane Ray
32	Why Don't You Believe Me	The Duprees

No.	Title	Artist
33	Desert Pete	Kingston Trio
34	Hear The Bells	The Tokens
35	Blue Velvet	Bobby Vinton
36	Linda, Linda	Rock Romano
37	Little Yellow Roses	Jackie De Shannon
38	At The Shore	Johnny Caswell
39	Girls In The Summertime	Paul Peterson
40	Treat My Baby Good	Bobby Darin
41	Then He Kissed Me	Crystals
42	Scarlet O'Hara	Claudie King
43	Something Old/Something New	Paul & Paula
44	Twist It Up	Chubby Checker
45	Teenage Cleopatra	Tracy Dey
46	Heat Wave	Martha and the Vandellas
47	The Key's In The Mailbox	Pat Zill
48	Saltwater Taffy	Morty Jay & Surferin' Cats
49	Another Fool Like Me	Ned Miller
50	Lana	George McCannon III

Chart X — WLAV Music Guide — July 26, 1968

No.	Title	Artist
1	Grazing In The Grass	Hugh Masekela
2	Turn Around, Look At Me	Vogues
3	Sky Pilot	Animals
4	Sealed With A Kiss	Gary Lewis
5	Born To Be Wild	Steppenwolf
6	Classical Gas	Mason Williams
7	Lover's Holiday	Peggy & JoJo
8	Hello, I Love You	Doors
9	Autumn Of My Life	Bobby Goldsboro
10	Hurdy Gurdy Man	Donovan

No.	Title	Artist
11	People Got To Be Free	Rascals
12	Alice Long	Tommy Boyce & Bobby Hart
13	Pictures Of Matchstick Men	Status Quo
14	Journey to The Center Of The Mind	Amboy Dukes
15	Sally Had A Party	Flavor
16	The Horse	Cliff Nobles & Co
17	I Need Love	Third Booth
18	Stoned Soul Picnic	Fifth Dimension
19	A Lover's Hideaway	Al Green
20	Love Makes A Woman	Barbara Acklin
21	Give Me One More Chance	Wilmer & Dukes
22	The Every Day Housewife	Campbell/Newton
23	You Met Your Match	Stevie Wonder
24	I Can't Stop Dancing	Archie Bell & Drells
25	Somebody Care	Tommy James & Shondells
26	1,2,3, Redlight	1910 Fruitgum Co
27	Dream A Little Dream Of Me	Mama Cass
28	You're All I Need	Marvin & Tammi
29	You Keep Me Hangin' On	Vanilla Fudge
30	Do It Again	Beach Boys
31	Give A Damn	Spanky & Our Gang
32	5 O'Clock	Fredric
33	Down At Lulu's	Ohio Express
34	Midnight Confessions	The Grass Roots

What stands out in the 1968 chart are songs romanticizing drugs: "Journey to the Center of the Mind," for example, and perhaps "Grazing in the Grass" and "Stoned Soul Picnic." Those, and others such as "Born to be Wild" by Steppenwolf and "Hello, I Love You" by the Doors, reflect a completely different social—indeed moral—universe than, let's say, "Judy's Turn to Cry", or "Please Don't Talk to the Lifeguard" (1963), or "Roses are Red" or "Little Red Rented Rowboat" (1962). In only four or five years, music shifted from such moral dilemmas as Ral Donner's being in love "with the girl of my best friend," such laments as James Darren's that "that mean fickle woman would make a crying clown out of me" in "Goodbye Cruel World," and such longings as Elvis Presley's, "are you lonesome tonight, are you sorry we drifted apart?"—to a world where Bob Dylan can sing that "everybody must get stoned."

Many of the best popular songs of the late Sixties no longer dwelt upon the sagas and personal moral struggles of young love. As the 1968 chart shows with "Sky Pilot" by the Animals and "People Got to be Free" by the Rascals, in the midst of the "bubble gum" and other inane music that always seems to show up on the hit parade charts of any period, *songs began to appear which voiced the deep social concerns of the Sixties.* In fact, because there was so much inane music, the album format (the "L.P.") became very popular among the Sixties Generation, replacing or supplementing the 45s in our record collections. There were several reasons for this. First of all, the album gave musicians an opportunity to develop an artistic theme, which the limited time of the 45 made extremely difficult (AM radio stations were reluctant to play long songs, which was why most 45s were under three minutes). Albums such as *Rubber Soul* by the Beatles and *Days of Future Passed* by the Moody Blues, were thematic wholes, not simply collections of songs, like most previous Rock and Roll albums. (In fact, I would argue that *Rubber Soul* was the turning point in the production of albums.) Secondly, the album gave the artist the opportunity to present "serious music," which in the field of Rock meant music expressing social and moral concerns, as well as expanding musical horizons. Bob Dylan's early albums and the Beatles' albums, *Revolver* (especially the cut "Eleanor Rigby") and *Sgt. Pepper's Lonely Hearts Club Band*, paved the way here. Dylan also showed the musical world that hit records could break the three minute barrier. His record "Like a Rolling Stone" was truly revolutionary in 1965, becoming an AM hit in spite of the fact it was over six minutes long. Afterwards, AM radio adjusted its air time schedule to accommodate other long songs such as "Hey Jude" by the Beatles. But this was a classic situation of "too little too late." FM radio stations had started to play album music, which further energized that recording format. It was these stations that the Baby Boomers increasingly listened to in the 1960s. This switch from AM to FM, and from 45s to albums, marked the decline of "hit parade" programing on AM radio. Indeed, it marked the decline of AM radio in general.

Social concerns in music are nothing new; after all, Pete Seeger and the Weavers had been singing social protest songs for years, and the whole folk music movement, then highly popular, drew upon a rich tradition of socially relevant music. However, during the height of the folk music movement in the *early* 1960s, it was such groups as the Kingston Trio and the Brothers Four who had the most commercial success. Why? Because of their rich melodies and smooth harmonies (listen to "Greenfields" or "The Green Leaves of Summer" by the Brothers Four, or "All My Sorrows" and "Tom Dooley" by the Kingston Trio); such groups paralleled the pop music of the day. The Kingston Trio symbolizes the pre-Beatles era as much as "doo-wop." Early Kingston Trio albums such as *The Kingston Trio, Live at the Hungri i, The Kingston Trio at Large, Here We Go Again*, and *Sold Out*, were rich in melody, and featured wonderful harmonies and great guitar and banjo playing. These memorable albums were commercial successes, and they truly reflect that tranquil era —at least tranquil for white suburban culture.

But, like "doo-wop," the songs on those albums did not grapple with current social issues, such as the horrible racism plaguing American society. That quickly changed, however, even in commercial folk music. The civil rights struggles, and then the Vietnam War, rapidly changed the concerns of both much folk music and many hit parade records from *personal* tribulations to *social* conflicts. (Although, interestingly enough, there were never, to my knowledge, any popular songs or folk songs which struggled morally with the use of drugs. Songs glamorizing drugs became very popular, e.g., "White Rabbit"; but songs were not written or recorded that condemned drug use—which is one more piece of evidence for how rapidly our culture was changing, and how rapidly our moral and religious traditions were eroding).

Numbers such as Scott McKenzie's "San Francisco," Peter,

Paul and Mary's "Blowin' in the Wind" (written by Bob Dylan), Elvis' "In the Ghetto," "Revolution" by the Beatles, and "Chicago" by Graham Nash were examples of hit records which were also social criticism. The English group, the Kinks, were particularly adept at this. Similar songs carried over into the Seventies: "Give Peace a Chance" by John Lennon, "Military Madness" by Graham Nash, and "War" by Edwin Starr (even Motown, along with Elvis, jumped on this particular bandwagon). The assassinations of John F. Kennedy, Robert Kennedy, and Martin Luther King also gave powerful impetus to song writing dealing with subjects other than romance—for instance, Dion's "Abraham, Martin and John" in late 1968 and early 1969. After President Kennedy's assassination, even the Kingston Trio released an album of songs (*Time to Think*) which focused attention on the moral problems of contemporary American society, a new turn for that group. Arguably, the great popularity of Barry McGuire's "Eve of Destruction" in the summer of 1965 led the way for others in this novel genre of popular music— "novel," in any case, for mainstream "hit parade" record charts.

As important as socially relevant music was for future musical trends, it was the romantic music of the early Beatles (e.g., "Anna," "All My Lovin'," "Not a Second Time," "If I Fell," "And I Love Her," and "That Boy") which helped us more than anything else in coping with the trauma of President Kennedy's assassination. The Beatles provided us with an emotional outlet just when our society needed one. They gave us a different focus in the midst of our cultural grief. They diverted us from our anguish to young love once again. The freshness and exuberance of their first music supported our cultural illusion that perhaps our Age of Innocence hadn't entirely disappeared after all, that it hadn't ended suddenly with the shot of a gun, that somehow we could wish our way back to the days before November 1963— after which we would never be the same again (nor, in the long run, would the music).

The Beatles, for a brief moment, took us all back to "Camelot," to a simpler way of life and a genre of music that reflected that life. Both were rapidly fading, as much as we tried to hold on. "Camelot," of course, was another illusion, but one we cherished. And many still do. The Beatles were soon going to change, as we all would in response to the turn of events. More than melodic romantic music was lost in that period, more than "doo-wop" would disappear. We lost our innocence, and the moral climate of America would never be the same again.

Conservative Religion and the Western

There is another phenomenon in the society of the Fifties and early Sixties which further substantiates my thesis about the influence of religion upon popular culture. Why were westerns then so popular on television and in the movies? When the Sixties erupted, these westerns pretty much died out. Clint Eastwood's "spaghetti" westerns, produced by Italians and filmed in Spain (take *For a Few Dollars More* and *A Fistful of Dollars*), were obvious exceptions— but these also fit my thesis, as we shall see. The genre of the western as the Sixties Generation knew it, has really disappeared. When growing up we regularly watched such television shows as "Gunsmoke," "Have Gun Will Travel," and "Wagon Train," or saw movies such as *Shane, The Magnificent Seven,* and *High Noon* in the darkness of our neighborhood theater amidst the smell of popcorn. Why were westerns then so numerous, and why aren't they now? Why were such TV shows as "Bonanza" part of our Sunday night ritual in the early 1960s, but not after those years? Here is a theory.

Conservative religious traditions of that period would not condone much expression of sexuality in movies and television shows. Here their power of censorship paralleled their effect upon popular music. (As I mentioned, if the impact was not direct, it was at a minimum indirect through a generalized influence of religion upon the culture.) On the other hand, violence was "permitted" in the mass media. Why was sexuality curtailed or criticized, but not violence? Here is one possible answer. Religion from its very beginnings, especially the Christian religion, has distrusted sexuality (e.g., the work of St. Augustine, which in turn was influenced by some of the teachings of St. Paul); religion has often viewed sexuality as its major opponent.

But time and time again in world history, religion has sanctioned the use of violence—the Crusades, the Inquisition, and its general support of World War II (especially the Lutheran Church in Nazi Germany) and the Vietnam War being only four of the most obvious examples. This religious sanction of violence—either explicitly, or implicitly by silence—helped to create the violence in both popular culture and the society into which the Baby Boomers were socialized. Religion certainly did not stem it. In response to all this, many of the Baby Boomers later revolted against their religious traditions.

Television shows such as "Gunsmoke" and "The Untouchables" (an urban western) were extremely violent, yet extremely popular. The media reflected society. Much of this violence was, I believe, a cultural projection of dark, highly powerful forces lurking in our collective psyche, forces which had a direct connection to religion. And it was those "forces" which explain some of the popularity of such TV shows. Let me elaborate.

First of all, the hostility and violence expressed outwardly in the movies and television shows of the period mirrored what many people were feeling inwardly—either consciously or, more than likely, unconsciously. Remember that this was the age of the Cold War. We were brought up to distrust, if not hate, Russia and China, and all Communists for that matter. Also recall this was the era when we were debating as a society whether or not we would lock out a neighbor from our fallout shelter if that would insure our own family's survival. Our hostility toward the Communist world was "blessed," even encouraged by organized religion, especially the conservative variety. Sermon after sermon from the era denounced Communism. After all, weren't all Communists atheists? Of course, that wasn't true, but it was our cultural projection, a projection in part instigated by religion. Conservative religion, right wing politicians, and the military-industrial complex were sleeping in the same bed, sharing the same fears, and suffering the same nightmares.

Secondly, the violence of these television shows also expressed, I believe, the latent and even overt hostilities of whites toward blacks, who rarely appeared on the television free of stereotyped roles, roles such as Sapphire and Kingfish on "The

Amos 'n' Andy Show," or Rochester on "The Jack Benny Show."
Television shows also reinforced stereotypes of other minorities,
e.g., Hop Sing, the Chinese cook on "Bonanza." Native Americans had an especially difficult time on westerns. Indians were
almost always portrayed as "savages," as inhuman, terrifying,
dangerous, drunken, or dirty. They were thus "expendable" on
those shows, rarely appearing more than once ("The Lone
Ranger" being the obvious exception, although Tonto also was a
stereotype, "the good Indian"). As a result, Indians were killed
in droves each week on television. They were rarely depicted in
a sympathetic light, something else that changed in the Sixties,
perhaps beginning with the movie *Little Big Man*. This breakdown of cultural stereotypes was a positive legacy of the Sixties.
As we now look back on the mass media of the '50s and early
'60s, it is difficult to believe we tolerated such stereotypes. That
is just an indication of how racist we were, and in most instances
we didn't even realize it! We hadn't yet learned as a society to be
sensitive to the feelings of those who were so often depicted in
such a simplistic manner.

For an even deeper interpretation of those television shows,
Freud's theory of group formation once again shows its brilliant
explanatory power. The white people (mostly men)—who controlled the mass media—were united by common moral and
religious ideals, including shared images of family values. Their
television shows reflected, or projected—and certainly protected—those ideals and values. But these same white people, who
controlled the mass media and the sponsoring corporations, were
also unified by a shared hostility—conscious or unconscious
—towards the "outgroups," whether they were Indians, blacks,
Mexicans, or Orientals. Again, recall how those groups were
presented by the media. Consciously or unconsciously, outgroups
were perceived as threats to the ideals and values upheld by the
television shows of the period, and here I am particularly
interested in the western. Those ideals and values were, in large
part, reflections of conservative religion, whether Jewish, Roman
Catholic, or Protestant. This conservative religion, of course, was
mostly white; at least this holds true for religion with cultural
clout.

The Ku Klux Klan, obviously, fits Freud's theory hand in glove, but the theory has a much broader applicability to American culture. In the Fifties and early Sixties, American society was largely segregated. Most white children were not in schools, neighborhoods, or clubs that included minorities (country clubs are still notoriously white, and the Gentile clubs discriminate against Jews, and the Jewish clubs return the favor to Gentiles). Such segregation reinforced the solidarity of the white ingroups and fed the distrust, even hostility, toward those who were "different," i.e., the outgroups. Thus it should come as no surprise that these groups were not portrayed sympathetically in movies and on television. There was precious little sympathy for those groups in daily life. It was a true disservice to the lives of those people that they were commonly depicted as direct threats to whites. The media both exacerbated the racial hostilities already existing in the wider society and reflected those hostilities. Here we have the classic vicious circle.

No doubt the television shows and movies of the period did offer the society a "safety valve" which released strong hostilities, both overt and latent. But at what a price! Moreover, the mass media permitted Americans to identify with heroes, but the heroes were usually the "guys in the white hats" in the westerns, and the "bad guys" almost always wore black hats, something, I believe, that further reinforced racial fears. "Black" was associated with "badness." Good and evil in these westerns were as simple to perceive as the color of one's hat! Or, in some cases, the color of one's skin. To reiterate, these television shows reflected deep divisions within the culture, divisions that we have not overcome to this day.

Television westerns and other types of shows reinforced another cultural myth, the myth that "America is always right."[4] If America was always right, then the Soviet Union and her allies were always "wrong." Television conveyed this "black and white" view of the universe. The "good guys" killed the "bad guys" in these westerns. The viewers thus vicariously shared in that simple moral victory of good over evil, right over wrong. Americans were provided with a handy outlet for their aggression and fear.

That simplistic view of life quickly changed in the late Sixties, however. Good and evil became blurred. During the Vietnam War, Americans no longer thought of themselves unequivocally as "the good guys." The movies and television shows likewise mirrored these new ambiguities and confusions creeping into American life. The "anti-hero" was born in the mass culture, such as the role of Benjamin Braddock created by Dustin Hoffman in the 1967 movie, *The Graduate*, or his character of Rico Ratso in *Midnight Cowboy* in 1969. Good and evil not only became blurred, they became far more complex, expressing our own moral confusion. As a result, the stark portrayals of good versus evil in the westerns of an earlier period seemed out of date and no longer true to life once the Sixties erupted. These westerns had reflected the view of life presented to the society by conservative religion, that life was a moral battleground, even a battleground between God and Satan. In the Sixties, this view of life seemed too simplistic, too naive. Moreover, this point of view seemed to exclude psychological understanding of the complexities of human beings. Suddenly, conservative traditions seemed "out of touch," as did the movies and television shows which were mirror images of those traditions. Many members of the Sixties Generation thus rejected those very traditions, and no longer watched the related movies and television shows. My generation knew, or discovered, that history was far more complicated than "good versus evil," and we knew that human beings were made up of both. We learned that by learning about ourselves, if in no other way.

There was something else that was curious about westerns in the pre-Vietnam years. There was so little sex. There was plenty of violence, as we have just seen, but why, do you think, there was so little sex? Again, the religious and moral climate of American culture provides the key to answer that question. Let's look at a few of these shows. Take "Gunsmoke," one of the most popular television shows of the day. Matt Dillon and Kitty were presumably "a couple," but did they ever kiss on the air? Did they ever spend the night together?[5] Was sex ever intimated? I am not arguing that it should have been, I am merely pointing out that it wasn't, in order to establish a contrast to what came after.

Maybe Matt and Kitty symbolized American society's own sexual dilemmas, inhibitions, repressions, conflicts, in short, our "hang-ups"—before the Sixties Generation rebelled against the moral and cultural restrictions of such relationships. Matt and Kitty always seemed to be waiting for something—week after week—and it seemed that we Baby Boomers were, too. We were waiting to grow up. Matt and Kitty waited for more than twenty years to consummate their relationship, and then they never did. My generation would not be so patient. My generation rejected the moral boundaries (and perhaps inhibitions) Matt and Kitty represented. (After the pill, we often rejected them on the first date.)

Remember "Bonanza"? Like so many of our westerns, this show upheld family values and other traditional values, such as the importance of hard work, loyalty and generosity to the community, the use of violence only when morally necessary or when one's life was threatened, and respect towards women. But where were the women? Like so many of these westerns, the show was essentially about men, in this case four men living together in the midst of their ghostly memories of their dead wives and mothers. No sex on that show (!), an occasional romance (highly sublimated), and more than occasional violence; but this violence was always clearly directed at evil.

There was also little or no sex on the "cops and robbers" genre of television shows, such as "The Untouchables." I don't think Elliot Ness's wife ever appeared on the show, and he certainly never came close to succumbing to the favors of the women who so often tried to compromise him. As Robert Stack portrayed Ness—and he was very effective in doing this—there was absolutely no libido expressed toward anyone; violence yes, but not libido, not even in the form of affection. This was also true of "Dragnet," in the way Jack Webb interpreted the character of Joe Friday.

Psychoanalysis has taught us that violence and rage often arise as a result of repression and frustration. Such TV shows raise the following questions: Were we as a society repressing libido to such an extent that the violence and sexual relationships of those shows reflected a frustrated society? Was violence a symptom of that frustration? Was the sexual revolution of the Sixties a reaction against both this frustration and violence? Moreover, wasn't it true that the television shows and movies of that era projected an ideal of family life that actually existed in far too few households? One thing is certain. Conservative religion, and the television shows of that time, together reflected a cultural world standing at the brink of total revolution, at the same time they worked to deny the real fragility of that world. What do we see when we turn to the western movies? Much the same thing. Consider *High Noon*. Again, we have violence but little physical affection expressed between the characters played by Gary Cooper (Sheriff Will Kane) and Grace Kelly (she played Amy, a Quaker pacifist, who in the end kills one of Frank Miller's gang). In *Shane* there is a hint of fantasized adultery between Shane, played by Alan Ladd, and the character played by Jean Arthur. But traditional religious values win out, along with the "good guys" who stage their inevitable victory when Shane guns down the gunfighter Wilson, played by Jack Palance. Like the sheriff in *High Noon*, Shane does this on his own, with little help from society. As in Protestantism, victory—even redemption—is attained after the lonely battle of the autonomous individual, embodying good, against the collective forces of evil symbolized by the hired gun. The battle is fought and won alone, and the moral conflict is crystal clear.

My intent here is not to argue or even intimate that traditional religious and moral values should not be portrayed in a favorable light, or as being victorious. I merely want to show the strength of religious and moral values in the era immediately preceding the Vietnam War. Before Vietnam, violence was sanctioned in popular culture, or at least tolerated, whereas relationships between men and women tended to be extremely sublimated, or celibate as with Matt and Kitty, or restricted to traditional marriages where men and women had clearly defined gender roles. The relationships that existed were barely affectionate, almost platonic, and certainly not steamy, as you quickly observe if you watch old "Dennis the Menace" reruns, or those from "The Donna Reed Show," "Father knows Best," "Lassie," or "Bewitched." Such shows did, however, express the religious and moral aspirations of the postwar suburban family—even if "true life" did not equal the ideal.

The westerns of the Fifties and early Sixties were predicated upon a very idealistic and romantic view of women and sexuality. When the culture changed in the late Sixties (i.e., when traditional gender roles were challenged, and when sexuality was much less romanticized, idealized, and sublimated in the society at large, when, in other words, sexuality became far less discreet and far less restricted to its traditional arena of marriage)—when this change "came to life"—westerns simply died out. Or like the popular music, their form, as we knew it during pre-Vietnam years, changed. Thus when we watch old westerns today on our VCRs, they seem rather corny, just as much of the same period's music seems sappy.

Interestingly enough, once sexuality was more directly expressed in the movies and TV shows of the late Sixties, there was more violence, too. But *there was a difference* between the violence of the Fifties and early Sixties from that depicted afterward. In movies such as Clint Eastwood's *For a Few Dollars More* and some of his other westerns, the battle between good and evil was not nearly as clear as it was in, let's say, *High Noon* or *The Magnificent Seven*. The important point here is that after the Sixties, *violence did not have the same clear moral sanction* in most movies that it had in the westerns of the 1950s. As I said, the movies of the Vietnam era were more violent; the body count was higher. And in recent years this violence has turned even more graphic. Having a war brought into our living rooms on TV desensitized us to blood, guts, and gore. All of this increased violence in our mass media indicates not so much society's sexual repression, as in the 1950s, but rather our increasing propensity to view people as objects rather than as real human beings. The Vietnam War and the sexual revolution are, in part, to blame.

The role of women in Eastwood's early westerns was minimal. Even though his Italian westerns did not depict sex, one comes to feel, after a dozen killings or so, that all of that violence was eroticized in the same way sadism is erotic for some, and one comes to see the six shooter in these westerns as a symbol for a loaded, aggressive penis. That is, perhaps, just a Freudian impression. In any case, Eastwood's later westerns and his series of "Dirty Harry" movies enlarged the role of sex. Once violence increased in the movies, and once moral ambiguity also increased, then the sublimated sexuality of earlier westerns, such as *Shane*, completely disappeared. In other words, in the movies of the late Sixties and afterward, sex was was more blatant. *This shift mirrored a change in the surrounding culture.*

But let me now sum up this discussion of the western. The movies of the Sixties reflected changes in us. These movies expressed our American tendency in the aftermath of Vietnam to accept more and more violence in our entertainment, along with more and more explicit sex. Most important, the movies since the Sixties demonstrate our resignation to moral ambiguity. They echo a widespread weakening of tradition. Religion in the Fifties and early Sixties still had enough influence in the culture to at least checkmate the sex, but now it has lost even that power. We have become secularized to that degree. Since the Sixties, and now into the Nineties, sex and violence have been running amuck in our media. There seems to be nothing in place—institutionally, psychologically, or morally—to hold them in check, least of all public taste, which now appears insatiably hungry for those things. To put it bluntly, the Sixties opened up Pandora's box. I am not calling for censorship, a highly dangerous road. But I am questioning America's taste in movies, and I do think this violence and blatant sex are symptomatic of some frightening spiritual realities in American society. Moreover, I mourn the loss of tradition which once had some influence on our taste, if not always felicitously. Good taste would be the best form of censorship.

Television Evangelism

Since the topic of this chapter is conservative religion, I want to insert an aside here about television evangelism, especially of the 1980s and 1990s variety. I said above that if sexuality is repressed, the ensuing frustration can find expression in violence and anger. That is a psychoanalytic truism. When I watch television evangelism, I sometimes question whether or not the constant suppression of sexuality implied, or advocated, by TV preachers is a cause for the angry tone of their sermons. Moreover, I have wondered if these preachers' own personal repression of sexuality hasn't contributed to their hostility towards various outgroups, such as "hippies," secular humanists, feminists, and homosexuals, a hostility heard so often in their sermons. Lastly, I wonder whether this repression of sexuality does not finally get its revenge in the frequent sex scandals so many of these television evangelists (and other clergy) have been entangled in recently. Television evangelism—in its nostalgia, in the values it upholds, and in its "black and white" view of the universe—is an atavistic residuum of the westerns of the Fifties. There is a similar outward aggression, and a similar inward repression of sexuality (television evangelism is as asexual as those westerns were). This should come as no surprise. As I said, the westerns from the '50s and early '60s may be best understood in the Protestant cultural matrix out of which they emerged—and it is that era which contemporary Protestantism yearns for.

However, let me add this caveat. Conservative Protestantism and Roman Catholicism have always had a very shrewd psychological understanding of the connection between religion and sexuality: both run on the same fuel—the libido—and thus are often competing forces in life.[6] For most conservatives, this knowledge, I would guess, is more subconscious, or subliminal, than conscious. Most of the Sixties Generation soon realized the same thing, but for us it was definitely a conscious awareness. Thus many opted for the "sins of the flesh" rather than the inherited traditions forbidding such sins.

I am not arguing that conflicts between sexuality and religious conservatism no longer exist for many people. They do, but the revolution of the Sixties drew up a new playing field for sexual ethics in the American culture of the 1970s, 1980s, and now into the 1990s. Moreover, the Sixties set new rules for the game— freer rules for a more open playing field. This situation has made it *very difficult* for organized religion to make a constructive response with its truths, such as those proclaimed by Christianity: that history has meaning, and life has purpose throughout; that people should never be "used" (as Kant said, a person should never be a means to an end); that God has a will for each one of us and a will for the communities and nations in which we live; that the Resurrection of Jesus Christ symbolizes hope in the midst of suffering and death; that self-love and fornication need to be seen in a moral context that includes warnings. Religion has numerous other truths to offer our sex crazed world (some of which are tied to particular religious traditions, and some are found in all religions). I will return to that claim toward the end of this book when I explore the retrieval of tradition.

Longing for the "Old Time Religion"

Religious conservatism's wholesale condemnation of all forms of sexual expression outside of marriage, joined to its frequent commendations of violence in both the mass media and in public policy (e.g., its support of the Vietnam War, and more recently, the Gulf War), has marginalized its message for many Americans, especially among the Baby Boomers. Consequently, the ability of conservative Christian traditions to interpret the Gospel to a secular society, for instance, has been greatly reduced. After all, our society is far more complex and varied than the way of life depicted in the television shows of the Fifties and early Sixties. The revolution of the Sixties—indeed, the permissiveness of those years—destroyed that way of life, or at least struck a serious blow.

Some religious conservatives embrace a literalist Biblical agenda in the attempt to combat secularization, but that effort is laced with nostalgia for an "old time religion" in a world that no longer exists. Biblical injunctions written down thousands of years ago don't easily translate into forms applicable to modern society; they need a great deal of interpretation. My generation learned that truth in the aftermath of the Sixties. Here I am not going to advocate any particular form of Biblical interpretation or religion which can speak to our age. I reserve that task for the concluding arguments of this book. Here I only wish to emphasize the complexity of the religious challenge of our time.

The conservative religious agenda is, obviously, embraced by many Americans. The phenomenon of the "megachurch" and the growth of the evangelical movement provide ample evidence of that. This agenda is also presented weekly on many televised church services. But it is this very agenda—basically Biblical fundamentalism (and here I include much of Roman Catholicism, because of its authoritarianism)—that was the target of the Sixties Generation's rebellion, especially when religion supported the state in its war policies. That agenda was anathema to many of us, and this fact cannot be overestimated for understanding the Sixties. The revolt of my generation during that period has made it impossible for conservative religion to speak to the majority of us. We have been too thoroughly secularized by what we went through during the war years.

Now we have one ball in the air, if you recall my image of the juggler. We have looked at the rebellion of the Sixties Generation against religious conservatism, a conservatism which was so often associated with parental authority. Some of this rebellion was, no doubt, part and parcel of the normal oedipal conflicts everyone experiences sooner or later.[7] For some people this rebellion was a temporary one. For many others, however, it was permanent. In any case, many people had to manage, on their own, the traumas of the Sixties we will be discussing later on. As we shall see, *without their religion many succumbed to excessive narcissism.*

To conclude this chapter, I am now going to toss up a related ball, one that perhaps has had even more social significance than the revolt against tradition. That ball can be characterized as follows: many of the Sixties Generation wanted to eat the "forbidden fruit" then offered. They didn't simply want to rebel, they wanted to indulge.

Desire: the Mother of Revolt

Self-sacrifice has always been at or near the heart of Christian ethics. This ideal has many sources in Jesus' teaching, but none as demanding as the form expressed in Matthew 16:24-27:

> Then Jesus told his disciples, " If any man would come after
> me, let him deny himself and take up his cross and follow me.
> For whoever would save his life will lose it, and whoever loses
> his life for my sake will find it. For what will it profit a man,
> if he gains the whole world and forfeits his life? Or what shall
> a man give in return for his life? For the Son of man is to
> come with his angels in the glory of his Father, and then he
> will repay every man for what he has done."

Self-sacrifice has been emphasized to some degree in all Christian
churches, indeed in most religious traditions. That being said,
conservative traditions, I think, have made that ideal more prominent in their institutional life than mainline Episcopal or Presbyterian traditions, for instance. Thus I include a discussion of
self-sacrifice in this chapter on conservative religious traditions
—although in varying degrees, what I am going to say holds true
for mainliners, too.

This is my hypothesis: many members of the Sixties Generation came to feel during the Vietnam War years, and then
afterward, that the Biblical teaching about self-sacrifice was far
too demanding. For many, that ethic had been greatly emphasized during their religious upbringing, but during the revolution
of the Sixties, it lost its emotional allure. It also lost its religious
authority in a culture moving farther and farther away from its
religious roots. The Church's support of the war, a support that
became associated in many instances with parental support for the
war, was particularly significant in this loss of authority. The loss
of religious authority undermined parental authority in general,
and vice versa (by the time many churches—and parents—
opposed the war, the distrust of authority had already set in, and
for many people it has never gone away).

Moreover, the Christian paradox that fulfillment in life lies in
self-sacrifice was not taught insightfully or skillfully by the
Church of the Fifties and Sixties. Thus the ethic of self-sacrifice
(in its Americanized form this is often spoken of as "service")
was not embraced with either enthusiasm or depth of understanding by the majority of the Baby Boomers. For many, ethics
were reduced to moral obligation, with little or no emotional content. In the institutional religion of the Fifties and early Sixties,

feelings were not deemed important within educational programs. Belief was what was important—and here I am particularly targeting conservative traditions. Feelings were not honored except, of course, when they were "religious feelings"—and even those were rather narrowly defined. (Since the Sixties, however, the Church has responded to this psychological need to feel—it simply had to during the upheavals of the Sixties—and relatively recent "renewal" movements in the Church cannot be understood, sociologically and psychologically, apart from the emerging emphasis on affect in the Sixties.)

Feelings were distrusted by many traditions, no doubt because of their close connection to the libido. Many traditions equated passion with sex. In consequence, sermons were overly dogmatic and cognitive (haven't we all heard far too many of these?). The upshot of all of this was a negative feeling about self-sacrifice and hard work; they were viewed by many in the Sixties Generation as a *suppression* of healthy narcissism. The flip side of the revolt against religion was a quest to rectify a perceived imbalance between self-love and love of and service to others. Conservative religious traditions, in particular, emphasized the latter at the expense of the former. *The Sixties Generation's quest for a healthy narcissism has contributed to the intensification of narcissism—both healthy and unhealthy— within institutional religion itself!* I will elaborate upon my meaning in the following section.

Kohut showed in his work (building upon Freud) that every person needs a certain amount of narcissism in order to have a cohesive self and a healthy level of self-esteem. The Sixties Generation transfigured the empirical "everybody needs" into a moral "everybody ought to have." Much of the narcissism within the Sixties Generation was a psychological and social reaction to the ethics of self-sacrifice and hard work which were so strong in conservative religious traditions. Put simply, many members of the Sixties Generation thought that this powerful emphasis upon self-sacrifice and hard work within institutional religion exacted too high a personal cost, that it forced the inner world to pay a terrific price. The moral values of self-sacrifice and hard work —with their once solid religious grounding in American culture

—became casualties of the Sixties. Their collapse has had incalculable consequences for American society ever since. The excesses of the Eighties (e.g., the tremendous acceleration of both personal and national debt, and the corruption in the savings and loan and junk bond industries) and the abuses of the welfare system are obvious manifestations. Part of many Americans' longing for the "old time religion" voices a yearning that self-sacrifice, honesty, and hard work may once again energize our lives and our society.

A Psychoanalytic Perspective

I will conclude this chapter on conservative religious traditions by summarizing my argument from a psychoanalytic perspective. Desire was indeed the mother of revolt in the Sixties, and that desire was oriented around the self. The balance between object-love and self-love—which religious traditions have always tried to inculcate—was lost during the upheavals of the Sixties, and in subsequent years. During the Vietnam War, there was a psychological reaction against religion, which then translated into a social reaction. This was part of the overall rebellion that we now associate with the Sixties. Many members of the Sixties Generation openly said that narcissism was not "sinful," that not all forms of narcissism were selfish or "bad." On the contrary, narcissism, it was argued, was healthy, even necessary, along with the self-indulgence that seemed to accompany it. Narcissism was considered by many as "good," even moral. It was thus "wrong" to neglect narcissism where the self then paid the price (all of this was what Lasch and Kohut saw in American culture). In the aftermath of the Sixties, many observed: "Didn't Jesus teach us to love ourselves as well as our neighbor?" Many in the Sixties Generation believed—and I think correctly—that their religious traditions emphasized the neighbor much more than the self. From this perspective, religion connoted a social ethic robbed of feeling. Churches did not seem capable of nurturing the inner world. Tradition was reduced to moral obligation without mystery, without "depth." The Roman Catholic Church is a good illustration of a tradition that has lost its sense of mystery since the Sixties, some would argue since Vatican II (I am thinking of things like the use of folk music in worship on a regular basis). Protestant traditions, however, are equally bereft of symbol and myth, and are equally guilty of eliminating pageantry and mystery in the name of "community," and "correct" dogma.

In reaction to dry dogmatism, the Sixties Generation cried out, "The inner world is worth nurturing!" Indeed, many of us became fascinated with the inner world and immersed ourselves in emotionality and spirituality. For some, psychology became the rage; for others, Eastern religions (e.g., Transcendental Meditation or the Hari Krishna and Vendantist movements); for yet others, drugs and sex filled the bill. All of those trends became popular in the Sixties because they focused on the inner world, the inner self that was home to spirit and feeling, the world of mystery and fantasy, the world of symbol, myth, and perhaps even magic. This great emphasis on what I have been calling a "healthy narcissism"—even if some of the manifestations of narcissism were not so healthy, as in the case of drugs, certain kinds of mental disorders, promiscuity, materialism, and cults— had a dramatic influence upon the entire culture, an influence still with us.

The Church realized in the late Sixties, perhaps too late, that indeed affect and the inner world had been neglected. The liturgical renewal movements in such denominations as the Lutheran, Episcopal, and Roman Catholic traditions, movements which accelerated during the Seventies and Eighties, can't be fully understood without realizing that these traditions were responding to weaknesses within their churches *and* the reactions of young people to those weaknesses. In the Sixties, many of the Baby Boomers turned away from their childhood traditions. Some Baby Boomers have now come back to those traditions in the 1980s and 1990s. They have children of their own, and want for them what their own parents wanted—a religious upbringing. But the Baby Boomers' attitude to religion often reflects a "pick and choose" mentality. They want the particular church that "meets their needs." Loyalty to a specific denomination has diminished in our secular age. It is now narcissism which largely fuels the religious quest, and that quest is usually for a church emphasizing fulfillment of the self (of which there are many). The Baby Boomers at the height of the Sixties said, "Self-sacrifice *is* important," but self-sacrifice turned out to be on our own terms. Why? Because what is *really* important to my generation is the way *we feel* (and think), and our own sense of our own significance. Just as Protestantism fostered an imbalance between self-love and object-love, the reaction to that imbalance on the part of the Sixties Generation has created another imbalance, but one shifted toward the opposite side—towards narcissism. And that is where we are stuck in the Nineties. A question I will raise when we come to the retrieval of tradition is how we can "turn the tide" of narcissism and shift some of our libido from love of self to love of others, thus restoring a more viable libidinal balance.

Conclusion

The first ball I threw up into the air was revolt, whatever the source of that revolt. Psychology and sociology are both important here. Certainly there was more than one reason for the revolts of the Sixties. Here, I have emphasized the rebellion against conservative traditions. A second but related ball we now have in the air is the Sixties Generation's quest for "healthy narcissism," a quest which often inspired unhealthy behavior and values. At this point, we will turn from conservative traditions to the more liberal, mainline denominations. What we will see there is not so much a revolt against tradition as its general neglect.

Notes

1. In high school we heard it said quite often (in the hallways and locker rooms) that the teenagers in these traditions had been so deprived of movies, dancing, card playing, television, and Rock and Roll, "that all that was left was the hayloft" (many of the pregnant teens were literally farmers' daughters).
2. They fit perfectly Max Weber's thesis in his book, *The*

Protestant Ethic and the Spirit of Capitalism; they felt—if only vaguely—that they were members of the "elect," and they worked obsessively to assure themselves that this was in fact the case. Moreover, their academic success assuaged any anxiety over the possibility that they might be mistaken in their assumption.

3. When Buddy Holly was killed, the producers of the show in which he had been scheduled to appear (in Moorhead, Minnesota) held a talent contest to find a band to add to the bill. A group from Fargo Central High, called the Shadows, won the contest. As Ed Ward writes, "Their lead singer, Robert Velline, chosen because he knew the words to all the hit songs, was catapulted into the spotlight, and soon found himself renamed Bobby Vee and being groomed for stardom. The next night, instead of Buddy Holly and Ritchie Valens, Frankie Avalon and Jimmy Clanton were on the tour." Ed Ward, Geoffrey Stokes, and Ken Tucker, *Rock of Ages* (*The Rolling Stone History of Rock & Roll*) (New York: Rolling Stone Books, 1986), p. 195.

4. In the Sixties it seemed that individual narcissism intensified as our cultural narcissism disintegrated, as if cultural and individual narcissism were sitting on opposite ends of a teeter totter.

5. In the Old West, a female operator of a saloon was usually a prostitute, and most likely a madam. To my recollection, "Gunsmoke" was silent about that issue.

6. See Idema, *Freud, Religion, and the Roaring Twenties*, pp. 11–12.

7. Ibid., pp. 26–35.

Chapter IV

The Withering Away of Tradition

Two Hypotheses about Mainliners

This chapter is the most important in my entire theory of the Sixties. (To return to my metaphor of the juggler, this will be the biggest ball of all.) It treats what I think is the most salient factor for an accurate interpretation of the Sixties Generation—the religious upbringing of the mainliners.

One way of understanding the sweeping cultural changes in any epoch is to uncover a common denominator within that group of people who brought about most of the changes, a common denominator powerful enough to account for much of what happened, or at least to explain some of the most important events and cultural transformations. My chief hypothesis, in brief, is this: the Sixties Generation, especially those of us who were raised in the mainline religious traditions, had a very weak religious background to rely upon for guidance and strength. The majority of the Sixties Generation were mainline Christians, if only nominally; but the majority of this majority had little knowledge not only of the Christian tradition, but also their own denomination's interpretation of that tradition. *The most important aspect of this overall ignorance was a glaring weakness in knowledge of the Bible.* (The weakness has endured. Most traditions

—especially my own, the Episcopal Church—continue to be very weak in teaching and interpreting the Bible, not to speak of teaching Christianity in general.)

One reason many conservative religious traditions have been growing so rapidly in recent years is that people flock to authoritarianism during periods of cultural upheaval and uncertainty, both of which have characterized our society since the Sixties. Secondly, people are drawn to churches where there is a Biblical emphasis, or the appearance of one. Actually, in most of these conservative traditions, usually only one Biblical lesson is read during worship, versus, for example, three in most Episcopal services (which rely upon a common lectionary). Thus, much of this "so-called" Biblical emphasis in conservative traditions is an illusion. Moreover, in many of those churches, the Bible is interpreted literally. However, this may be a distinction in Biblical interpretation that is more a clerical concern than one shared by the average churchgoer. The truly interested person in the pew may very well be more worried about the overall weakness in a church's Biblical education program than the particular presupposition which underlies that education (though this does not mean that people should not be concerned about the errors of fundamentalism and its anti-intellectualism).

A knowledge of the Bible is, obviously, the central foundation of religious faith in both Judaism and Christianity, as is knowledge of the Koran in Islam, or the Upanishads in Hinduism. Without a sound knowledge of the Bible, a Christian or Jew's religious house is built on sand—exactly the foundation upon which the Sixties Generation's religious house was built. We apparently preferred sand—or quicksand. We fit perfectly into Jesus' parable in Matthew 7:24-27:

> Every one then who hears these words of mine and does them will be like a wise man who built his house upon the rock; and the rain fell, and the floods came, and the winds blew and beat upon that house, but it did not fall, because it had been founded on the rock. And every one who hears these words of mine and does not do them will be like a foolish man who built his house upon the sand; and the rain fell, and the floods came, and the winds blew and beat against that house, and it fell; and

great was the fall of it.

The last verse of that parable is especially appropriate for my generation in light of what happened to us: "and the rain fell, and the floods came, and the winds blew and beat against that house, and it fell; and great was the fall of it." Without knowledge of, and emotional ties to, a religious tradition, my generation was deeply affected by traumas.

Let me recall my first hypothesis about my generation: we had a very weak religious background. A second hypothesis ties in with the first: as a direct result of weaknesses in the religious socialization of the Sixties Generation, or even its complete absence, traumas unduly threatened the self. These traumas threatened the self not only literally (in the case of Vietnam, for instance) but also figuratively, i.e., spiritually and psychologically. And what is the normal psychological reaction to threats to the self? Anxiety and narcissism!

Sometimes narcissism in this book means self-preoccupation, even self-absorption. At other times it means a healthy feeling of high self-esteem (and its deprivation is devastating for the personality, a deprivation that sometimes is misinterpreted as "excessive narcissism" when in truth it is being craved[1]). I am even sometimes using the term "narcissism" in reference to my generation's selfishness (as witnessed by our vanity and materialism, for instance). Freud thought of it as emotional investment in the self, and for him the term was value free. But at times he used another word for narcissism; he sometimes substituted the term "self-preservation," a very helpful substitution when interpreting the Sixties Generation. For Freud then, narcissistic libido helps to preserve, even protect, the self—its integrity, cohesion, safety, and identity. And it does this in the face of both internal and external threats.

Early in his career Freud had discovered that anxiety is a normal reaction to traumas. But then later on, he found that narcissism may be a common reaction as well. Sometimes this reaction is healthy, and highly positive in light of the circumstances. At other times, narcissism may be excessive, even inordinate. For instance, if we have an injury to our body, that often becomes our chief focus. Similarly, psychic wounds within the Sixties Generation brought about our self-preoccupations. We *did* respond to traumas with anxiety (and then repression, often thereby causing neurotic symptoms in the desperate attempt to bind that anxiety[2]). *Narcissism, however, was our most prevalent reaction.* That will be my chief argument. *The most important point I will be making is that there was direct connection between regression to narcissism and secularization.*

Before detailing my two overall hypotheses about the mainliners, let me summarize the central thrust of my theory of the Sixties. I have pointed out that religion, if it functions efficaciously, not only helps the believer bind anxiety, but it helps him or her curb narcissism as well. That dynamic in the psychology of religion lies at the heart of my theory. Since the religious socialization of the Sixties Generation was so incredibly weak, or even non-existent, religion played a small psychological, social, and moral role in the experience of many (my first hypothesis). As a result, my generation was highly vulnerable when the traumas of the 1960s began to seriously threaten the self (my second hypothesis). When narcissism was unleashed—which *is* the normal psychological reaction to any threat to the self—religion did not have enough strength to channel the libidinal currents away from the self, or at least a portion of that libidinal energy (enough to establish a healthy balance between object-love and self-love). In other words, there was not a solid religious and moral foundation underneath the personality structure, a foundation strong enough to prevent or modulate narcissism before it overwhelmed an entire generation. Let us remember that this generation was the largest, by far, in American history. So we are observing something here that was—and is—highly significant for the course of American history.

Narcissism and Idealism

Perhaps the reader is now wondering, "What about the 'famous' idealism of the Sixties, doesn't that prove that the Sixties Generation was 'religious'?" Maybe in the broadest sense. I am arguing, however, that this idealism even further highlights the weaknesses of religion, at least in its institutional form. Let me explain. First of all, the idealism of the Sixties did not have a Biblical base, for most of my generation anyway (it obviously did for some, such as many of the followers of Martin Luther King, Jr.). This idealism was, for the most part, *grounded not in religion but in narcissism.* Even the ideal of self-sacrifice, which *was* strong for many, was rooted in narcissism. For many, idealism merely served the self and fulfilled its needs for hope and identity, needs which became intensified by the surrounding social upheaval. The Sixties' idealism did help many of us to maintain a semblance of self-cohesion in the midst of the turmoil; that was very important to us psychologically. Moreover, the idealism provided meaning and direction in life when the traditions and institutions of society failed to do so. No doubt, some people were forever changed by this idealism (e.g., the movie director, Oliver Stone, Tom Hayden, who started his political activism at the University of Michigan in the early Sixties, Senator Bob Kerrey, and numerous others). And we should not underestimate the continuing influence of that idealism. In most instances, this has been among the positive effects of the Sixties. But most of the idealism I witnessed had shallow psychological, social, moral, and (especially) religious roots.

The movie *The Big Chill* captured that shallowness. It portrayed—very accurately—a group of University of Michigan graduates from the Sixties (in fact, from my own class, 1969, or one close to it) who gather at the funeral of one of their classmates in the 1980s. During the weekend depicted by the movie, the characters explore their own loss of idealism, their regrets and compromises. No doubt Lawrence Kasden, the writer and director of the movie, was drawing upon his own experience as a Michigan student during the Sixties, especially his recollection of the disillusionment and the abandonment of cherished ideals which so stamped the era's aftermath.

One of the historical functions of religion has been to anchor a society's ideals, both socially and psychologically (for example, a religion's marriage ceremony so functions). The loss of this function of religion was one of the Sixties' most significant casualties, as witnessed for example by the acceleration of divorces. To substantiate my point about the shallowness of the Sixties' idealism—its secularism—permit me to ask the reader two questions. What happened to this idealism after the Sixties? It collapsed like a deflated balloon. But why? Because when the traumas of the Sixties ceased to be threats to the self—particularly the Vietnam War—this idealism drifted away like the fading smoke of a dying "joint," to use another metaphor, one from the times.[3] Most of the idealism ended when the Vietnam War ended. The next set of traumas to hit the Sixties Generation occurred in the Seventies, and they were economic in nature (hyperinflation caused by the bills from Vietnam coming due, the oil crisis, the necessity of, finally, getting a job, the shock of learning the cost of diapers for the Baby Boomers' burgeoning families, etc.). These economic traumas did threaten the self, as did Vietnam, but the response was so vastly different. The response was not idealism, or organized marches, or collective rage, or outcries about injustices. The response was self-preservation, and that response took the form of accumulating money.[4] Economic traumas, more than anything else, hastened to transfigure the Sixties' idealism into materialism. After all, both this idealism and materialism had a narcissistic base; thus it is easy to understand how such a psychological and cultural transformation could occur, and then become a social trend for the 1970s, 1980s, and on into the 1990s. Perhaps the death of self-sacrifice, an ideal so important and so "alive" for the parents and grandparents of the Sixties Generation (who endured the world wars and the Depression), was the greatest loss of the Vietnam War.

Obviously, I have been generalizing about cultural trends, as all interpreters must. However, my two overall hypotheses about the mainliners (centered upon [1] the weaknesses of their religious socialization in the Fifties and early Sixties, or its complete absence, and [2] the failure of tradition to protect them from traumas) are, I believe, an accurate interpretation of my generation's narcissism. They might very well be the chief explanation for it, if such a thing could ever be proved empirically. To repeat, my theory of the Sixties emphasizes the lack of religious preparation for an entire generation, a void which left its members rather defenseless when facing such powerful traumas as Vietnam. Put in simplest terms, *the Sixties Generation did not manage threats to the self at all well. And judging from my generation's materialism, I am not sure we have improved in this regard since the end of the war.*

I have offered two hypotheses about the Sixties Generation in synoptic form. I will now expand upon them, flesh them out, so to speak. First of all, let's consider the childhoods of the Baby Boomers, at least those who were privileged enough to have grown up in the prosperity of the suburbs (mostly segregated) and were college bound. This was the group that changed American culture more than any other. Was there ever a generation in American history which had been given so much and then expected so much?

The Childhood of the Baby Boomers

I preached a sermon recently in my present church (St. John's Episcopal Church in Grand Haven, Michigan) where I argued that the Sixties Generation (mostly its white constituency) was the most spoiled generation in our nation's history. We were spoiled, in large part, because our parents gave us what they themselves did not have materially while growing up during the Great Depression. The prosperity of the Fifties, I argued, shows how successful they were.

One of my parishioners—who was in my high school class, my college class, and who lived up the street from me in the Fifties on Pinecrest Avenue in East Grand Rapids—come up to me after the sermon and offered this critique: "We weren't the spoiled ones, it was our younger brothers and sisters. And they are now the real materialists, they are the true 'Me Generation'" (both of us were the oldest children in our families). Perhaps. It did seem that there were some clear differences among the various age groups within the Baby Boomers back then and even now. It did seem to me, in the 1970s for instance, that my younger siblings' peer groups were more devastated than my own age group (born around 1947) by some of the things that happened in the Sixties, or emerged out of those turbulent years, that, for instance, the use of illicit drugs was widespread, having by then filtered down to the high schools and even the junior highs. Moreover, it did seem that promiscuity was more prevalent among the younger Baby Boomers, a legacy they in turn passed on to today's youth, who have excelled us all on that count! In high school, I didn't know what a joint of marijuana was, and my peers seemed to be prudes when their sexual activities were compared to the behavior of those who followed us. Perhaps our younger siblings are more materialistic, but all that can be debated within any family. Judging from the number of my contemporaries who are now AA, I would have to say that my peers did not go through the era unscathed by drug abuse. And judging from how many of us drive BMWs and Mercedes Benzes, I can't say we are innocent of materialism either. In addition, our sexual behavior was not particularly virtuous in the 1960s, being held in check more by fear of pregnancy than by moral values. Moreover, divorce afflicts all of us, along with the ensuing emotional problems. A generation is a generation, and all of its members, I think, are far more alike in their quirks, problems, and emotions than they are different. They are certainly more alike when compared to their parents! While there indeed may be some differences in the age strata within each generation, such as which rock groups are the current rage, or which songs are memorable, I am not concerned with such fine distinctions in this book. At least, I am more interested in what the Baby Boomers have in common, however significant the differences among age groups may be within any particular family.

Having said all that, let me offer this caveat: wasn't it the oldest child who was the most likely candidate for being the most spoiled, not the younger siblings, because the oldest had the most bestowed upon him or her, both in terms of love and worldly goods? Moreover, the oldest were the guinea pigs for the parents' initial attempts at child rearing, and they then fine tuned their skills with each successive child. So after spoiling the oldest child, they then, perhaps, backed off with the second child, and so on down the line. Even Freud said the oldest child expects the most from life because the mother instills images of grandeur. Freud himself was the apple of his mother's eye, and her oldest. Oldest children not only have the greatest expectations of what life should bring, but the greatest pressures to succeed, being the first from the family to launch out into life. Thus they also expect a great deal from themselves. I think it was the oldest children in the family among the Sixties Generation who found it particularly difficult to leave home for college. It was harder for us, I believe, than it was for our younger siblings who followed in our footsteps. We were also perhaps more homesick. So as I think about it further, my old friend was right, there are more than "fine distinctions" among the age groups in a generation. But I am going to treat the Sixties Generation as a whole, and you, the reader, can make your own age group differentiations based on your own experience.[5]

Be all of that as it may, most members of the Sixties Generation had wonderful childhoods in the Fifties (unless they were living in a ghetto). Our childhoods were relatively peaceful, relatively stable, and relatively affluent and innocent as compared to what came after, and in some cases, what came before. The nostalgia for that "golden age" is an ongoing dynamic of my generation. If you were fortunate (and most of us Baby Boomers were fortunate enough, at least those of us who were white and/or middle and upper middle class), you grew up in neighborhoods where you can still drive up and down the streets and name which family lived in which house, and point out which backyard you prowled around in as a youngster; perhaps you can still remember particular trees and bushes where you hid. On Pinecrest Avenue, my own street until 1961 (when we moved to the more staid Cambridge Boulevard), there was the Bennett house up the street from us; and Dan Aument, my friend at Ottawa Beach, lived up a few doors from us. Dave Nelson, another childhood friend with whom I was always getting into fights, lived up at the top of the street, and the Holstes lived right across the street from him, and the Yules still live next door to where the Holstes lived before moving to Lake Forest, Illinois. And there was "the gum lady," with her immaculate lawn and her endless supply of Juicy Fruit;

the Stiles lived right across from us, and the Bellaires lived next door to them, and next to the Bellaires lived Jim and Jean Johnson with their white 1958 Impala convertible. Back of their house there was a black water tower, over ninety feet high, that we used to climb, scared to death. Next door to the Johnsons lived this old man we were always afraid of, and on and on.

You get the picture. Pinecrest Avenue in the 1950s was a magical kingdom, or sometimes an enchanted forest. We lived at 821, that was my place of safety and warmth on a blustery winter day or during a scary Halloween night, or in the midst of Christmas joy. My childhood friends and I knew every yard in the neighborhood by heart, every tree, every configuration of bushes, every nook and cranny. After rainstorms, we would look for that pot of gold at the end of the rainbow which we knew lay in one of those yards, somewhere. We built countless forts, some above ground with lumber we "borrowed" from houses under construction nearby, and some underground with a labyrinth of dark tunnels lit up with candles, which cast an eerie glow as the light from their flames flickered off the earthen walls. We played capture the flag, and the entire neighborhood was our warring kingdom.

To understand the Sixties Generation, you must grasp the importance of such close knit neighborhoods for our psychological development; you must appreciate what it felt like to grow up in such places. We inherited a sense of safety, a sense of time, place, and order. We experienced a web of relationships we could rely upon. I think some of the movies of the Fifties, such as *The Invasion of the Body Snatchers*, *The War of the Worlds*, *Them*, *The Blob*, *The Creature from the Black Lagoon*, and all the other countless "invasion" movies then so popular, were gripping because they threw a pall of fear, even terror, over this sense of community and safety, because they drew forth anxiety that these things could be lost, that even your next door neighbor might be some "alien" now inhabiting the body of that familiar person you could always trust. These movies, and television shows such as "Twilight Zone," played upon our deepest anxieties, all of which coalesced into a threat to our home, family, neighborhood, and even "the American way of life" (one of the most powerful of all the myths we inherited). Of course, the Baby Boomers had lively imaginations, too, made livelier by the threat of nuclear war. Recall, this was a period when schools such as mine had regular air raid drills, and I can remember having vivid fears about what fallout would do to my skin (would it fall off, or turn into slime?).

I will conclude this discussion of neighborhoods in the Fifties and early Sixties by emphasizing some things which may, at first, not seem terribly important for the psychological make-up of the Sixties Generation. They illustrate many of the sweeping changes in American society since World War II. I will begin with my school buildings.

For my kindergarten year and for five of my six elementary school years, and for two years of high school, I attended classes in the oldest buildings in the entire East Grand Rapids school system. For one year of elementary school, my sixth grade year at Lakeside Elementary School, for two years at the junior high, and for my final two years of high school I attended classes in the newest buildings. The psychological—even spiritual—contrast was profound! For my freshman and sophomore years I was in the same high school building my mother graduated from in the 1930s. This old high school on Lake Drive was a red brick structure, built in accordance with the typical Georgian architecture of the period, with its smidgen of classicism that gave the whole structure its dignity of line and its atmosphere of higher learning. This old war horse had wide hallways and dark brown wood window moldings, which were always shiny. Overflowing trophy cases lined those hallways, and the place always smelled musty.

I often walked down those hallways late in the afternoon when nobody was around. My footsteps would echo down the corridors, and the sun would cast fleeting shadows all around me, shadows created by the branches of the old elm trees outside that looked like black lace against the fading sky. There I felt ghosts, the ghosts of those listed on the war memorial, the ghosts of the Class C state championship basketball team from the early Fifties, the ghosts of all those classes preceding mine, the ghosts of those who had lived and died but who had once laughed and loved in those same hallways, and studied hard or not so hard under those high ceilings in the same classrooms.

Speaking of classrooms, there I studied such subjects as Latin with Miss Hill, ancient history with the rather ancient Mrs. Robinson and math with "Ma" DeJonge, who had taught my mother. Such teachers were the last of a now almost extinct breed of incredibly dedicated teachers (at the time, however, we called them "battle axes"), whom we thought must have been old even when they were young. But they gave their lives so we could learn our Latin, or know our Roman and Greek history, or whatever we were studying. We worked our butts off for a B or that rare A (no grade inflation among that group, which would later become prevalent in higher education, beginning when grades preserved one's student draft deferment during Vietnam).

During our physical education classes in that antique school, we played basketball in its tiny gym, which always reeked of sweat and old tennis shoes. This gym had once been the home of a state champion, but it had been silenced long ago when the varsity games were moved to the new and larger junior high gym adjacent to Reeds Lake. (This remained the team's home until the new high school was ready for the 1963–64 season.) If we didn't play basketball, we swam in our aging swimming pool, which almost asphyxiated us with its chlorine. Our teacher, Carl Nestor, would make us do jumping jacks before getting into the freezing water. Of course, we were all in the buff, and he would bellow out, "Don't laugh, you all look equally ridiculous!" I think he was alluding to the syncopation, up and down, of that part of our anatomy which rarely sees the sun.

We also had wonderful dances in that smelly old gym, where the music would echo in every corner. We danced to such songs as Neil Sedaka's "Calendar Girl," the Crests' "Sixteen Candles," "Once in Awhile" by the Chimes, and "The One Who Really Loves You" by Mary Wells, or we would dance to the music of such local groups as the Kingtones, playing their regional hit record "Twins," or my own Rock and Roll band, the Renegades, which was just getting started in 1962. Such music would stir young hearts and heat up already throbbing libidos.

This gym was also the place where I forever ruined my knee in wrestling practice. The sport of wrestling was the worst choice

I ever made of a way to spend my late afternoons and garner glory for the East Grand Rapids Pioneers (Carl Nestor was also the wrestling coach, and the football coach, and my algebra teacher; so I associate him and his Fifties flat top haircut and his varsity jacket with those impressionable—and for me literally painful—years). Many years earlier I had taken social dancing in that same gym, during the fifth grade, wearing my brand new white suit and white bucks that I had hounded my parents for, until they finally relented, but then warned me, "You can look like a fool if you want to." However, after putting gobs of white powder on those shoes, and gobs of grease in my hair, I thought I look rather "cool" in that suit, I thought I looked like a cross between Pat Boone and Elvis Presley.

Many of you probably have your own memories of such venerable old schools before their post-World War II demise, when glass and steel replaced brick and wood. When that happened, our feeling for tradition diminished; our knowledge of the past declined; and our appreciation of a community's heritage—symbolized by its old school building—was weakened. After my sophomore year, we moved into a brand new "modern" high school several blocks away. I felt severed from the past, even my own past. I felt cut off from tradition. Now everything was so new, so bright and sparkling clean. It also smelled different, so fresh. We had dances in the new glassed-in cafeteria, but they weren't the same as those in that sweaty old gym. One important link to the past had been forever broken. The following is an unsigned letter to the editor of our student newspaper, the *Flintlock*, in the October 30, 1964 issue, expressing some of the same sentiments:

> Two years have passed since the students of East Grand Rapids migrated from that old worn building which they used to call East High. The juniors and seniors infrequently think about it in a blurred vision and the younger students sometimes see an apparition from the past which never really belonged to them.
>
> Did we leave something behind—something intangible, almost indefinable?
>
> It can be expected that moving from one building to

another can effect some loss of spirit and shedding of traditional events but a total lack of these things is frightening.

As for specific events, for all practical purposes we left the
pep jug, old clothes day, hall monitors, and sports assemblies
back in the old building. But it is more than that, something
invisible which haunts us. The product is a total lack of cohe-
siveness, pride, closeness, or whatever you want to call it. We
have successfully produced an aseptic, clean, white, brittle
school with a student body and faculty to match. There seems
a deficiency of co-operation or any attempt at co-operation
between the administration and students. It is almost as if a
fight exists over who shall put the highest obstacles in the path
of education.

We are flooded by a deluge of red tape which exemplifies
the inflexibility of our system. This shows a lack of basic confidence in the students.

The final mystifying question in this quiz is what happened to the spirit which carried us to the state finals in basketball only three short years ago. Where is the feeling of
fraternity, the electrifying spark, the drive which engulfed the
entire community?

Perhaps our wealth of fine athletic teams has made us fat
with confidence, and maybe a little shocked by anything less
than victory. This fatness, this lack of spirit, could gauge the
gradual deterioration of East High which began with our
migration from the old school to the new.

— A Reader

These old school buildings had an aura surrounding them that
can't be duplicated by modern architecture. My Victorian kindergarten building—once perched majestically upon a hill and standing sentinel over the abandoned football field of the old high
school (a new stadium had replaced it years earlier)—dated back
to the nineteenth century. Reportedly, it had been part of the underground railroad for escaped slaves seeking their freedom in
Canada; that is what we heard as kids, anyway, and it added to
the building's mystique. Sadly, it was torn down in the aftermath
of the Sixties when so many other old stately buildings were destroyed around the country, especially in our downtown areas and

on our college campuses (including my own in Ann Arbor). Here we see once again our society's abysmal sense of history. Americans are ignorant of how the past shapes us spiritually—hence the ease with which we tear down physical embodiments, "traces" of that past.

Let me offer yet another illustration of how venerable buildings help us appreciate what has come before us. Our old high school had an auditorium with a stage and theater seats, which our new high school could not afford (we used the large new gym). The names of those who had appeared in countless plays and musicals were etched or painted on the walls behind the curtains, including my own because I played the drums in numerous musical productions, and my Rock and Roll band played there a few times, too. As a sophomore in one of the annual musicals called "A Night of Rhythm," I played in a raucous "battle of the drums" in that auditorium with several juniors—including Tim Corl and another I will leave unnamed because he is now serving a long prison sentence for drug trafficking. After those shows the cast parties were always wild, and we would, in Sam Cooke's words, "twist the night away."

Here I am not referring only to old buildings, but their traditions as well. When I was in elementary school, on the night before the annual East Grand Rapids-Ottawa Hills High School varsity football game there would always be a gigantic bonfire, right below the kindergarten building and near that old abandoned football field. On the top of a ten foot high tepee of wood, a dummy of an Ottawa Hills football player was thrown, to the accompaniment of much cheering. The flames would engulf that dummy, helmet and all, and the sparks would fly up into that early autumn sky. The sound of crackling wood and the smell of burning leaves mingled with the night air. The trees surrounding that old Victorian kindergarten building standing up above us—a building which looked very spooky silhouetted against a harvest moon—would sway back and forth, buffeted by the wind. Those trees were releasing their leaves to that chilly harbinger of winter. Down below, we would huddle together drinking cider and eating fresh doughnuts. That bonfire was an annual autumn ritual of my childhood. As a culture, we have lost so much of that kind of ritual, ritual which brings structure and rhythm to our lives. Thus we have lost the ensuing emotions which mark time and build community.

As long as I am on the subject of buildings, I will quickly mention several other types which have largely disappeared from our communities, leaving additional spiritual voids. When I was in elementary school and junior high, we used to have a daily ritual of eating lunch in a little cluster of stores on Wealthy Street near the schools. We ate hamburgers and french fries at a diner, a type of restaurant which has almost completely disappeared from the American landscape. For lunch I would get what was called an "East High Special," which consisted of a hamburger, fries, and a phosphate (now almost extinct) for the grand total of 50 cents!

Then after school, we would return to the same stores and order sodas at Remes Drug Store. Remes, like most drug stores in the 1950s, had a soda fountain. Drug stores that served malts and sodas as you sat on those little round leather and chrome stools, that spun around and around while you talked to your friends, are about gone. Also gone are the juke boxes controlled by those little red song selection boxes (lining the soda fountain) which you would flick through to find the latest Elvis or Chuck Berry recordings. Now the full service gas station and the neighborhood grocery store and movie theater also face oblivion. (The dance halls that my parents' generation flocked to in order to hear Benny Goodman, Artie Shaw, or Duke Ellington had largely disappeared before the Fifties.)

When I was very young, an amusement park, Ramona Park, was still standing across the street from the stores I just mentioned. The park overlooked Reeds Lake. Our little town, East Grand Rapids, was originally a resort for amusement and cottages, long before it became the relatively affluent suburb it is today. Ramona Park was a childhood haunt for all the kids growing up in the area, and we especially enjoyed the bright orange excursion boat, the "Ramona Boat," which took us out on wonderful summer evening cruises around Reeds Lake. The smell of roasting popcorn filled the air on the decks, and when we leaned over the side, exploding colors from the amusement park were reflected up to us from the dark water. Sometimes the sunset would turn the lake into a sheet of fire.

The boat was scuttled and the park was torn down in the early Fifties, giving way to a shopping center and apartment complexes. These now cover the ground where, for example, the pavilion once stood where the Swing bands from the 1930s entertained hundreds of summertime dancers with such numbers as Bunny Berigan's "I Can't Get Started With You" and Artie Shaw's "Nightmare." My grandmother lives in one of those apartments, and when I visit her in the very space once enclosed by that pavilion, I sometimes think I hear, faintly, the refrain from Glenn Miller's "Moonlight Serenade" or "Perfidia." A supermarket now stands over the spot where the "fun house" and the "house of horrors" equally amused and terrorized us. The roller coaster, with its sounds of screaming kids and banking cars, is long gone, too, silenced by the wrecking ball. I have heard that "cat houses" also once stood there, somewhere, although as youngsters we could never find them.

Near the park there was a popular record store where we often hung out. This shop had those little booths that you could go into to listen to the records you might buy. I loved to fondle the 45s, and look at the colors of their labels. Some of the first 45s I bought in the mid-Fifties were Frankie Laine's "Moonlight Gambler," Jim Lowe's "The Green Door," Guy Mitchell's "Singing the Blues," and Elvis' double hit, "Too Much" and "Playing for Keeps." You would listen to ten, and buy five, that's how records were sold in the Fifties.[7]

Diners, drug stores with soda fountains, musty record shops with creaky wooden floors, neighborhood gas stations, movie theaters, grocery stores, and community amusement parks with excursion boats that could take you out on a lake on a summer night with the tinkling of a piano in the background, all of these things are pretty much gone from our society. But let me offer one final illustration. I refer to inner city churches. Many, once stately and architecturally significant, are today abandoned or neglected. Without question, the decline of the inner city church crystallizes the feeling I am trying to convey about our overall loss of tradition.

Most of these inner city churches were victims of migration to the suburbs (the Roman Catholic tradition, in particular, has had to shut the doors of many churches in downtown areas because the ethnic neighborhoods which once supported those parishes have disappeared). The church buildings which have replaced them in the suburbs are, however, in most instances rather sterile, usually as sterile as the suburbs they mirror. These churches are also as white as these suburbs (in most dioceses in the Episcopal Church there are always one or two congregations which are known as the "black congregations," and they are usually located in the inner cities, such as St. Phillip's Episcopal Church in Grand Rapids).

The downtown parishes which still exist more often than not are having financial struggles. Yet there is something grand about worshipping in a building where, perhaps, your great-grandfather worshipped, where the stained glass windows are of deep blue, bright red, and lush green, not the pale modern variety. In these old churches, polished dark wood abounds, and there are real pews, not chairs. The whole structure most likely has a certain kind of dank smell you can't describe, but that will forever remind you of childhood and your grandma's house (e.g., St. Mark's Episcopal Church in downtown Grand Rapids).

Grace Episcopal Church—the church I was baptized in, and my parents were married in—was once such a downtown parish. In the late 1940s, it was located on Cherry Street in Grand Rapids. The only thing I now can remember about this church is its magnificent rose window. The church was torn down in the early Fifties, its sacred space giving way to the more mundane space of a hospital parking lot. The parish followed most of its members out to East Grand Rapids, and away from the encroachment of an "undesirable" neighborhood (i.e., black, although the word used back then was "colored"). No doubt this migration also helped seal the doom of Ramona Park, which was then getting pretty seedy and attracting an "undesirable" element, hoods (not the Mafia type, but the "greaser" variety) and the blue collar beer-guzzling crowd.

Our consideration of what vanished in church ambience, when old structures were abandoned for new, provides entry into the climax of my theory: an evaluation of institutional religion in the Fifties and Sixties. We are turning from the Baby Boomers' childhoods, seen broadly, to one specific aspect of those childhoods—our religious upbringing.

Mainline Religion and the Sixties Generation

I will begin with a paper sent to all Episcopal clergy in 1990 by the national church office of my denomination in New York. It is entitled "Statement of Church Membership," and it was written by Donald W. Kimmick and Robert I. Bonn. This paper briefly documents religious decline in the mainline traditions, and then offers an explanation for this decline. The authors observe that "the period from 1965–75 was a 'baby bust' and church membership declined." [8] They then argue that this membership decline can be explained by dwindling birth rates and smaller families in the mainline traditions. They conclude that "the rapid growth in the smaller churches can be attributed to high birth rates."

In any discussion of religious decline (both loss of influence in American society and actual loss of membership) demographics must be considered; but this explanation does not fully account for the devastating membership decline many denominations and individual parishes have suffered since the Sixties. Moreover, demographics do not do justice to the psychological and sociological complexities of the problem. It is no coincidence that *the* pivotal year in the Kimmick and Bonn report is 1965, when American troops began to enter combat in Vietnam. The symbolic significance of that year did not dawn upon the authors! The fact that the turning point in mainline traditions was 1965 suggests other factors at work besides demographics. Of all the reasons for religious decline, the most important were some glaring weaknesses in the institutional Church of the Fifties and Sixties (weaknesses which to a great extent have not yet been rectified). Moreover, the Church supported the Vietnam War far too long, or remained silent. (This was particularly true in the war's early stages; although later on many clergy and denominational groups condemned the war—and even actively opposed it—the Church *as a whole* remained supportive of the federal government's war policies. This was especially evident among the *adult male laity*.) The Church's support of the war put it into a political and moral position contrary to the majority of the Baby Boomers. For now, though, let's take up the weaknesses, one by one.

A Weakness in Knowledge of the Bible

First of all—and perhaps most important in terms of its long range effects upon the culture—there was the widespread weakness in the Baby Boomers' knowledge of the Bible. This weakness, in turn, contributed to a weakness in their overall knowledge of religion, including the history and moral positions of their own denominations. Most churches in the Fifties and Sixties did a very poor job of teaching, preaching, and interpreting the Bible. Nor did churches do much to inspire their members to read it. The Bible, obviously, is one of the cornerstones of Western culture. It is necessary to know the Bible if one is to read, intelligently, Shakespeare or Milton, Fitzgerald, Hemingway, or Faulkner, not to speak of countless other authors, poets, and playwrights. To fully grasp the history of philosophy one must know the Bible. To understand the roots of modern psychology with such originators as Freud, Jung, or Watson, or more recent interpreters such as Rollo May and Carl Rogers, one must know something about the Bible and the religious traditions it fostered. To appreciate the great originators of sociology, such as Max Weber and Karl Marx, to name just two, one must know the Biblical tradition which inspired such thinkers. To understand the history of art, architecture, and classical music, one must know the Bible or be absolutely lost. Obviously, to know anything about Western religion, one must know the Bible. Its importance in the field of ethics—and in the creation of our own moral values—is immense. These are just some of the ways the Bible impinges on any well-rounded education, our own spiritual development included. The Sixties Generation, for the most part, was not raised to understand, inwardly digest, appreciate, and incorporate into their own experience, or even read, the great texts of Western culture. But it was *particularly* unprepared to read the Bible. I would also argue that one must be familiar with the Bible, and understand its central tenets (e.g., its proclamation of a God who works through history for redemptive purposes; its emphasis on social justice, particularly for the poor; its command that we do specific acts of mercy, such as visiting prisoners and the sick) in order to appreciate the great texts of Eastern cultures, including the sacred scriptures of their religious traditions. Why? Because we *must* know our own intellectual and emotional roots before understanding those of another culture. This is something Americans have not been very good at, with tragic consequences, such as Vietnam or, more recently, events in the Middle East. Many turned to the East in the Sixties and immersed themselves in Eastern religions, or such offshoots as Transcendental Meditation. Some, however, lost their bearings because they did not first have a foothold in their own tradition before they embraced a foreign one.

On the other hand, as I have said, during the Fifties and Sixties, churches—especially the mainline churches—didn't do a very good job of teaching the Bible. Here I am not referring to a mindless "the Bible tells me so" fundamentalism, nor am I referring to the memorization of Biblical verses out of context in order to impress parents or throw them at people like poison darts. I mean teaching the Bible on its own terms as story, myth, theology, symbol, history, poetry, literature, and wisdom.

Moreover, the churches of the Baby Boomers' upbringing had, in many instances, very weak preaching. This preaching did not enliven or illuminate the Bible in its original context, nor did it effectively correlate the Bible with (1) everyday experience (2) the pressing moral issues (e.g., civil rights, war, and nuclear weapons), or (3) a range of world events. When the Vietnam War escalated, this institutional weakness became even more noticeable, especially when so many clergy lent the war their support—a support which helped to undermine the authority of both the Bible and the Church within the Sixties Generation (many clergy later opposed the war, however). Many members lumped their parents and the family's religious tradition together because both supported the war. Thus many of the war-protesting youth rebelled simultaneously against the religion of their upbringing and against their parents. Here the Oedipus complex, with all of its rage, revolt, and rejection, combined with animosity towards the war—like gasoline with fire—to create an explosion in the culture. And the mainline traditions took the full force of the blast. They have never totally recovered.

This weakness in the Sixties Generation's knowledge of the Bible, and religion in general, has a long history, probably beginning with weak Christian education programs in churches. Postwar suburban churches were flooded with new families. Just as mass education was coming into its own following the Second World War (in order to accommodate the hugh new generation coming along), the Church faced its own equivalent onslaught. There were more Episcopalians, for instance, attending church in the Fifties than ever before—or ever since. Because of secularization, some of the Sixties Generation were not socialized into any religious tradition, but this was not the majority, by any means. The majority had some exposure to religion. However, the typical Christian education program in the typical parish of the 1950s was not very effective in *teaching the youth* about the tradition (Sunday school teachers were usually parents who themselves knew very little about the Bible).

Moreover, many churches had no adult education, or very little. Thus the parents of the Sixties Generation were allowed to languish educationally; this had a deleterious effect upon their children, both in churches and at home. How many families—as families—read the Bible together?

Preparation for the Sacraments

The preparation for baptism, confirmation, and marriage was very weak and often perfunctory. Take confirmation, for instance. It is, supposedly, the time in our lives we reaffirm as adults the baptismal vows said for us as infants. Confirmation strengthens our discipleship to Jesus Christ. Confirmation grafts a person psychologically into the Christian baptismal promises (e.g., forgiveness of sins, the gift of the Holy Spirit, redemption and liberation, the hope of resurrected life). Moreover, through confirmation one joins the Church (the catholic Church, i.e., the universal Church) as a full-fledged member with all the rights and privileges therein. So confirmation, obviously, is highly important, perhaps the most important decision we ever make as Christians (if we were baptized as infants).

But, having said all that, what was confirmation, *in actuality*, among the Baby Boomers (and here I am drawing upon my own experience in the Episcopal Church)? "A joke," as many of my friends put it, and many clergy still agree. Confirmation was an eighth grade rite of passage; as an event, it was more social than religious. It occurred at a time in our lives when we were too young and too distracted by other things to learn very much about the Christian tradition. We certainly did not learn very much about the Bible.

You could take just about every one of the Church's sacraments in the mass culture of the Fifties and Sixties, and if you examine how it was treated, it would fit like hand in glove Dietrich Bonhoeffer's scathing indictment of the Church in his essay "The Cost of Discipleship." There he coined the term "cheap grace" to refer to the Church's failure to link responsibility to the sacraments. As Kierkegaard (who influenced Bonhoeffer) emphasized, for centuries the Church—like a harlot—has been whistling to the culture to come into her confines so she could bestow upon it her favors. But then the Church betrayed both her profession and her sacraments by requiring little or nothing in return as "payment," either in terms of commitment, or attaining even a basic knowledge of what the sacraments mean. As a result, *most of the Baby Boomers grew up without associating religion with sacrifice and responsibility.* As an adolescent in the Episcopal Church—and I think my experience was fairly typical —I never learned that to be a Christian, a disciple of Christ, requires discipline, hard work, living a moral life, knowledge (and wisdom!), and self-sacrifice.

President Kennedy's 1962 Inaugural Address had a great effect upon me and my generation, especially his remark, "Ask not what America will do for you, but what together we can do for the freedom of man." But in my youth I never associated religion with that kind of idealism, that kind of sacrifice. My church did not help me make that connection. While growing up in the Church, I never truly understood what sacrifice meant from the Christian perspective, a perspective grounded upon the Bible that I and most of my contemporaries failed to learn. I grant that the Baby Boomers also failed, and continue to fail, their inherited traditions through neglect, laziness, and rejection. *But our traditions also failed us*, especially in the late Sixties when we could have truly used their help. So the failures of institutional religion in the Sixties were located on both sides of the altar rail; both the clergy and lay people can share the blame.

The Clergy of the Fifties and Sixties

Since I am talking about both sides of the altar rail, permit me to make a couple of observations about clergy of the Fifties and Sixties. I have already mentioned their support of the Vietnam War, especially during its initial stages. That certainly alienated many Baby Boomers.

Another major reason organized religion has failed so many people is the simple fact that, since the late Fifties and early Sixties, the Church has not been able to attract to its ordained ministry enough talented, well-educated, and psychologically stable people to fulfill its needs. There are many reasons for this. The compensation (in real dollars), training, and prestige of the clergy have been eroding for years, and this has taken its toll on the ordained ministry. The best minds and talent in American society since the Fifties have been carrying out their callings—not in the Church's ordained ministry—but in professions such as law, science, technology, business, and medicine. There the prestige and financial rewards are so much greater. This has not always been the case. The ordained minister used to be the best educated person in town, and the most respected, but those things are no longer true.

Many of the clergy of the Fifties and Sixties were not

particularly effective. One example illustrates this. When many of the Sixties Generation turned to the religions of the East, and then talked to their own clergy about those traditions, a conspicuous weakness was brought to light. Most clergy didn't know very much about religions other than their own! That was—and remains—a kind of intellectual myopia. Now let's take up another aspect of the Church that "turned off " the Sixties Generation.

The "Cold Church "

In many of the large suburban churches in the post-World War II era there was little sense of community.[9] Many Americans perceived—often correctly—that the Church was more of a "social club" than a true house of prayer, that it was a place where commitment to Jesus Christ was secondary to the social contacts one made. In addition, many churches, then as now, were felt to be "cold." (This was an accusation that much of the Church has responded to with liturgical revision, women clergy, various renewal movements and church interiors redesigned to accentuate community feeling.)

Not only was the Church experienced as cold as far as being a "community," but also in its social ethic. Churches were sometimes even bigoted. Many Americans saw their local churches doing little in the way of demonstrating that they had a social conscience. This was particularly evident in the *early* days of the civil rights movement, especially within white suburban churches.

The Sixties Generation saw this weakness, and it became the Church's Achilles' heel. The Sixties Generation's rage at the Church for its inertia and insensitivity in the realm of civil rights was, then, intensified by the support of the Vietnam War on the part of many Christians (especially parents!).

As the war began to tear American society apart, some churches dusted off their social ethic and began to speak to the weighty moral and social issues of the day. Many clergy started to oppose the war and work for civil rights, even if most of their parishioners did not. (This caused much friction in many congregations.[10])   But before the revolts of the Sixties forced the Church's hand—one more example in history where the Church was a follower of culture rather than its prophetic leader—many churches supported the political ideology of the power structure in control of the government and corporations of America.

To sum up, the "white" church failed to fight for civil rights and against the Vietnam War, racism, and sexism until it was absolutely embarrassing for congregations not to do so, although many never have. The Sixties put a spotlight on the Church's moral weaknesses. There were some obvious exceptions, particularly in the "black" church where such leaders as Martin Luther King, Jr. used the Bible and the Christian tradition to articulate and ground their battles for civil rights and against the Vietnam War. But white, affluent, mostly suburban churches in general— *the majority of whose members were the Sixties Generation's parents and grandparents*—did not take courageous moral positions for civil rights and against the war. Many members of the Sixties Generation regarded this failure as organized religion's unpardonable sin.

Television and Education

I will close this chapter on "the withering away of tradition" by pointing to several social forces which, although external to the Church, contributed to the Baby Boomers' lack of knowledge of religion. One is television. When the television set entered into American life in the Fifties, it became a competitor to the written word not only by replacing reading time, but also by influencing what the family did with its shared time. Families once sat together and read, either reading as a group or individually, but they were together, putting aside the time it takes to read because reading does take time. Television changed all of that.

It became the new focal point for the family; families hovered around the TV to watch their favorite shows, or any show, even eating their family meals in front of it! The family meal that began with a prayer or a Bible reading was left behind in the TV's wake. Moreover, a blaring television set made it very difficult, if not impossible, to sit in the same room and read. Television also competed with church activities. (In my church, once in a while someone will say at an important meeting, "Let's get this over with, my favorite TV show is soon going to start," or "The football game has begun.") Television, and now the VCR, have made us a culture more oriented around visual media than the printed word, especially the classic texts in the history of civilization (and here, of course, I am thinking particularly of the Bible).

Another social factor in this ignorance of both the Bible and religion has been the separation of church and state in American society. The churches were not effectively teaching the Bible and religion in the Fifties and early Sixties, but neither were the public schools, including public universities. The Bible and religion were not taught either as literature, history, or powerful social and cultural forces within both world history and American culture.

Moreover, most public schools have not dared to touch upon religion and morality in their course offerings because of the fear of controversy—a very real fear in many communities. Amazingly, American history has been taught for decades with narry a word said about the Bible, which then leaves out an essential part of the story of the founding of America, e.g., the source for the ideals, motivations, values and hopes which shaped our history. Consequently, an ignorance of the Bible and religion has been compounded; it has become an ignorance about the basic facts of American history itself, or at least the essential ones (those pertaining to the meaning of events).

It seems that the one "safe place" where religions and their sacred scriptures could be taught in public education—without controversy—would be in courses on the history of civilizations. But, sadly, religious traditions are often not even taught there.

Conclusion

The main argument of this chapter has been that teaching the Bible and religion in general, including world religions, has not been enough of a priority in the Church, the family and schools.

It is unconscionable that we don't understand our own traditions. But it is also a sad situation that we don't know—and appreciate—the religious traditions of other cultures, the knowledge of which would be a powerful force for world peace and mutual understanding.

My generation's abysmal knowledge of tradition left us highly vulnerable during the traumas of the Sixties. "There are no atheists in fox holes," they say. Well, we were in fox holes under siege during Vietnam. Maybe we weren't atheists, but we had a very difficult time coping. And it is this particular story about my generation to which we now turn.[11]

Notes

1. Kohut's "bad" narcissism is the inadequate narcissism that often gets misinterpreted as "excessive narcissism" in our culture. John Jacobs, my editor, made this observation to me in a written communique: "It may be more blessed to give than to receive—yet the capacity to receive may, paradoxically, take the form which makes the exercise of that capacity a profound gift."

2. Idema, *Freud, Religion, and the Roaring Twenties*, pp. 74–75, 86–86.

3. A "joint" is a marijuana cigarette, whose smoke was inhaled, held for as long as possible, and finally exhaled, usually with a gag. Then you were supposed to feel better, i.e., "higher."

4. On the role of money and its psychology in American culture, see my chapter "F. Scott Fitzgerald: From Religious Symbols to Symbols of Affluence" in *Freud, Religion, and the Roaring Twenties*.

5. However, I am curious to know whether the instigators of the revolts of the Sixties tended to be oldest children in their families. Were the campus radicals and creative artists of various kinds, who contributed so much to social change, the oldest children? Was it the oldest children in particular who used rock music to free themselves from the authority of the father? Was it the oldest children who were the most rowdy and the most obnoxious on campuses? Was it they who started the constant fist fights and egg throwing battles between my fraternity at Michigan, Alpha Delta Phi, and the "jock house" next door, the Sigma Chi's? The police got as tired of breaking up those fights as I did of cleaning the egg shells off of my car. Lastly, did the

high expectations of the oldest children, in particular, turn into rage, and then disillusionment? Intriguing questions. I will leave their answers in the hands of some future dissertation writer!

6. See ibid. for a theory of ritual, pp. 166–169.

7. Not only have record stores been disappearing, but the records themselves. They have given way to the CD. What we have gained in sound we have lost in album cover art work.

8. Donald W. Kimmick and Robert L. Bonn. "Statement on Church Membership," prepared for the Office of Evangelism Ministries, Education for Mission and Ministry Unit (New York: Episcopal Church Center, 1990), p. 4.

9. On the loss of community in American society, see my chapter "Ernest Hemingway: From Religious Communities to the Privatization of Religion" in *Freud, Religion, and the Roaring Twenties.*

10. These wounds have not healed to this day in many congregations. In the search process for new clergy, some churches make it very clear in the literature they send to prospective candidates that they do not want a minister who will be a social activist.

11. In *Freud, Religion, and the Roaring Twenties,* I concentrated on the increase in neurosis, featuring the younger generation following World War I. Here, treating another war-torn generation, my theme will be narcissism.

Chapter V

Three Traumas of the Sixties

Narcissism and the Sixties Generation: a Thesis

In the last chapter we discussed the loss of tradition within the Sixties Generation, particularly among the mainliners. Here we will be facing the consequences of that loss. I am arguing that the loss of tradition meant that the Sixties Generation was ill equipped, either psychologically or morally, to master a series of traumas. I will concentrate on three: (1) sexuality; (2) leaving home and the concommitant responsibility to prepare for a career; and (3) Vietnam.

That list, obviously is not exhaustive. It certainly does not represent the sort of trauma one would encounter almost daily within inner cities or on an Indian reservation. But those were the crises which most affected those of us Baby Boomers who were college bound around 1965, who had come from privileged backgrounds, and who were the driving force behind the bulk of the cultural changes in the Sixties (by the sheer force of numbers if nothing else!). The heart of my argument is that narcissism was our principal, shared reaction to these traumas.

Recall that earlier I argued that one of the chief functions of tradition is curbing narcissism. Here I will be emphasizing that there was little or no tradition in place—both collectively and psychologically—to limit that narcissism and, thus, help us balance the two currents of the libido. I will also discuss some of the effects these traumas (especially Vietnam) have had on American culture. With that synopsis of my overall argument, I will now turn to the first of the major traumas the Baby Boomers faced, sexuality.

Forbidden Fruit: the Trauma of Sexuality

My generation was betwixt and between. We were more secularized than our parents, but not nearly as removed from tradition as those who followed us in the Sixties' wake. For most of us attending high school during the early Sixties, morality still had plenty of power to prevent sex and cause a lot of havoc. Part of what we experienced was the fear of pregnancy, but we also had a fear of sex itself. Moreover, tradition had enough residual power to cause guilt, lots of it—if not for our actions then for our fantasies! When we were being raised, we had no doubt where the Church stood on sexual matters, even if sex was not widely talked about in the churches.[1] The Baby Boomers didn't pay as much attention to their religious traditions as their parents had during their own youth, but the younger siblings of older Baby Boomers paid even less. They knew less, and they cared less! But for us, tradition still had some pull during our adolescence, as we stood at the precipice of "the Sixties"—with the heyday of mainline church growth in the Fifties behind us, and the onslaught of social change in front of us. This was change unlike anything our culture had ever seen before (or will ever see again, during our lifetimes anyway).

So what was the trauma in this murky realm of sexuality? It was this: our sexual desires were at their peak, or felt that way, at a time in our lives when in Biblical days we would have already been married. Yet the Baby Boomers had no sanctioned outlet for those desires. That was the trauma—no satisfactory outlet for all concerned. This situation of frustration and conflict was, in large part, what the revolt of the Sixties was all about.

Religion was no help to us, absolutely no help. The Church

could have at least explained to us the complexity of the problem (especially since our parents didn't!). Even masturbation was wrong in the eyes of the Church, and—although the Sixties did precipitate the gay rights movement—I can't imagine the psychological horror of being a homosexual in the climate of the Church at that time (not that it is all that much easier today, with the increasing prevalence of both AIDS and prejudice).

So what were we to do? Play sports? Yes, we could sublimate our libido into sports; we were even encouraged to do so. (And maybe that is why our society has been so sports crazed for so many years.) And we could take cold showers, lots of them. Our frustration was very real, and much damage was caused by sexual repression and suppression. As I pointed out earlier, those Baby Boomers who did have sex as teenagers usually felt so much fear and guilt during sexual intercourse that they didn't enjoy it anyway.

Some of the Baby Boomers married at eighteen or so, but this was a tiny minority, and I doubt they knew very much about the institution of marriage, either sacramentally or psychologically. Most of the Baby Boomers did not marry young, however, another social change brought by the Sixties. Thus, according to the church and society, we had to cope, somehow, with our sexual urges until much later, when we did marry. But, of course, many of the Baby Boomers have never married, and of those who did, many are now divorced (all of this was part and parcel of the sexual revolution of the Sixties). So we coped (or tried to!). As the Rolling Stones sang in 1965, "I can't get no satisfaction." (Satisfaction was what the ensuing years would be all about!)

The Church, even to this day, has not offered much of a guiding hand in this whole morass of sexual morality, where too often ethics are "made to order" for the great variety of living situations people have found themselves in since the 1960s. So, sexuality remains fraught with fear and anxiety, over and above the dread of disease and pregnancy. Here is the basic problem.

During adolescence, the emotions are not mature enough for people to engage in sexual intercourse and yet maintain that delicate balance between the sensual and affectionate currents of the libido. If a couple enters into a sexual relationship in their teenage years, or even in their twenties outside of marriage, there is a real danger that sensuality will dominate affection, establishing a dangerous pattern for life (even beyond the twenties these dangers remain, of course). Tremendous guilt is incurred when a person realizes that his or her own narcissistic needs are predominant in the relationship. The spiritual and moral tragedy of such situations is that an insidious pattern of "using" another person to satisfy one's own needs begins very early in life. Narcissism may then dominate all subsequent relationships, as we have seen so often since the Sixties. Narcissism may also lead to the feeling of "being cheap," or to feelings that relationships are not what they should be, or what one had hoped. Dreams shatter, and disillusionment permeates the soul like a poison.

Much of the narcissism of the 1970s, 1980s, and on into the 1990s was a by-product of the sexual revolution of the 1960s, a revolution that was, in reality, *secular*; yet, perhaps paradoxically, it is weaknesses in the institutional Church that have been a major cause of immoral and destructive sexuality. Let me explain.

Narcissism was both a product *and* a cause of increased sexual activity. Narcissism and the sexual revolution fed off of each other like wounded sharks. The sexual revolution fed the insatiable demands of narcissism, and narcissism helped instigate the sexual revolution. Certainly narcissism has had causes other than increased sexual activity, but nowhere else, during the Sixties anyway, do we see narcissism so clearly, so vividly. The narcissism which arose from other causes, such as from the threat of the war, attached itself to sex like a leech. And indeed, many felt like they had been sucked dry after they had been used, abused, and dispatched.

Adolescents are simply too young, too immature, to know very much about self-sacrifice. They are too young to know very much about the paradox (prominent in Christian thought) that personal fulfillment is discovered in the joy and fulfillment of the other. Under the impact of secularization, many Baby Boomers were not exposed to such ideals. Thus in much of our adolescent and post-adolescent sexuality, the needs of the self dominated relationships. It should come as no surprise that narcissism emerged as the dominant psychological dynamic.

When narcissism dominates a relationship, altruistic and tender feelings toward the other—the feelings fostered by religion—are extremely difficult to feel. The sensual current of the libido overwhelms the affectionate current. As a result, the Biblical "hardness of heart" often comes to the fore, especially when there is no commitment.

Lack of commitment has become a pitfall of promiscuous sexuality for all age groups since the Sixties. "Living together" outside of marriage has been the outward and visible sign of this inward lack of commitment. Break-ups in these kinds of relationships are often as traumatic as divorces; moreover, the property laws are not protective, adding to the trauma.

For all of the above reasons, institutional religion upholds the standard of marriage (since the Sixties, however, some—including many clergy themselves—have questioned that standard). The Church has traditionally argued that only in marriage can sexuality have the necessary security to be fully experienced, both emotionally and physically—without jealousy, fear, and rage.

The Baby Boomers inherited from their own families very high ideals of what a marriage and a family should be. Our difficulties in achieving what we had in childhood, or what we hoped for, have been a cause of much pain and guilt. The sexual revolution left in its wake broken hearts as well as broken dreams, and it overwhelmed many with deep feelings of betrayal. We acted in ways that would have been devastating for us had our own parents acted in the same way, either in their own youth or during our childhoods.

Sex for the Sixties Generation was, and for many remains, an escape from a brutal reality. Like the drugs people abused, sex eased the pain, especially the pain from Vietnam and the racial, social, and economic injustices of society. But very few people were truly able to handle the emotions intertwined with all of that sex. Few of us were psychologically, morally, and spiritually equipped to handle intimacy. (I don't think many people who lived through that turbulent era will take issue with my observation.)

Let me now summarize this section on the trial and tribulations of sexuality. Many members of the Sixties Generation did not make sensitivity to the feelings and needs of others a higher priority than the needs of self. This was one effect of secularization (arising from our ignorance of traditional religious teaching about self-sacrifice). Narcissism was thus a strong dynamic in many relationships, and feasted upon many a person. Few truly experienced commitment from a traditional religious perspective, where sex was put off until marriage. Just as the idealism of the Sixties was not religiously grounded for many people, similarly, many relationships were not grounded upon much of anything either—except desire and narcissism. Consequently many of these collapsed once that desire waned or was sated. It was not simply that relationships among the Sixties Generation were bad —although, God knows, many of them were—it was that far too many were not adequately grounded. Far too many relationships were not enriched, protected, or sanctioned by symbols and rituals, especially those found in religion. This failure of religion —and our failure toward our religion—paved the way for some of the inordinate narcissism which crept into so many relationships.

Nor did the Church articulate the complexity of the sexual problem. It didn't face the basic issue—the "biological trick of nature," which causes such passion at an age when the consummation of that passion does even more damage than repression or frustration. We were either guilty or unsatisfied much of the time, and in many instances we felt both all the time. The Church did not respond to this "Catch 22" pastorally. It didn't speak to us with real wisdom and guidance, along with firmness and compassion. "Thou shalt not" was not enough for us in the presence of the forbidden fruit. We were left to figure it out on our own, and many of us never did.

The Trauma of Leaving Home

Another trauma the Sixties Generation faced, en masse, was leaving home, whether it was going off to college (my main interest here) or Vietnam, or leaving home for some other purpose and destination. Our parents, whose childhoods seldom included the material abundance we enjoyed, worked hard to give us what they themselves did not have (most likely during the Great Depression). But I am not at all sure my generation truly appreciated the sacrifices our parents made for us. We took a lot for granted. To be frank, we were spoiled.

Education was one of the things presented on the proverbial silver platter, one of those things many took for granted. Indeed, I wonder how many truly appreciated that gift at the time, and how many took full advantage of it. Our education was given to us, but we had to leave home to attain it (most did anyway). And that separation was one of the first major shocks of our lives! We were not psychologically prepared.

The one song from the era which captures best all of our feelings connected with both separation from the home and our responsibility to prepare for adult life is "She's Leaving Home" from the Beatles' *Sgt. Pepper's Lonely Hearts Club Band*, an album that more than any other spoke to the Baby Boomers in 1967 (particularly during its incredible "summer of love" when all hell broke loose, especially in our inner cities, drug use accelerated, the Doors' first album came out with songs such as "Light my Fire," "The Crystal Ship," "Alabama Song," and "Break on Through," and we all were freaking out!). Paul McCartney caught our sad mood in his haunting vocal, which reverberated through the rooms of many a late night party when the lights were low, everyone was mellow, and it was about time to call it quits.

The Sixties Generation did not know how to handle such feelings of separation constructively. It was the warmth of our own homes that made our separations particularly difficult. In psychiatric jargon, the Sixties Generation was "acting out" its rage and depression (in psychoanalytic theory, rage and depression are flip sides of the same coin) on college campuses, in reaction not only to war and injustice, but also to separation from home (this included the related developmental traumas of loss and abandonment). Thus American society had on its hands a generation that was both the largest in its history *and* the most explosive. (Or, to put it in more technical language, members of the Sixties Generation were regressing to feelings of narcissism at the same time—a shared reaction to shared traumas.)

As a component of that regression, other primitive (i.e., developmentally early) feelings surfaced in conjunction with our feelings of self-preservation—for example, desires for merger and deep longings for security. All of this entered into the sexual behavior of the Sixties Generation. Other aspects of my generation's regression were revelling in dirt, even feces (more than one college administrator had turds deposited in his or her office), being rude and slovenly.

Our childhoods, often idyllic (remember once again all those television shows mentioned earlier, such as "The Adventures of Ozzie and Harriet," "Father Knows Best," and "Leave it to Beaver," with their idealistic portrayals of the postwar home), created very high expectations of what life should bring. The fact our childhoods were so good, was what made it so difficult to leave. For leaving home meant that we were leaving our childhoods behind. Many of us grew up in families where our mothers were still at home, not yet forced by economic circumstances (or by greed) to bring in that second paycheck. Thus it was a real jolt for us to separate from that secure, nurturing, warm home—to adapt to the relatively unsheltered life at a large state university, for instance.

There is no question about it, many Baby Boomers had privileged childhoods, which in a sense carried right on through adolescence, and sometimes even beyond college graduation (although that was the symbolic end of childhood for most of us, if not the literal one). Let's admit it, we were given so much. There were summers on the beach when we didn't yet have to work. (We were the generation the Beach Boys sang about, the generation who, if we weren't on the beach, fantasized that we were, the generation whose daddy took the T Bird away if we got too far out of line.) We were given plentiful toys to play with, and then, later on, nice cars to drive (more expensive toys!). We were given trips to exotic places. We were offered dancing lessons, riding lessons, and encouraged to get some culture with music lessons, and we were given the musical instruments to go along with them.

Up through college I spent my summers on Lake Michigan, most of them at a little resort called Castle Park, near Holland.

There I had the opportunity to establish a wonderful peer group, friends such as Carol Blossom, Doug Veech, Tom and Andy Watling, Kay, Nancy, and Elizabeth Zeller, Susan Beebe, Dick, Amy, and Chris Muzzy, Morgan and Holly Hall, Gray, Katie and Ted Lerchen, Gay Barber, Bill Parks, Steve and Suzy Nobel, Betsy and John Clarke, Baker Moore, Rick Steketee, Nancy Redding, Carol Hedbloom, John Kunkel, Ernie Kelly and many others, including a whole raft of southern kids who came up north to work in the summer hotel, the Castle. They stayed out in back of the hotel in living quarters called "the Shack" and "the Henhouse." The latter, of course, was where the women lived, and thus the place where we had numerous parties. Most of the names of these kids have escaped me, excepting a few such as Trish Rose, Andy Cyrus, Tommy Flowers, Dick Shepherd, Dale Irwin, Del Sutton (who, as I remember, was a very pretty blonde, unfortunately pinned to some ATO from a southern university).

Just about every southern school was represented one summer or another down through the years. Both the personal names of these southern kids and the names of their schools, along with the school's colors, were painted for posterity on the walls of the Shack and Henhouse. (The schools included Georgia, Auburn, Alabama, Mississippi, Tennessee, Florida, and Vanderbilt.) For me, the names of those schools still have a romantic ring; they evoke William Faulkner, the taste of bourbon, the smell of pipe smoke and curing hams, and the mystery of a different way of life, slower and more genteel. In fact, the Castle was modeled on southern resorts, being owned by southerners, the Carter Brown family. All the traditions surrounding the hotel echoed times long past: formal dances, formal dining, Labor Day pig roasts, horse shows, stables, stories about ghosts in the tower of the Castle, the legend—and possibility—that the Castle was the model for the Wicked Witch's castle in Frank Baum's *The Wizard of Oz* (the author had summered nearby in Macatawa Park, and he was seen gazing at the Castle towers many years ago; the Oz Society met annually at the Castle until the hotel was closed). The Castle exuded southern charm. The blacks on the staff had their own separate living quarters, I should add, preserving a less attractive aspect of that cultural past. Indeed, the Castle represented a way of life rapidly passing away, and not just in our little resort on the shore of Lake Michigan.

Every summer those of us whose families rented or owned cottages would eagerly await the arrival of the fresh batch of southern kids coming up north to wait on hotel tables or work in the kitchen. We wanted to know who was new, and who had returned for yet another summer of parties. The males (and females!) in my group were particularly interested in those southern belles whom the hotel called "pixies." We were enchanted by their accents. These southern kids brought charm, vitality, and pulchritude to our little resort. Their lively renditions of "Dixie" in the shows they put on in our buggy Greek revival amphitheater still haunt my memories and evoke long forgotten dreams of summers past.

During those Sixties summers, my group had college draft deferments in hand to protect us from Vietnam's hells (and guilt plagued us, for we knew that others from less privileged backgrounds, especially blacks, were doing most of the fighting). During those summers of escape, we had numerous beach parties, often with kegs of beer. Many of these parties were held at the foot of "Baldy," a majestic sand dune south of the park. We also had cookouts with fresh corn steamed in the husks, and we held many lively dances on our "dance dune" overlooking the lake. My band played at many of these, and the music drifted across the entire park.

From time to time we took early evening excursions to the dune scooters in Saugatuck, a charming resort a few miles south of Castle Park. I had bought a 1962 Lincoln from a friend's brother, who was going into the military. It was burgundy, but I always thought of it as my "purple Lincoln." It had real leather in the interior, and a generous supply of wood on the dash and door panels. (I could cruise at ninety coming home from Ann Arbor and nobody in the car would know it.) I would pile about twelve kids into that Lincoln for the adventure of driving the bumpy road from Castle Park to Saugatuck. Dune scooters were hot rod cars from the 1940s and 1950s, with open tops and balloon tires. These old Mercuries and Fords tore up and down and in between the white sand dunes north of the pier, where the Kalamazoo

River flows quietly into Lake Michigan. During those soft summer evenings at sunset, the sky was often flushed with red, as if from a wound.

During those same summers, many times we ventured far out into Lake Michigan in beautiful wood speedboats (Centuries and Chris-Crafts), now a rarity. There we would party, go swimming, and drink beer on that blue sheet of glass (if the lake was calm). The glistening white sand dunes stood at attention far off in the distance. They were partly covered with beach grass, and were crowned with lush green trees: pine, birch, poplar, and beech. Then later on, having had enough of the hot summer sun, we would water-ski back to shore, accompanied by the blaring music of the We Five's first album, *You Were on My Mind*. Songs such as "Beyond the Sea," "Love Me Not Tomorrow," "Softly as I Leave You," "If I Were Alone," and "I Can't Go Home Anymore" mingled with the spray from the boats and the roar of the powerful engines. One of my good friends, Susan Beebe, would cut through the water on her slalom ski, making figure eights far out in the back of the boat, throwing water high into the air and making dozens of rainbows in the bright sun. She would dance, skip, and jump over the waves with her long blond hair flying in the wind.

During those summers we drank beer all season long—on boats, in cottages, on the beaches, in the Henhouse, in the Shack —while others, without deferments, were dying in Vietnam.

On rainy days, we would sit in our cottages and play bridge to the plaintive music of Ian and Sylvia's albums, *Play One More*, *Four Stong Winds*, *So Much for Dreaming*, and *Early Morning Rain*.

Indeed, many of the Sixties Generation had privileged upbringings (varying in degree, of course). Some of us went to high schools where we were "popular," where we had boyfriends or girlfriends, were good at sports, or, like me, had a well-known Rock and Roll band which played in teenage night clubs throughout Michigan. The Sixties Generation was especially blessed with close knit "circles of friends." This was the group we shared so much with—pain as well as joy; these were, and are, the friends we often still value as our best (and if we no longer know where they are, that is a deep source of regret). "Home," "summer," and "friendship" were powerful symbols for my generation. But what did many of us leave all of that behind for after graduation from high school? We left it for the alienation of life at a large state university, where we went from being known and secure in our identities to being a number and a nothing—unless, of course, we played varsity sports and were thus "jocks," as we called the members of that elite fraternity at the University of Michigan. Freud said leaving home is one of the most difficult of all the developmental hurdles to master. For the Sixties Generation, this was particularly true because when we left home for a very uncertain future—especially for those who went to Vietnam —we left more comfort and security behind than any previous generation in American history. No generation had it so good while living at home. And no generation had more difficulty leaving it all behind.

Something that was very evident among my generation was the "sophomore slump." For some reason, my friends and I felt little homesickness during our first year. It was during our second year, when we fully realized that we could not go home again. It was then when we knew that high school, with all its pomp, romance, security, and glory, was finally over. It was then that we knew we could not hang onto our high school sweethearts any longer. They were at their own schools, and they were going through the same things.

Many high school couples did try to stay together through college, not without difficulties and not without fear, anger, jealously, and sometimes even depression. But most of us knew instinctively that in order to "mature," we had to move beyond wonderful memories, long cherished dreams, and old girlfriends or boyfriends for something new. But what? It was that uncertainty about the future (sometimes symbolized by our uncertainty about whom to ask out for a Saturday night date, and whether we would ever find a relationship at a large university as meaningful as the one we had left behind)—coupled with nostalgia for high school or even childhood—which created those sophomore slumps. Vietnam didn't help, either. And we drank too much or used other drugs. We were mourning our lost childhoods, rapidly disappearing behind us. In short, we were experiencing grief. We were making the same separations from our past as a bereaved person. According to psychoanalytic theory, mourning instigates deep regression. As we "work through" our current separations, earlier childhood fears and traumas are revived (concerning separation, loss, and abandonment). It was the Sixties Generation's mourning for the past—our regression—which became one of the chief conduits through which narcissism flowed, like a surging river, into American culture. It was difficult for us to look ahead, especially in the midst of Vietnam. So we regressed to the past. And powerful feelings, originating from childhood, were relived. During the Sixties—and especially during those sophomore slumps—we almost drowned in the emerging narcissism, which was so often a very sad feeling (one that further fueled our nostalgic mood). I used to sit up late many a night with my close friend, David Huff, who had lived next door to me in my freshman dorm, Winchell House of West Quad, and we would talk for hours about the past. We would go out for hamburgers at Crazy Jim's, a little joint near West Quad which served scrumptious, if greasy, food. Or we would order pizza from Domino's or the Cottage Inn, and we would listen to such songs as Johnny Rivers' "Poor Side of Town," Buddy Holly's "True Love Ways," and "Cherish" by the Association, or the haunting music of Smokey Robinson and the Miracles ("OO Baby Baby"). We would then reminisce about our high school girlfriends and how good things were back then. We were mourning for what we had lost. That aching, sad, weepy feeling in your gut during a sophomore slump was horrible to endure. It was extremely hard to make it go away. It was often coupled with regret—and sometimes rage—at our own stupidity for breaking off a relationship for the sake of the maturity that we knew we needed but didn't especially want. My own nostalgia always seemed to be intensified by the waning four o'clock sun and the shimmering leaves in an Indian summer breeze. When everyone else seemed to be scurrying around campus—through the Diag (the open grassy area in the center of campus, carved up by sidewalks leading to a large brass "M," which you were never supposed to step upon), in and out of the libraries or the Michigan Union—I wondered if I were the only person in the world feeling that way.

Many Baby Boomers were homesick during the fall of '66 (or whatever year, or season, it was). But yet those of us who felt that way did appreciate things more. We appreciated things more because our emotions were so raw. We hadn't yet become hardened. We hadn't yet become the cynics we would become when the war was so prolonged. We were not yet agonizing about Vietnam and its horrors. In technical language, we had not yet repressed our feelings, which so many would do later at the height of the Sixties. The emotional intensity became more than we could endure. Before that happened, however, for a brief period in our lives we felt the autumn air and saw the Halloween pumpkins as we never had before, and we heard the music drifting through the October nights from dorms and frats and smelled the cigar smoke at football games as we never would again. It was truly magic.

For some, the problem was simply one of confusion. In high school, life was so clearly mapped out, but now we were faced with the whole world, and we were faced with the rest of our lives. Talk about being overwhelmed! And then our parents began to exert pressure, around the time of our sophomore year: "Don't you think it is about time to decide what you want to do in life?" "What are you going to do when you graduate?" "Don't you think you better plan ahead?" Plan for what? Plan for what when you might get your head blown off in Vietnam! "Nag, nag, nag, life is a drag," was a poetic line of my roommate's that he intermingled with his profanity. But that indeed was how many of us felt. The movie *The Graduate*, with that famous line, "plastics," accurately caught our mood, our uncertainty, our alienation, that pit in our stomachs when we felt paralyzed, unable to act, unable to move. Like Benjamin Braddock in the movie, we floated on a raft, drifting around drinking beer. Or we escaped the world by smoking some grass and listening endlessly to the Moody Blues' song, "Nights in White Satin," or by blasting the Temptation's "Get Ready" and "Girl, Why do You Make Me So Blue" and the Chambers Brothers' "The Time Has Come" (the long version) on our stereos for all the world to hear. Let me now bring religion to bear on these issues.

Max Weber showed in such sociological works as *The Protestant Ethic and the Spirit of Capitalism* that religion had once inspired work. Work was a calling, a "beruf" in Luther's terms. The Christian worked for the glory of God and in obedience to God's will. Work was a sacred duty. Work was grounded upon religious faith. But, as Weber discovered, when secularization seeped more and more into Western culture, work became less and less of a calling and more of an obligation, one with almost all the religious emotion washed out. Weber also discovered that when a society becomes secularized, work is viewed not simply as an obligation but drudgery. As we put it in our fraternity bull sessions, "Work is a pain in the ass!" In other words, work was an adult responsibility few of us looked forward to. So our response? Have another beer! Any possible religious grounding for our future plans had completely disappeared by the time the Sixties Generation faced that dreaded hurdle of, God forbid, a job.

In sum, the religious context for work had collapsed under the pressures of secularization. Obligation remained, but it no longer had the glow of religious inspiration; it no longer had religious force. We *were obligated* to do what our forefathers wanted to do. That was the central difference between us and our parents, and especially our grandparents. Education for the Sixties Generation did not serve goals and ideals grounded in religion, nor was our education inspired by our religion. Those of us who grew up in the Fifties and early Sixties had little ability to co-ordinate goals in life with our education, and then unify it all with a philosophical or theological world view. Here we have another serious failing of our religious socialization.

Our attendance at large, secular universities did not rectify that situation either. There, many of the professors were more interested in their own research than in teaching—or inspiring—undergraduates. Much of the teaching fell into the laps of doctoral students who, likewise, were more absorbed in their own programs than in teaching. The goals and ideals animating that environment did not touch upon spiritual issues; the purposes motivating the students, faculty, and entire university community were usually materialistic, mostly self-centered, and certainly secular. There was definitely no overall philosophy in that secular education to inspire the Sixties Generation to much of anything beyond doing the work and getting good grades in preparation for a job, which would then provide us with the material things of life we were accustomed to.

Universities and colleges served a paradoxical social function. They kept the Baby Boomers out of the work force while preparing them to join it. These institutions prevented massive unemployment. For far too many of my generation, a school was a "babysitting" institution, not a place of scholarly pursuit. The religious ideal that sees work as a sacred duty or a calling had been reduced to material advancement in life. Education, and the instrumental reason it relied upon, were a means to an end, not an end in and of itself. The quest for wisdom and knowledge in the classic sense of becoming a better person, or learning the meaning of life, or entering into life's spiritual mysteries, inspired far too few. Consequently, many of us turned against our education, deeply enraged and bitterly disappointed. We were not overly enthusiastic anyway about a job in a society which supported the Vietnam War. Moreover, we were unwilling to sacrifice what our parents had sacrificed to attain the material things we had anyway—because our parents had given them to us! Work as a means of attaining something we already had, in fact, did not appeal to us.

Our complacency about work, however, changed when the inflation of the 1970s threatened us. Suddenly, it dawned upon my generation how difficult it was going to be to have what our parents had, especially when we no longer could rely upon them to provide for us. But work looked boring, if not frightening. Our horror at adult responsibilities was one more reason why many of us turned within and became self-absorbed. Many of us escaped from reality, that is, we regressed, and we did this through various vehicles: drugs, sex, mysticism, cults, and psychosis. Some even committed suicide. Several of my friends did, and these deaths were not unrelated to what was happening in the culture, and the desire to escape from it.

One of the traditional functions of religion has been placing, or integrating, a person into the social order. It was that function especially which broke down in the Sixties; so if one became interested in religion, it was usually the mystical, inward elements of it which had great appeal.

Religion also did not help the Sixties Generation in another crucial way. The British psychoanalyst, David Winnicott, in his book *Playing and Reality*, shows the developmental importance of what he calls "transitional objects" (e.g., teddy bears, blankets, dolls, etc.) for making the transition from total dependence upon the mother and the home environment towards independence. We all know that children love to sleep with their dolls or stuffed animals, and that they find comfort in these objects when they are separated from their parents or leave home. We are careful not to laugh when our children take their well-worn blankets to the supermarket or on a trip. Psychologically, they are filling up the space between their inner world and that all too frightening outer world. As transitional objects, religious symbols serve the same function. They enable us to make the break from home. They offer us guidance and security as we stumble our way into adult life and begin to establish our own autonomy. The fear of separation is one reason we internalize comforting religious symbols, especially during those childhood years when separations are so difficult.

Because of the Sixties Generation's weak religious socialization, the Church did not function at all well in helping us— through its transitional objects—cope with our separations. Religion didn't ease the emotional trauma of breaking away from the home. In our struggles with loss and separation, religion could not prevent or mitigate unhealthy regression. Religion did not help us look ahead in life with anticipation, concrete goals, and ideals that could outlast the Vietnam War.

For many members of the Sixties Generation, their transitional objects were a bottle of beer, a joint of marijuana, a girlfriend or boyfriend to whom we were sometimes in bondage, or the symbols and offerings of popular culture. Our emotional energies, i.e., the currents of the libido, were not effectively balanced and channelled by either religion or education. Those currents thus became diffuse. We were not focused on concrete goals when we moved away from home. Few of us had definite vocations in mind as we went off to college. Consequently, many of us wanted to move back home; we wanted to restore the safety and glory of our high school years. This was a form of regression which became a powerful cultural theme during and after the Sixties. The 1930s gave us the movies, *Gone With the Wind* and *The Wizard of Oz*, with their strong theme of returning home (a theme that no doubt spoke to the Depression era in the midst of its own traumas). The Sixties Generation would later give us *E.T.* with its own variation on the theme of returning home. It became the biggest money maker of all time, which says something about the power of this particularly Sixties theme. To put it succinctly, religion did not protect the Sixties Generation from the traumas of separation and the necessity of preparing for adult life. Religion didn't help us in establishing goals, nor did it protect us from the pain of loss and separation. As a result, we regressed, we regressed like no generation before us, or after (at least thus far). For some people, this regression became very deep, far beyond nostalgia and sadness. Many demons were let loose: drugs, promiscuity, violence, rage, disillusionment, withdrawal from society, and materialism. The trauma of separation—working in conjunction with the loss of tradition—caused some of our narcissism, but undoubtedly its greatest precipitator was Vietnam, and to that we now turn.

The Trauma of Vietnam

The Vietnam War was *the* major trauma for the Sixties Generation, there is no question about that. This is the event which has shaped us the most, the event which has twisted our collective psyche more than any other. Vietnam is the psychic wound that has never completely healed. Vietnam has had more of an impact upon American culture than anything since World War II because it was the chief catalyst for the revolution of the Sixties. The Baby Boomers were too young to be affected by the Korean War. It was Vietnam which enraged us, it was Vietnam which incited us to violence and the rejection of authority.

Black rage has always existed in American society for the injustices people of color have had to endure for so many years. But Vietnam, because it also threatened whites, touched off an explosion of white rage never seen before, and one which hasn't been seen since. The war exposed white people, especially the younger generation, to cruelties and injustices which had been mostly hidden from view during childhood, a childhood that was, most likely, very sheltered. My main hypothesis concerning the war and the Sixties Generation is that Vietnam was a threat to the integrity and preservation of the self. It was a trauma which affected the currents of the libido in so many people, and to such an extent, that narcissism (especially self-interest and self-preservation) became a widespread social phenomenon. Many people also turned inward and became self-absorbed in reaction to their pain. Just as a person becomes preoccupied with the self when sick, many became similarly preoccupied because they hurt so much inside, as I alluded to earlier. Others reacted to Vietnam more outwardly, with intense rage, even violence. In short, Vietnam ripped us apart not only socially but also psychologically, exposing the society to a flood of powerful libidinal currents. These, in turn, initiated vast social and cultural changes. I will now examine that hypothesis in less broad strokes.

The Assassination of John F. Kennedy

I don't think we can truly appreciate the spiritual devastation of Vietnam without first recollecting the disillusionment and pain caused by President Kennedy's assassination on November 23, 1963. What the media called "Camelot," and all it represented, was forever shattered. The innocence of our youth was lost. Most people who can remember the assassination can also remember exactly where they were when first hearing the news. That fact alone shows the severity of the trauma.

I first heard of the assassination while sitting in the East Grand Rapids High School library with my girlfriend. Our high school broke the news to us by putting a radio broadcast over the

PA system. We all sat there stunned, even mesmerized. Eventually, school was dismissed on that bleak November day. Students were crying in the halls. Teachers had pale, bleached-out faces. Such memories are forever seared on my generation's psyche. Who can forget being glued to the television set for several days watching the swirling events? Who can forget all of that sad, even lugubrious music on the radio? I spent hours with my girlfriend driving through town in the blowing rain in my father's 1960 black Bonneville. Antonin Dvorak's "New World Symphony," played so often on the radio, still reminds me of those moments, sitting there in that car and looking through the windshield at the cold November rain.

Bitter disillusionment began to pervade my generation like a plague. Deep in our psyches that feeling has never truly disappeared; it has never been exorcised. It may now be covered over, but it is still there. And it still affects my generation spiritually. "How could such a thing happen?" we naively asked of life. But life was cold then and unresponsive. And it didn't get any better afterwards. (Maybe my generation is still looking for an answer to that question, after all of these years.)

Only a few months earlier, during the previous summer, my friends and I had been driving around Grand Haven, Grand Rapids, and Saugatuck in convertibles, chasing the girls to the music of the Beach Boys blaring on our radios. All of a sudden, that seemed frivolous, yet it wasn't, and it should not have felt that way. The destruction of our innocence shouldn't have been so violent, so quick, so final. The assassination robbed us of what was left of our childhoods. The Fifties were over, the "Sixties" were now beginning. Suddenly, we had to face life, in all of its brutality, before our time. And that made us angry, and that anger would be expressed in myriad ways throughout the decade.

In order to adequately explain our disillusionment and anger, I need to quote an excerpt from President Kennedy's Inaugural Address. Think back to that moment if you can, and recall how you felt when you first heard these words (or maybe they are new words for some of you). It was January, 1961:

Let the word go forth from this time and place, to friend and foe alike, that the torch has been passed to a new generation of Americans—born in this century, tempered by war, disciplined by a hard and bitter peace, proud of our ancient heritage.

To those new states whom we welcome to the ranks of the free, we pledge our word that one form of colonial control shall not have passed away merely to be replaced by a far more iron tyranny.

To those peoples in the huts and villages of half the globe struggling to break the bonds of mass misery, we pledge our best efforts to help them help themselves, for whatever period is required.

To our sister republics south of our border, we offer a special pledge—to convert our good words into good deeds—in a new alliance for progress—to assist free men and free governments in casting off the chains of poverty.

Finally, to those nations who would make themselves our adversary, we offer not a pledge but a request: that both sides begin anew the quest for peace. . . . We dare not tempt them with weakness. But neither can two great and powerful groups of nations take comfort from our present course—both sides overburdened by the cost of modern weapons, both rightly alarmed by the steady spread of the deadly atom, yet both racing to alter that uncertain balance of terror that stays the hand of mankind's final war.

Let us never negotiate out of fear. But let us never fear to negotiate. Let both sides, for the first time, formulate serious and precise proposals for the inspection and control of arms. . . . Let both sides seek to invoke the wonders of science instead of its terrors. Together let us explore the stars, conquer the deserts, eradicate disease, tap the ocean depth and encourage the arts and commerce.

Now the trumpet summons us again—not as a call to bear arms, though arms we need—not as a call to battle, though embattled we are—but a call to bear the burden of a long twi-

light struggle . . . against the common enemies of man:
tyranny, poverty, disease and war itself.

Will you join in this historic effort?

In the long history of the world, only a few generations
have been granted the role of defending freedom in its hour of
maximum danger. I do not shrink from this responsibility—
I welcome it. I do not believe that any of us would exchange
places with any other people or any other generation. The energy, the faith, the devotion which we bring to this endeavor
will light our country and all who serve it—and the glow from
that fire can truly light the world.

And so, my fellow Americans: ask not what your country
can do for you—ask what you can do for your country.

My fellow citizens of the world: ask not what America
will do for you, but what together we can do for the freedom
of man.

For a brief moment in time, American society shared the
idealism expressed in that Inaugural Address. The Kingston Trio
sang of "The New Frontier." There was optimism in the air.
Vaughn Meader's album, *The First Family*, was selling like crazy, pushing its way to the top of the charts. When Americans
heard that Inaugural Address—and young people in particular—
they felt a sense of hope and pride, a sense that something new
and better was coming for *all* the people. We were touched by
the ideal of self-sacrifice embodied in that address, an ideal rooted
in our nation's religious heritage and historical experience.
The idealism inspired by Kennedy's Inaugural Address was
not grounded in narcissism in the same way it would be later on
in the decade. Once the war threatened us, idealism took over the
additional burden of helping preserve a sense of self. Idealism
became a life raft to hold onto; it was a way to escape from pain,
or transcend it. Idealism then became far too deeply intermingled
with our self-interest and our self-preservation. On the other
hand, idealism was one way we channelled our most powerful

feelings. (It was these deep currents of emotion which singers such as Simon and Garfunkel were able to tap so effectively in such songs as "America," "Sounds of Silence," "Old Friends," and "I Am a Rock," or Bob Dylan in "Desperation Row," "Blowin' in the Wind," and "I Shall be Released.")

The idealism of the late Sixties (so often associated with our music—and expressed by that music) was also one of the principal ways we externalized our rebellion. It was one of the ways we dealt with our rage at Vietnam, and one of the ways we coped with our sadness; we were sad, profoundly sad, because we felt betrayed by our country. We felt our country had betrayed us by betraying those very ideals expressed in Kennedy's Inaugural Address. The sadness we felt was a hybrid of narcissism, rage and depression, dashed ideals, and abandoned good intentions.

In the late Sixties, there was an all-too-brief period of time when privileged whites were empathetic to the plight of blacks and those who were poor. And many of us did join the Peace Corps, or VISTA, and we joined with high hopes. But how long did those hopes last? About as long as Vietnam kept us angry, and otherwise emotional. Our ideals lasted about as long as we felt threatened by the war. Corporate offices and law firms are now loaded with former VISTA volunteers who traded in their ideals for dollars.

The idealism of the early and mid-Sixties—that very idealism captured in Kennedy's Inaugural Address—had a purity about it, an innocence and naivete which our later idealism lacked. Maybe that is because this early idealism was not yet overloaded with narcissism and our self-concerns. This "overload" eventually doomed our later idealism. Once the threat of the war ended, most of this idealism was crushed, leaving a heavy residue of guilt and regret. As I mentioned earlier, the idealism of the Sixties changed into the materialism of the Seventies and Eighties. This happened almost instantaneously; it happened when the threat from the war turned overnight into a threat from harsh economic realities like the price of a gallon of gasoline. (These "realities" were created in large part by the deficit spending for Vietnam.) It was then that our insidious materialism truly accelerated, even if it wasn't particularly intelligent. Even if, in reality, most

Americans did not benefit significantly from the revised tax codes in the 1980s, for instance. Since then, the gulf between rich and poor (and the middle class) has widened sharply, although the media during that period led us to believe that everyone could afford a BMW.

Compare our culture in the 1980s to that of the early Sixties, and immediately you can see the differences between a culture inspired by ideals and one driven by greed. In the early Sixties, you see a culture beginning to change because of high ideals, as compared to today, where we have a stagnant culture because shared ideals no longer exist, beyond making money and enjoying "the good life." Sadly, much of the idealism of the Kennedy years, which were such a brief breath of fresh air in American life, collapsed with the man who helped inspire it. A spiritual vacuum was created in American society, one which has never been filled in the same way. Other things have filled it, however: a shallow patriotism, materialism, and hedonism. There we see so clearly how devastating the loss of tradition has been! However, we long for the inspiration that idealism, rooted in tradition, can bring. I think Americans crave hope, even faith, which we had before Vietnam. This longing lies underneath much of America's nostalgia for "Camelot."

Kennedy was not a great president as great presidents are rated by academic historians; we know that now. But Kennedy was a great inspiration, and that counts for a lot in the world of politics. He was the first president to successfully utilize the medium of television. Perhaps we saw in him what we wanted to see, or needed to see. We overlooked his troubled marriage, and most of us didn't know of his many affairs. Kennedy's importance for American culture was not so much legislative as psychological, even spiritual if we consider the inspiration and meaning he provided our lives. His influence, most significantly, was social, because so many people were affected by his aura in a shared way, especially the Baby Boomers. This is highly important for understanding the years following November 22, 1963. Historians, when they rate presidents, fail to stress adequately the importance of a leader's aura, how a leader makes us feel. Historians fail to consider the importance of such feelings for stability or change. They do not appreciate that the destinies of certain leaders are intertwined with our own destinies (and stages of development) because *we internalize those people.* We are thereby deeply affected. Once they become internalized, and become symbols (self-objects), they influence our emotions, fantasies, identities, and actions. Considering all of that, Kennedy's presidency was unique in the collective psyche of my generation, and his death was a prelude for what followed. Or try another way of stating it. His death was the opening act of the "Sixties"; Vietnam then followed, continuing the tragedy. Mindful of this, we will now consider the war's tremendous impact upon American culture.

The Effects of Vietnam

Vietnam has had at least three devastating effects upon American culture, all from which we are still reeling. First, there was the narcissism—the feelings of self-preservation and self-absorption—which so many felt. This was the psychological reaction shared by an entire generation to a genuine threat. Vietnam was not only a threat to life itself, but also a spiritual assault upon the American soul. Our government did not have the will to win the war, nor did our politicians have the political courage to pull out. As late as 1967—after countless protests and countless deaths—only 10% of all Americans favored immediate withdrawal.[2] Some Christians, including clergy, were opposed to the war and did something about it, but for the most part the Church reflected its constituents and supported the war. Or if, in some instances, churches did not support the war, they certainly did not favor total withdrawal in 1967. Collectively, Christians, Jews, and secularists, could not make up their minds about the war. So we remained stuck in Vietnam like a dinosaur in a tar pit, year after traumatic year. The fear, agony, fury, and despair caused by this prolonged war can not be overestimated, *ever*, in any assessment of the Sixties. When *Life* magazine finally put on its cover pictures of dead soldiers from one week's combat in Vietnam, that, I think, more than anything else symbolized a turning point in American sensibilities. When the river of blood turned into a torrent and was given a human face, support for the war began to rapidly erode. Emotionally, that one issue of *Life* affected more people than countless demonstrations.

Many of the Sixties Generation are still deeply scarred by the waste and carnage of Vietnam, especially those who were over there, and then returned to an unappreciative, cold, and even hostile society. Nor should we ever forget the anguish and pain of the families and friends of those who served, or were wounded or killed. The meaninglessness of the cause (especially when weighed against the cost), the lack of a clear purpose (North Vietnam was certainly no threat to the shores of California), the fact we were unwilling to win the war and unwilling to lose it, and the length of the war, all combined to tear us apart emotionally and socially. As Jesus predicted in terms of his own ministry, families were divided (Matthew 10:34–37). The civil war in Vietnam became a civil war for us, too.

The pain from Vietnam was so intense that, after a while, many people became emotionally numb. They repressed their feelings, which has had untold psychological repercussions ever since, affecting numerous relationships. This repression also heightened the need to feel through bodily sensations. As a result, people turned even more to drugs and easy sex (sex without responsibility, sex without commitment).

My generation was like Humpty Dumpty, and many of us have not been able to put the pieces back together again—even to this day. Vietnam's assault on the psyche was the real crime of the war, for both Americans and Vietnamese. The Sixties Generation's response to this assault was narcissism, a narcissism which was intensified by the other traumas of the era. As a result, for many people the currents of the libido became unbalanced or even failed to coalesce.

The second tragic effect of Vietnam returns us to my main theme: the loss—perhaps forever for some—of my generation's loyalty and attachment to the institutions and traditions of society. Todd Gitlin, who was at the University of Michigan when I was, writes of this loss in his provocative study, *The Sixties (Years of Hope, Days of Rage)*. When appraising the New Left, he writes:

Little by little, alienation from American life—contempt, even, for the conventions of flag, home, religion, suburbs, shopping, plain homely Norman Rockwell order—had become a rockbottom prerequisite for membership in the movement core. The New Left felt its homelessness as a badge of identity by now; damned if it was going to love what it had spiritually left.[3]

What Gitlin says about the New Left (the chief concern of his book), was equally true of other Baby Boomers. Our feelings about *all* forms of authority were soured by Vietnam. Our disgust with government—and our pervasive mistrust of it—have been hard to eradicate. We have become deeply disillusioned with the entire political process. And, for some, the disillusionment hardened into a posture: anti-institutional cynicism. The assassinations of the Sixties combined with the war to wreck our enthusiasm for politics. (I should also add that in the eyes of my generation, there have been precious few candidates in recent years to get excited about.)

Moreover, as Gitlin states, many of us did sever ties to our churches (in large part because of their support of the war, or their inertia in working against it). Yet others did return to the Church when it began to take a more active stance against the war.

Along with a decreased respect for the Church during Vietnam went a decreased respect for its rituals, such as marriage. Divorce skyrocketed throughout the Sixties and then afterwards, a trend which has not been checked. (This is an area of American life where one can see, very clearly, and very dramatically, the extent to which tradition has weakened.) More and more, people chose to live together rather than face the responsibilities of marriage and children. Many couples put off having children for so many years (with the help of the pill), that when they finally decided they wanted children, their bodies were not able to respond. Consequently, many have remained childless or have adopted. Again, we must bring the narcissism fostered by Vietnam into the picture to fully interpret what has happened to the institution of marriage and family since the Sixties. Then, living together fit the times; and for many, it still does.

The government, the Church, and the family were not the only institutions to suffer during the Sixties because of Vietnam. Allegiance to fraternities and sororities on our college campuses greatly weakened. Many houses went begging for members, literally. As some of the members of my house put it, "We have to take in 'lunch meat' to survive." At the University of Michigan, many houses folded (although the Greek system has made a strong comeback in recent years). Some of these houses finally paid the price for being racist. For many people, allegiance to the colleges themselves disappeared.

Vietnam also brought to America a general disillusionment with the military. People lost respect for the various branches of the service. On campuses, ROTC buildings were bombed or burned. Morale diminished within the military itself. The recent Gulf War supposedly restored morale, and removed the "Vietnam syndrome." But our failure to remove Saddam Hussein from office, and weaken his military to the point where it could no longer pose a threat, has simply renewed the Vietnam syndrome. We didn't complete something we had started; we didn't stay with a campaign long enough to bring it to a successful conclusion in the case of the Gulf War, whereas in Vietnam we lingered, once we made the mistake of entering into the war in the first place. Thus the Vietnam syndrome has hardly been eradicated; it has been reinforced! And disillusionment because of war and governmental policies has now affected a new generation.

Vietnam also created disdain for the business world. The businessman was mocked. When large corporations, such as General Motors and Dow Chemical, came on campus to recruit, few would listen, in Ann Arbor anyway. (That dramatically changed, however, in the Seventies in the midst of hyper-inflation and the oil crisis.)

The Vietnam War, in conclusion, ushered into American society a widespread distrust of institutions and traditions, even a revulsion. Since the Sixties, it has been extremely difficult to restore confidence in our institutions. There still exist a widespread distrust and disinterest. That is most obvious in the case of government, but it is equally true of the Church. As a result, it has been extremely difficult to revitalize our traditions, and here I have the mainline denominations principally in mind. Mainline religion has been hemorrhaging since the war, and no one has been able to figure out yet how to stop the flow of blood. Without tradition, a society fragments and turns within (the topic of the following chapter). Without tradition, a society spins out of control, which pretty much characterizes American society since the Sixties. We have had no clear purpose, no clear direction. Our governments can't seem to accomplish much of anything. The national debt seems uncontrollable, and is a horrible legacy for our children. Organized religion has splintered into a vast array of competing ideologies: those from the Right, those from the Left, the feminists, the charismatics, the evangelicals, the fundamentalists, the homosexuals. Even the growth of conservative religion, which has been dramatic, is not having much of an effect on restoring high ideals to American life. Conservative religion is more of a reaction to the disease, even a symptom of it, than a cure (it is too divisive). We only need to look at the sort of morality displayed, and upheld, in our culture if we want to substantiate my claim of religious and moral decline and assess its devastating effects. We have lost our ideals, we have lost our bearings, we have lost our souls. The problems are much deeper than simply having forgotten God. Repeating the tragic pattern of human history, we have put ourselves in place of God, which in the Bible is called "idolatry." Since the Sixties we have thus suffered almost a complete moral breakdown, in the board room, in the bedroom, and perhaps in the school room.

The third tragic effect of Vietnam is related to the previous two: in American society there has been the disappearance, or nearly so, of the belief that history has meaning and direction. Who today believes that we have a role to play in the ebb and flow of history? As I said above, the chief tenet of the Bible is that history has meaning, that history has a redemptive purpose and God works through that history, revealing his purposes through people and events. Moreover, the Bible teaches that we, as individuals and members of a community, even of a nation, have a purpose given to us by God, a purpose to be carried out in history. But how many people—even Christians and Jews— believe those things anymore? Who stands for those Biblical tenets any longer? Vietnam killed that Biblical perspective for

many during a time when history appeared to be absolutely mean-
ingless and without direction.

Because of the Sixties Generation's weak religious socialization, probably few of us had much sense of that Biblical perspective on history in the first place—but most of us had at least
an inkling of it in weakened, secular versions. We grew up, for
instance, with the myth of "progress." Remember Ronald Reagan on "The General Electric Theater" telling us each Sunday
night that, for G.E., progress was its most important product?
Progress is a watered down Biblical perspective on history.
Moreover, the Sixties Generation was raised to believe that
"America is always right," and that "we are the best country in
the world." In addition, we believed that "America has never lost
a war," and never could. Many people during the Vietnam era
tried to cling to those illusions, and put bumper stickers on their
cars such as "America, love it or leave it."

Much of our cultural narcissism in the 1950s had its origins
in the Biblical idea of a "chosen people," but stripped of its
original meaning and its historical context. In Puritan New
England it had taken the form of America as a new "city upon a
hill," a beacon of light to the world, a beacon of faith. In the
1950s, our image of ourselves was certainly far removed from, or
ignorant of, the additional Biblical perspective that God judges
both individuals and nations for the justice and mercy shown by
their behavior. The Bible warns that God judges everyone—
including nations—for their narcissism if it becomes inordinate
(read I–II Kings). When our cherished secular myths about ourselves and our national self-love were severely damaged by Vietnam—a divine judgment upon a society if there ever was one (!)
—our cultural narcissism then shifted to individual narcissism.
New slogans arose to replace the old ones: "if it feels right, do
it "; "live for today "; "do your own thing "; "let it all hang out ";
"don't trust anyone over thirty"; "hell no, I won't go." Sometime
during the Vietnam War, at some point, the Sixties Generation
turned from without to within and took much of America with it,
which is the topic of our next chapter.

Notes

1. In the 1990s, of course, that is no longer true; who knows where some denominations or their clergy stand on issues of sexuality in our present era. And the Church is certainly no longer reticent on the subject!

2. Todd Gitlin, *The Sixties (Years of Hope, Days of Rage)*, (New York: Bantan Books, 1987), p. 273.

3. Ibid., p. 271.

Chapter VI

The Effects of Narcissism on American Culture

My General Thesis

In times of social turbulence, when history seems to be out of control and life appears to have little meaning, people tend to turn inward. They become preoccupied with their own psychological processes.[1] Indeed, they often become interested in psychology itself, as witnessed by the popularity of doctoral programs in clinical psychology since the Sixties (at many universities they are far more difficult to get into than medical school). This interest in interiority, to the point of self-absorption, took a variety of forms and showed up in the culture in a variety of ways during the Sixties (some of which we are presently going to explore). My thesis is that this turn *inward* had a direct connection to a weakness in emotional ties *outward* to the traditions and institutions of society. I will show that *without the lens of narcissism*, a great deal of what has happened in our society can neither be clearly seen nor accurately interpreted.

This chapter will develop some ideas already alluded to, but it will also introduce fresh ideas. To begin, we will examine something now closely and distictively associated with the Sixties: popular culture.

Popular Culture: a Substitute Religion

During the Sixties popular culture became a sort of religion. As society's institutions, one by one, lost both their authority and their capacity to evoke emotional allegiance, *popular culture (especially music) took over many of the functions traditionally associated with religion.* In particular, it took over the functions of developing and nurturing the inner life, the life of the spirit. Many people looked away from institutions, especially the Church, for guidance, ritual, meaning, psychological integration, community, magic and mystery, spiritual and moral leadership, and deep emotion. The youth, in particular, found what they were looking for in popular culture.

Remember when John Lennon made that notorious flap that the Beatles were more popular than Jesus? And remember the reaction, especially in the American South? Many clergy had denounced Elvis Presley in 1956 for being a threat to "the American way of life," but that was nothing as compared to their reaction to Lennon's remark. The Beatles' records were smashed and burned; radio stations banned their music; and the group was castigated from the pulpit, and elsewhere, as blasphemous. But Lennon was misunderstood. What he was implying, I think, was an irony, an irony that a Rock and Roll group had, seemingly, more adulation, popularity, influence, and attention among the younger generation than the central figure in the world's largest religion.

Lennon had a point. Jesus had become "routinized" for many people within institutional religion, which explains the popularity of *Jesus Christ Superstar* and *Godspell*, as well as other fresh interpretations of Jesus, such as those found in various "Jesus movements." Significantly, they were usually distanced from the Church. The Jesus of the Baby Boomers' upbringing—in that very Church—was overly familiar, taken for granted. Yet his mission and message were little understood, in part because of poor preaching and poor Christian education (both in churches and families). Thus the tradition representing Jesus in the culture —the tradition which was now the target of Lennon's jibe—had become stodgy, even irrelevant, and certainly ineffective in articulating Jesus' message of love and justice. In other words, the

Church failed to show American culture the relevance of Biblical texts to its moral, psychological, and social conflicts. The Church neither stirred the imagination nor inspired the soul—at least for many people.

The upshot of this was a situation where increasing numbers of people did not find stability within institutional religion. To be blunt, it had become a bore to the Sixties Generation, and an ineffective one at that. Moreover, in our eyes the Church was supportive of a war in the name of the Prince of Peace. Thus Lennon was not making anything more than an empirical observation, and a rather critical one at that. He was not trying to brag. He was merely suggesting that popular culture had become a substitute religion. And he seemed a bit whimsical, even sad, when he made his remark.

Lennon had a point. Many people did find more spirituality and "wisdom" in popular music, for instance, than in their own inherited traditions. And many did discover richer layers of meaning being explored in movies than in their own churches. It also seemed that American society found more pageantry in spectator sports than in the Church's rituals. In many denominations, rituals had been stripped down to nothing, one of the less desirable legacies of the Reformation. And then, centuries later, Vatican II, as important and necessary as it was, robbed Roman Catholicism of much of its majesty. As a result, many people turned to what were, for them, new forms of religion, with fresh rituals and exotic symbols, especially in traditions imported from the East. These traditions were perceived—and experienced— as having more mystery than Christianity, and more of an emphasis on the inner world. Most important, these traditions were far removed from the taint of supporting a war. They were not associated with parents and their authority.

It is particularly here—in the great popularity of new forms of religion and creative expressions of pop culture—where we see, as if under a glaring light, the extent to which mainline religion was weakening. Considerable blame falls upon the clergy themselves, who, in many instances, supported the Vietnam War, and were often ineffective. Many hurt their religious institutions. But, in most churchs, clergy only mirror their congregations (the parents of the Sixties Generation!), who call them and pay their salaries. The inability of churches to minister to the Sixties Generation—their inability to address significant traumas— accelerated the migration away from tradition. Here we only need to examine mainline religion, and its loss of much of its own youth, to highlight the damage inflicted by the Sixties' upheavals. Popular culture, in part, filled up the void, along with the twin demons, drugs and promiscuity.

But if young people turned away from their traditions—and sociologists have substantiated this, especially vis-à-vis the mainliners[2]—the pastoral issue that then becomes salient from a psychoanalytic perspective is this: without the resources of tradition, how do people balance the two currents of the libido? How do people integrate affection and sensuality? How do people balance thought with feeling, and self-love with love for others? It is in these areas, especially, that so many members of the Sixties Generation have had tremendous difficulties. *The failure of tradition to help so many people balance the two currents of the libido, and then safely walk on that tightrope between self-love and object-love, has had far-reaching consequences for American culture.*

One of the principal themes of this entire book is that religion in the Sixties did not have enough of a psychological hold on people to influence their self-absorption and sensuality. It did not help people to balance those things with social attachments and ethical commitments. Thus many turned to popular culture as a sort of religion. There they sought direction and wholeness, excitement and spirituality, wisdom and grace, and community. But here is the rub: *popular culture accentuated narcissism.* Of course, that was part of its attraction! Its promises were ephemeral, however, as were its fulfillments.

During the Sixties, narcissism was already becoming prominent in American society because of the traumas we have already explored, along with tradition's failure to help people cope with them. But popular culture threw salt into the wounds. It bombarded people with stimuli, stimuli that both aroused sensuality and strengthened tendencies to turn within and withdraw from society. Popular culture did this in everything from advertising to "pop" psychology, from movies to best selling books and popular music. There was not enough moral structure in American society—nor enough internalized moral structure within individuals—to stem the excesses of popular culture. Since the Vietnam era, tradition has had a very difficult time controlling both narcissism and raw sensuality (which has been becoming rawer all the time!). Not surprisingly, then, affection and love for others have so often been casualties, as relationships descend into the dark chasms of inordinate narcissism and sex without emotion.

In sum, popular culture dovetailed with the narcissism then emerging; each supported the other in the midst of weakening traditions. It was popular culture that spoke to the needs of the Sixties Generation—not tradition. And we listened! Our narcissism in turn fed popular culture, reinforcing its appeal. Even the ideal of helping others—once so strong in the Sixties—eventually disintegrated to the point that it served the needs of the self far more than those of others. Empathy was becoming less and less the primary psychological dynamic operative in social activism as the Sixties wound down. In its place, there was a preoccupation with making the self feel good, meaningful, and relevant. Many members of the Sixties Generation helped others to help themselves. And they have been helping themselves ever since—to a disproportionate amount of society's goods and services! That is how narcissism has affected an entire generation, my generation, which once prided itself on its ethics, but eventually neglected them in its quest for gold, self-improvement, and self-fulfillment. Popular culture both reflected that shift in values and helped to bring it about. As Todd Gitlin points out when discussing the failures of popular culture as a religious substitute:

> Early in 1970 the Beatles released "Let It Be," which in the season of the townhouse explosion seemed a plausible alternative to the Rolling Stones' "Let It Bleed." Before 1970, no serious rock musicians could have sung straight-faced about "whisper[ing] words of wisdom." For comfort, the Beatles had moved from the Maharishi to Mother Mary, and she was only a last stopping-off point. To the youth culture's passionate spectators, the Beatles' breakup was traumatic in the way the breakup of SDS had been for the student movement. Then, in

1971, John Lennon racked the Sixties' heart with the stunning "I-don't-believe" chants of "God," renouncing everyone and everything from "Kennedy" to "I Ching" and "Beatles" in one dying fall after another, ending with the therapeutic afterthought, "I just believe in me," and the privatized "Yoko and me, that's reality." In the fall of 1970 Jimi Hendrix and Janis Joplin dropped dead of drug overdoses, and a few months later Jim Morrison collapsed and died, perhaps of drink, perhaps of drugs—all at age twenty-seven. Celebrity, one of the Sixties' headiest drugs, was evidently not so tonic. For eighteen- or twenty-year-olds seeking signs of grace in popular culture, the promises of deliverance had worn to a shine. Woodstock Nation's symbols peeled away from their Aquarian meanings and became banal with popularity. Joints of marijuana were served at dinner parties. Drugs and long hair fanned out from the middle class into the working classes; southwestern truckdrivers who sang along with Merle Haggard's "We don't smoke marijuana in Muskogee" began wearing ponytails.[3]

To illustrate how popular culture and narcissism reinforced each other, and drew upon one another for their own power, I will offer several brief illustrations.

"Go Where You Wanna Go"

One way of interpreting popular culture is visualizing it as analogous to a nocturnal dream. Like a Freudian dream, popular culture expresses a society's wishes and fantasies. But just as a dream is quickly forgotten once we wake up, and the morning sun shines brightly into our bedrooms, similarly a song, television show, best selling book, or movie is dismissed from our minds once it is over. This is not always true, of course. Sometimes a book, such as *Gone With the Wind*, or a movie such as *Casablanca*, becomes lodged in our collective psyche, which shows the power of its theme. But, for the most part, popular culture quickly loses its impact once we close the book, or leave the movie theater, or turn off the TV set. Yet, for a brief moment— that moment we are completely immersed—popular culture resonates with our desires, hopes, and fears. Or it expresses—even projects—our deepest conflicts, including unconscious ones.

In the Sixties we had movies, such as *Bonnie and Clyde* and the Clint Eastwood westerns, which depicted the autonomous individual with no social ties, no ties of any sort to a community, a religion, or to any other institution of society, including family. The characters are alone, and lonely. They are adrift, outside of any routine, regimen, or moral restrictions. These people are violent, but with no apparent remorse. Society seems to have little claim on these people. In the movie *The Collector*, the psychopathology of violence—a sickness in large part caused by the character's complete isolation—is depicted as symptomatic of a social world devoid of moral values. In the movie we actually participate in the killer's private amoral world. *The Collector* was a Sixties specter of a society without emotional ties, or any of the bonds which hold institutions together. It depicted human beings as objects to be used for the satisfaction of a sick mind's needs, a scenario that has been tragically played out since the Sixties in a profusion of serial killers in America, such as Jeffrey Dahmer. *The Collector* was, indeed, a chillingly prophetic film.

In *Dr. Strangelove* sick minds had nuclear arms to play with. For that is what those weapons were in the movie, toys, toys in the hands of narcissistic politicians and generals, each acting like a greedy little boy. They all envied the weapons of the other side, like boys fighting over toys, and at the end of the movie those "toys" were used to blow up the world.

In all of those movies—and certainly others could have been named—the theme is alienation from society, and a concomitant self-absorption. They show a world whose institutions no longer function effectively or meaningfully. They show a world devoid of tradition. The Sixties Generation flocked to see these movies in droves because they expressed what so many of us were feeling, what so many of us were fantasizing. Movies reinforced our own isolation from church and society, especially from our government which supported a war we could not support (in the way it was being conducted, anyway). Movies explored our own estrangement, thereby penetrating deep into the collective unconscious. Movies mirrored back to us our own preoccupations with our private, inner worlds.

Perhaps popular music, more than any other medium, expressed our feelings. Two examples will suffice. The first is the song "Different Drum," recorded by the Stone Poneys with Linda Ronstadt singing the lead (Mike Nesmith, of Monkee fame, wrote the song). There, the undesirability of commitment is the theme (e.g. "I'm not in the market for a boy who wants to only love me. . . I'm not ready for any person, place, or thing to pull the reins in on me"). Or, in a similar vein, examine this from "Go Where You Wanna Go," another signature song of the period (sung by the Mamas and the Papas): "You've got to go where you wanna go and do what you wanna do. . . you don't understand that a girl like me can't love just one man."

Such songs reflected weakening traditions. Self-absorbtion and doing what one wants are the themes. These songs paralleled the catch phrases of the day, injunctions such as "if it feels right, do it," and "do your own thing."

In sum, as in the larger social world, in popular culture we encounter the autonomous self, the self without strong ties, the self without allegiance to the institutions of society, the self more concerned about its own feelings than those of others. Narcissism is a common thread, a common theme.

The Turn Eastward

Exotic forms of religion were also extremely popular during the Sixties and became part of the counterculture. Some turned to cults, some turned to the East. These forms of religion facilitated our journey within, although, ironically, they also created the communities so many of us were starving for, a tragic-comic community of like-minded explorers of private psychological states. We were longing for the religious community we did not find in our own churches. A camaraderie was thereby created in movements such as Transcendental Meditation, which I participated in myself during the late 1960s and early 1970s. I and my fellow meditators would sit around in a dark room with incense burning, listening to Indian music or meditating as a group.

"OM" was the word of the day, and the music of the day was definitely George Harrison's triple album, *All Things Must Pass*, with such lyrics as "you don't need no church house." That album, heavily influenced by the religions of the East (e.g., the hit "My Sweet Lord"), spoke to us with power. Harrison expresses so well what we then felt, and the religious imagery of the album (Christian amalgamated with Eastern) shows the nature of our inward journey.

We not only immersed ourselves in George Harrison's music, but in exotic books as well, especially the Bhagavad-Gita, the classic text of Hinduism. I have selected three passages to show its appeal to us in a world we wanted to escape from:

> Only that yogi
> Whose joy is inward
> Shall come to Brahman [God]
> and know Nirvana.

> Self-controlled,
> Cut free from desire,
> Curbing the heart
> And knowing the Atman [the individual soul],
> Man finds Nirvana
> That is in Brahman,
> Here and hereafter.[4]

> For, when a man loses attachment to sense-objects and to action, when he renounces lustful anxiety and anxious lust, then he is said to have climbed to the height of union with Brahman.[5]

One version of the Gita, the one with which I spent a lot of time, was translated and commented upon by Maharishi Mahesh Yogi, the founder of Transcendental Meditation. Here I quote a pertinent verse, and then his commentary on it, to even better explain what we escaped into:

> *He whose happiness is within, whose contentment is within, whose light is all within, that yogi, being one with Brahman, attains eternal freedom in divine*

consciousness.
This verse is the crest of the teaching of this chapter on renunciation. It presents a state in which life is wholly converged upon its innermost aspect, and declares that state to be eternal freedom. Furthermore, it brings to light the sequence of stages on the way to realization: as the practice of transcendental meditation advances, inner happiness grows. With this, contentment grows, and at the same time the experience of Being becomes clearer—the inner light grows. With this, inner awareness grows, and with it the ability spontaneously to maintain Being during activity. When one naturally begins to maintain the state of Being in all states of waking, dreaming and deep sleep, then one has attained eternal freedom in divine consciousness.
'He whose happiness is within': . . . this implies that the outside world is not the field of happiness for a realized man . . . If his happiness does not lie in the outside world and yet he is happy, his happiness can only be within himself. The mind wanders in search of happiness but when, through Union with the Divine, the mind is transformed into bliss consciousness, *it finds the goal of its search within itself* (my italics).[6]

We also used to sit around in a group and read *Be Here Now* by Ram Dass, thinking we were reading something really profound. It wasn't, but paradoxically it communicated a spirituality missing in our own inherited traditions.

This obsession with our own psychological processes was a social force that later re-emerged in my generation's passion for privacy. Our quest not only to experience but to understand our inner world is a legacy from the Sixties that continues to have social consequences.

Drugs and Promiscuity

The role of drugs and promiscuity in the Sixties Generation's self-absorption and self-destruction cries out for analysis and anecdote. I link drugs and promiscuity because they were so often part of the same experience. I can remember many a party in my fraternity that ended—at least in terms of meaningful conversation—as soon as people brought out the pot and rolled the joints. Then they would mill around in their own private worlds, "grooving," stoned out of their minds. Eventually couples would peal off, one by one, and wander off to the privacy of their own bedrooms. I still have this surreal picture in my mind of a "hippie" party my fraternity held in 1968. We started out with Ripple wine, and then switched to pot. After a while, people were floating around the house like a phantasmagoria of ghosts, or zombies, silent, dressed up like hippies (parodies of themselves in many instances), with music such as the Doors' "People Are Strange" or the Strawberry Alarm Clock's "Incense and Peppermints" blaring away on the juke box in our basement party room. And I remember someone blasting the Turtles' "Happy Together" in one of the upstairs bedrooms, but you could still hear the bed squeaking out in the hall.

That night the only illumination in the entire place came from black lights, which transfigured the white of our clothes and teeth and the whites of our eyes into a blue and purple glow. A rainbow of colors descended upon us from the psychedelic posters on the walls, casting an eerie spell over the whole house, which by late evening reeked of marijuana and incense.

Parties were our escape during an Ann Arbor weekend. Students at Michigan studied extremely hard during the week, and then partied equally hard on the weekends. My fraternity specialized in theme parties, such as the one just described. Two themes, in particular, stood out on our liturgical calendar. The first was our annual pajama party. We mixed vodka, Hawaiian Punch, and dry ice in a large old bathtub, which we had hauled down to our basement party room and kept for this purpose. People proceeded to get crocked at a record pace. The vapor from the tub, reflecting the red basement lights, billowed out onto the dance floor in large clouds, which we wove in and out of. We clung to each other for stability, vainly attempting to dance to such songs of the evening as "Woman, Woman" by the Union Gap, "Born to Love You" by the Temptations, and the Animals' "We Gotta Get Out of This Place."

Soon the community bathroom was flowing in rivers of red vomit, which splashed all over the walls, leaving little red dots.

We turned our study into one big bed with mattresses from our bedrooms. It wasn't an orgy, but it wasn't a slumber party either. My final surreal image of that party is of a cute high school girl, who shouldn't have been there, being chased around and around the house by a group of my fraternity brothers, in a single file, with their arms outstretched; they grinned and salivated, baring their wolfly fangs as they pranced after her. It was by then four in the morning, and the Left Bank's "Walk Away Renne" was now alternating on our juke box with "You Didn't Have to be so Nice" by the Lovin' Spoonful, and these songs reverberated throughout the cavernous rooms on the first floor of the house, now mostly empty. All of this went on until one of the few sane and relatively sober brothers left locked up this girl in his own bedroom, "for her own protection," he said. That was our typical pajama party.

Our other famous theme party at the Alpha Delt house was our Viking party. We all, of course, dressed up like Vikings (using garbage can lids for shields, etc.). We prepared a scrumptious meal of turkey legs, bread, fruit, mashed potatoes, and plenty of gravy. The one party of this genre that stands out was when some idiot suddenly yelled out "FOOD FIGHT!" right in the middle of dinner. I was hit in the head by a drumstick and a large piece of coconut simultaneously. The evening from then on out was a blur, although I do vaguely remember pitchers of beer being poured upon some people, while others wrestled on the wood floor in mountains of grease and discarded food.

My generation drank *far too much* in college. Moreover, we drove far too often under the influence. Drinking has deeply scarred my generation, and many are now recovering alcoholics. My own career with the grape began the night before going off to college in August, 1965. Here's how that went. (I tell this story, along with some other escapades, to illustrate just how destructive the drinking actually was.)

I never had so much as a beer throughout high school. I didn't need alcohol to have a good time. Moreover, I didn't particularly relish the taste of the stuff. My girlfriend and I, along with my band members, enjoyed life without the need of stimulants. I developed somewhat of a reputation as a prude, I have to admit.

Many of my friends did drink, however, especially at Castle Park during the summers. I held out. My friends kept working on me, figuring I was virgin material. They saw me as a challenge, so they tried to corrupt me.

Well, the night before going away to college, there was a big party at a friend's cottage in Castle Park. Doug Veech, the host, put a big neon sign in front of his cottage whenever he had a party (which was often). It blinked "Club Veech," in big red script. Cases of beer were piled high in the kitchen, and smoke from countless cigarettes drifted throughout all the rooms. "Come on," my friends begged, "it is the night before you are going off to Ann Arbor! This only happens once. Have a beer!" I did. I had thirteen of them.

There are two things I recollect about that night. One is sitting in the woods, next to my friend's cottage, throwing up. I moaned to one of my corrupters, Tommy Watling, "Why did I drink so much? Why did you let me?" Tommy sat there calmly, munching on a box of pretzels. Finally I seized that box and tore it apart and threw its contents against the side of the cottage. That was my rather feeble attempt at revenge.

The second thing I remember about that night is rolling down the hill in front of the cottage, and then looking back up at that blinking neon sign.

Apparently, I also threw up on my dob kit back in my own cottage's bathroom because the first thing I noticed the next morning was the dried vomit, with little pieces of meat, which covered my toothbrush and razor.

I then tried to get ready for the three hour trip to Ann Arbor with my grandfather, of the class of '18. I was supposed to be at my dorm, West Quad, that evening. In the morning, I said to him, "Grandpa, I don't feel particularly well; I am a bit under the weather. Perhaps I have a touch of the flu." I added, "Perhaps I should take a wastepaper basket with me in the front seat of the car, in case I throw up." So we left, but a mile outside of Castle Park I reported, "Grandpa, I don't think I am going to be able to make the trip. I need to lie down a bit." So we drove back, and immediately I deposited my breakfast of blueberries on our front lawn.

Before trying once again to leave, I had enough time to walk around the park to curse my friends, who merely laughed at my plight. By then I was armed with a bottle of Pepto-Bismal, which I carried around with me for two days, even swigging it a few times during registration. After that infamous episode, I didn't drink for a whole year, not once. When I was a pledge, and thus required to clean up after Friday night beer parties at the fraternity house, I about "lost it" on a few Saturday mornings because of the smell of all that stale beer. The music of the Buffalo Springfield, along with that of the Mamas and the Papas, still reminds of those crisp winter mornings, because my pledge class so often played their music while we mopped the floor in our pine paneled party room. Songs such as "Sit Down, I Think I Love You," "On the Way Home," and "Do I Have to Come Right Out and Say It?" will be forever associated (for me anyway) with our fraternity dances, our basement party room and its juke box—and three inches of stale beer on a cold cement floor that needed mopping.

The second time I tried to drink something alcoholic was also a fiasco. I mixed gin with red Kool-Aid, and proceeded to get so intoxicated that I almost started a riot with our next door neighbors, the Sigma Chi's. I kept on yelling out of my window, facing their house, "I hate Sigma Chi's." A large contingent of them quickly gathered beneath my window. Many of the Sigs were football players. I was convinced that these "animals" ate raw meat for breakfast. My brothers threw me into the shower rather than throwing me to the Sigs.

Alcohol was definitely a problem in our lives. Soon after the Kool-Aid incident, I bit the vinyl dashboard of a friend's car (his father's brand new Mustang) after a particularly wild party. My teeth left a perfect imprint on that dashboard, like you see in a dentist's office when you are being fitted for a crown. I still don't know how he explained that imprint to his father.

Drinking also cost me a weekend in the Ann Arbor jail when I was crazy enough to tear down a "no parking" sign on the way home from a party. I was with one of my fraternity brothers, Jack Kleene, who was several years younger than me. I put that sign in from of me like a lance, yelled "CHARGE!" and then ran down

State Street, right in front of the Michigan Union. Before reaching my fraternity house on the corner, a car swerved out of traffic and ran up onto the curb. A man leaped out of the car, and made a mad dash toward me. I thought he was a Sigma Chi, so I swung that sign at him, hitting him squarely on the leg. Unfortunately, he was a cop. The next thing I remember is being in handcuffs, with police cars all over the place, their red lights flashing.

They proceeded to book me (after finger printing me) on assaulting a police officer (a felony), possession of municipal property, drunk and disorderly, and contributing to the delinquency of a minor. I forgot to mention, my friend also had "ripped off" a "no parking" sign; his jaw dropped to the ground when I charged down State Street. He stood there, frozen, on the steps of the Michigan Union with his "no parking" sign still in his hands. Thus he was easily identifiable—and he was arrested, too.

I was accused of being one of the most obnoxious prisoners in the jail's history. I kept on calling the police "pigs," "fascists," and I even accused them of being poorly paid. When I finally realized that I was in "big trouble," I had a bright idea. I threatened them with a major law suit, telling them that my father was a famous lawyer, hoping that those lies would save my neck. They did. As it turned out, the policeman I had hit with the "no parking" sign was a rookie; in fact, as I pointed out that night, he hadn't properly identified himself before tackling me (so it was understandable that I thought he was a Sigma Chi). All charges were dropped except the charge of drunk and disorderly, which I was happy to plead guilty to. Soon after my weekend in jail, I had a court appearance where I paid a $30 fine.

What happened to my friend? He was fined $60 because he was under the drinking age. Plus he had that sign (which mysteriously disappeared from my litany of charges). As a result, he had to work a number of Saturday mornings in community service, on the "chain gang" as he put it, while I slept in.

Alcohol was the great attraction at all of our parties during the Sixties, whether they were large and featured a lot of dancing, or small parties in the woods and sand dunes bordering Lake Michigan.

A favorite pastime of my circle of friends was buying a case of beer and holing up somewhere, in a cabin or a cottage, and listening to the music of the Temptations and Four Tops (or other Motown groups), and then dancing the "Temptation walk" with candlesticks for mikes. We would sashay to "You're My Everything," "Baby, I Need Your Loving," or "I Can't Help Myself" until we dropped from exhaustion. Together we would sing the refrains of such records as the Spinners' "I'll Always Love You," Jimmy Ruffin's "What Becomes of the Brokenhearted" or Smokey Robinson's "My Girl Has Gone" as we danced in syncopation.

In my fraternity house, an engineering student designed a beer machine, so that for a quarter you would get a 16 oz. beer from a keg locked up in a refrigerator with a spout fastened to the side. Availability was never a problem.

Luckily, I didn't smoke much pot. The second time I ever tried it was during my junior year of college, the same night I learned how to play bridge (getting fabulous hands). I didn't much like the stuff. It was painful to hold down, and I always ate far too much under its spell. The first time I had tried it was during the previous summer, with a Castle Park friend from California. We did it in my father's green 1965 Pontiac, parked out in the woods near the park. The trees looked different that night, that was all, but upon returning to a large party, I giggled all night, and repeatedly reported to my friends gathered in the Henhouse (who hadn't tried it yet), "It's a whole new world!" It wasn't.

Since drug abuse and promiscuity were so prevalent during the Sixties—and perhaps their worst legacy—it is worth considering the meaning of "addiction." An addiction is a habitual inclination to use a drug (or anything) because the feelings it arouses have not been structured into the personality. The same desired experience can't be generated on one's own, in other words. Psychological addictions thus reinforce physical addictions.

One of my friends, now an alcoholic, is a classic illustration. He started drinking bottles of red cough medicine in junior high; then graduated to Wild Turkey bourbon in high school. On many a Sunday morning during our college years I saw him drinking Bloody Marys to nurse a hangover, which is a withdrawal symptom. So "a little hair of the dog that bit you" becomes part of a vicious circle. One of the dangerous consequences of such abuse is that it escalates.

I have an additional theory of drug abuse and addiction which you won't find in a psychiatric textbook. It is a theory I verified while leading my church groups out to the Wind River Indian Reservation in Wyoming. There I discovered that among the Arapaho close to 100% of the adult males are alcoholics (many of them, fortunately, are recovering). In fact, the section of the reservation where we were (St. Michael's Mission in Ethete) was an "alcohol free" zone (which was not easy for some of my own people to put up with for over a week). One night I asked a prominent member of the tribe, "Are drinking problems among the Indians connected in any way to the loss of a way of life?" (I knew that there was also some genetic evidence for their alcoholism.) He replied, "Most definitely." And then we went on to have a lengthy conversation about the loss of tradition. He believed Indians were depressed about the loss of their ancient way of life (in the case of the Arapaho, the loss of the nomadic life as warriors and buffalo hunters). He pointed out that Indians were also suffering from the loss of many of the rich traditions which once sustained them.

The experience of the Arapaho and other Native Americans substantiates the overall theme of this book, that the loss of tradition is catastrophic for a culture: its spiritual life, its mental health, vocational drive, and unity. This raises another crucial issue pertinent to narcissism: the moral dimension of symptomatology.

Symptoms and Morality

Earlier in this book I pointed out differences in psychopathology that have turned up in the history of our culture. I showed that narcissistic disorders have been more prevalent in recent years than the transference neuroses. And then I explained why, by referring to changes in Western culture.

Some psychiatrists dismiss the role of culture in psychopathology—a serious error in interpretation, as we have just seen with the Arapaho. Drug abuse, sexual problems, anorexia, and bulimia, for example, are obviously connected to the nature of a culture.

If culture is linked to psychopathology—and narcissistic disorders in particular—then a moral critique of our social world should be part of any overall explanation and plan of treatment. In other words, to fully contexualize psychopathology, such as excesses or deficiencies of narcissism, culture must not only be understood but morally judged. Why? In order to make the cultural changes that are necessary to cut down the frequency of the pathology. If anorexia, for instance, can be shown to be linked to a destructive vanity as well as unrealistic goals for one's weight, then to combat the malady society itself must be changed—the very society giving rise to such unrealistic expectations in the first place!

My point is that psychopathology—and all mental phenomena for that matter—do not occur in a cultural and social vacuum. If societies are destructive to the mental, physical, and spiritual health of people, then we must critique those societies, and make the changes that are required to mitigate pathology. These are, obviously, moral (and political) issues.

Symptoms are thus clues to the moral as well as the mental health of a society; they indicate the character of a culture. For instance, the destruction of Arapaho traditions and the imposition of an alien culture, created a deficiency of healthy narcissism among that once proud people. That was certainly an immoral act. And when the media foster inordinate narcissism in our contemporary culture, that, too, is an immoral act (e.g., the cigarette and beer advertising which entices young people to use such products through the manipulation of their self-esteem). In both illustrations, the culture must be morally evaluated as part of any complete explanation of pathology because the pathology arose, in large part anyway, *due to the very nature of the culture itself.* When considering the narcissistic disorders of the Sixties, one must include a moral (as well as a social-scientific) interpretation of society.

The health of our circumstances (both social and physical)

affects the intrapsychic world, and "what is going on in the head" in turn affects the outer world. Psychopathology shows how linked we are to the moral health of our society just as our physical pathology shows how linked we are to nature. If society and the physical environment are sick, we will be, too. And if we are sick, we will create a sick world. The environmental movement (focused on our "natural" circumstances) emerged from the Sixties and has been one of that era's greatest legacies. We *finally* realized how interconnected we are, both to each other and to our natural world—thus our "raised consciousness" about diet, drugs, exercise, weight, smoking, pollution, and conservation (e.g., recycling).

To sum up, the moral dimension of symptoms not only has a *cultural* and *social* ingredient (linked to our collective behavior) but also an *individual* ingredient (linked to our personal behavior). Consequently, in any discussion of narcissism's effects on American culture we must look at both the individual and society. Moreover, we must consider how the nature of our culture has accentuated that narcissism.

Since the Sixties we have become emotionally invested with our environment, seeing it as an extension of ourselves. And, today, environmental issues are being emphasized in schools far more than when I went through the educational pipeline. So let's now turn to education to see some additional effects of narcissism.

The Demand for "Relevance" in Education

One of the first emotional shocks my generation experienced after leaving home and enlisting in "mass education" was the typical large undergraduate survey course, often containing hundreds of students. These courses were held in large lecture halls. The professors rarely knew your name. The format was a lecture by a tenured faculty member, and then a smaller recitation class taught by one of his or her graduate students (whom at Michigan we sometimes thought of as lackeys). Our reading assignments were usually from thick text books, not from primary sources.

In this system of mass education, many people received degrees but without much of a knowledge of the great thinkers in the history of civilization, even in one's own field. Majors in psychology, for instance, rarely read Freud—they read *about* him in textbooks, but they did not as a rule read Freud's own writings, or those of other seminal thinkers such as Jung, Rank, or Adler. Mass education was cold, impersonal, and rightly called "irrelevant," even "fraudulent."

The narcissism of the Sixties Generation had far-reaching consequences for education. We demanded that courses address not only our own emotional and intellectual needs, but also the moral issues of the day which we identified with, such as the Vietnam War, civil rights, or the pollution of our environment. Courses, in the word of the day, had to be *relevant*! A positive effect of this demand was that the entire impersonal system of education began to change. My generation challenged the mass education of the Fifties and early Sixties, which ended up being one of the most important contributions we made to American society. Residential colleges were set up within large universities. Courses were offered which met some of our demands, classes in such areas as women's studies, black studies, and religion. Professors made more of an effort to teach lower level courses, and even learned a name or two.

However, there were some negative aspects of these changes. Some courses and their reading materials were judged to be "relevant" only according to the highly personal needs of those doing the judging. And then later on, education was shaped—to a dangerous degree—by my generation's various ideologies. They became the lenses through which we viewed the world. We invested much of our narcissism in those ideologies. They were part of our souls, part of our being, part of our identity. However, some very "questionable" courses began to be taught, with questionable reading assignments (on both intellectual and artistic grounds). Many of these courses were what we called "gut" courses—an "easy A" without much work to do and without much of an intellectual challenge.

Furthermore, numerous schools dropped or eased their academic requirements. For instance, foreign languages were often eliminated, as were courses in math and science. Ideologies emerging from the Sixties played the crucial role here. The upshot has been a denigration of Western civilization itself. What we used to call a "general liberal arts education" has been undermined in some institutions by ideologies. Many of the "classic texts" of Western culture have been relegated to the junk heap of "irrelevance."

Narcissism infused the various ideologies emerging from the Sixties, whether these ideologies were from the Left or Right, from feminists or homosexuals, blacks or Hispanics, fundamentalists, environmentalists, or secular humanists. This was not always positive. Ideologies created an affirmative action strategy that turned into a quota system. Ideologies brought the straight jacket of being "politically correct" to our campuses. The impact of ideologies on free speech and a well-rounded education has in some instances been devastating. It is no longer our common history that is important, but rather "my history." This stress on our own experience easily slipped from a healthy ethnic pride into "bad" narcissism. Such narcissism "privatized" our understanding of experience itself.

In sum, very little of the current debate on education, which both the late Alan Bloom of the University of Chicago (*The Closing of the American Mind*) and Dinesh D'Souza (*Illiberal Education*) have presented, can be fully understood apart from the traumas of the Sixties. It was from them that narcissism surged with such force into the debate.

Narcissism and the Abortion Question

As a final illustration of contemporary issues which can not be fully understood without considering narcissism, let me close by making several observations about the abortion debate. First, the perimeters of the debate emerged from the Sixties. Roe vs. Wade was based on "the right to privacy," and that idea, as it was presented in the case, was shaped by the social currents of the Sixties. Much of our concern—even obsession—with privacy emerged from that era. Secondly, in the debate precious little is said about the parents' responsibilities for the unborn child. Many remain silent on this issue anyway, which again reflects social changes brought by the Sixties, especially the *undermining of those very traditions which once made that responsibility self-evident.* Often we hear the outcry, "I can do with my body what I want." Such pleas can't be understood apart from the psychology of narcissism. Responsibility in sexual behavior is also not emphasized enough in the arguments. The right to have an abortion is part of the Sixties' sexual revolution. Loss of that right is the dominant fear of those who applaud the sexual revolution. However, as someone put it, "The real choice involved in abortion is the choice to get into bed." I don't agree with that remark, but sometimes it fits the situation.

Thirdly, to appreciate the emotions stirred up by the abortion debate, we must grasp the degree of psychological investment which people have in ideologies. The amount of narcissism which both sides bring to the question is blatantly apparent, and it has become much like a set of blinders. Each side is so invested in its own position that it can't empathize with, or even hear, the important arguments and truths the opposing side is articulating. The Left seems to dismiss any rights of the fetus, and they don't want to discuss sexual ethics too much. On the other hand, the Right doesn't seem to have any empathy for the mother of eight whose birth control failed. Or for parents who can't possibly cope with the serious medical problems of their coming child. The Right has so much narcissism invested in its rigid ideological positions, that it can't empathize with a family where a daughter has been raped, even by her own father.

Narcissism has solidified—sometimes in concrete—each wing of the polarity, which makes it difficult for someone in the middle—as I am as a minister—to bring together fanatics on both sides. To understand fanaticism, one must understand narcissism, including the social upheavals that gave it such strength in modern times.

Conclusion

Narcissism has become a powerful current in contemporary American society. We have examined a variety of its manifestations. Narcissism can be both a highly positive and an equally negative phenomenon when it emerges. It is even difficult to use the word without making moral judgments. My concern, however, has been to understand narcissism as both a social and psychological force, and then look at some of the changes it spawned within American culture. The narcissism that the Sixties produced was—and is—powerful indeed.

My theory of the Sixties, which sought to explain why narcissism has been so prevalent among the Baby Boomers, has focused upon traumas, traumas we reacted to with exceptional depth of feeling. The loss of tradition left us if not completely defenseless against those traumas, then at least highly vulnerable. Now we will consider the retrieval of tradition.

Notes

1. See Idema, *Freud, Religion, and the Roaring Twenties*, pp. 196–200.
2. Ibid., pp. 223–231.
3. Gitlin, *The Sixties*, p. 429. The "townhouse explosion" refers to the following incident as described by Gitlin: "On March 6, 1970, Cathy Wilkerson's father was vacationing in the Caribbean. In his West Eleventh Street townhouse, a group of Weathermen were manufacturing pipe bombs and bombs studded with roofing nails— makeshift copies of antipersonnel bombs like those the United States was dropping in Vietnam. Someone connected the wrong wire. The house blew up, igniting the gas mains. Cathy Wilkerson, Kathy Boudin, and several other Weathermen staggered out of the rubble and disappeared. That night, Ted Gold's crushed body was identified. Diana Oughton's had to be identified from the print on a severed fingertip. There wasn't enough of Terry Robbins's body left to identify; only a subsequent Weatherman communique established that he was the third who died. Enough dynamite was recovered, undetonated, to blow up a city block. The police claimed that the roofing-nail bombs were intended for use at Columbia University; the Weathermen deny it, but have never said—

they insist they will never say—what the target was going to be" (pp. 400–401).

4. Bhagavad-Gita, translated by Swami Prabhavananda and Christopher Isherwood (New York: Mentor Books, 1944), p. 61.

5. Ibid., p. 63.

6. Maharishi Mahesh Yogi, Bhagavad-Gita (A New Translation and Commentary With Sanskrit Text) (Middlesex, England: Penguin Books, 1969), p. 371.

Part II

The Retrieval of Tradition

Chapter VII

How to Revitalize Our Traditions

An Evaluation of the Sixties

We have taken a lengthy journey back to the Sixties. For me, that era didn't actually end until the Vietnam War was over, Watergate had ended, and President Nixon was out of office. Because of the vast social changes that occurred in the Sixties, we might say that they have not yet ended. They have certainly not ended for the generations that lived through them. To this day we have not put President Kennedy's assassination and the Vietnam War behind us. Moreover, the music from the period heavily populates the FM band in most areas of the country, whether it's Simon and Garfunkle's "Scarborough Fair," "Punk's Dilemma," or "Bridge Over Troubled Water" that is being played or the Beatles' "Hello Goodbye," "Your Mother Should Know," and "Fool on the Hill" from their album *Magical Mystery Tour*, whether it's "lite rock" or "heavy metal." And a few of us even dig out our old Kingston Trio or Journeymen albums from time to time. We will begin our evaluation of those seminal years, the past which is still present, by referring to some of their positives.

The Positive Aspects of the Sixties

The Sixties gave us the civil rights movement and the revolutionary legislation passed by Congress soon after President Kennedy's assassination (something he could not accomplish in life but, ironically, only in death—with the help of LBJ's strong arm). The Sixties also accelerated feminism and the whole women's rights movement. Moreover, the gay rights movement is rooted in the Sixties. One of the most positive legacies from the Sixties is the quest for equal justice for everyone, regardless of race, gender, religion, or sexual preference.

During the Sixties males discovered greater freedom of expression. They felt less threatened by their feelings. They wore their hair longer, and became more "feminine" in a variety of ways. Women, on the other hand, became more "masculine," if I may be permitted to use those fuzzy terms. Women asserted themselves in the work place. They also tried to balance careers with families. In short, gender roles were revolutionized. John Lennon announced to the world that he had become a "house husband," and many have followed him in this, even if that only means pitching in more around the house. It was also far less of a stigma to be single in the Sixties, even when approaching middle age. We became more tolerant of each other's life styles. We also wanted to explore our affective nature more. We entered into our inner worlds; we became psychological, even spiritual. And we certainly became more sensitive. For the most part, all of that self-expression was a "healthy narcissism" asserting itself, although women have had an especially difficult time balancing family, career, and personal fulfillment. Even with that caveat, these new freedoms and challenges have been positive for American culture.

The music of the Sixties was highly creative, and memorable, even if there was a lot of junk, too. I have a theory about culture and creativity. When cultures go through waves of suffering, as we did during the Sixties, creative juices flow. Artistic energies are tapped by traumas, in other words. When suffering afflicts us, powerful emotions surge into consciousness. In creative people, these emotions empower their art. I think such a theory accounts for much of the Sixties' creativity. Just think of the body of music that was produced, from the musical *Hair* to the great variety of music created by the Beatles, e.g., "Michelle," "A Day in the Life," "Here, There and Everywhere," "In My Life," "Not a Second time,"and "While My Guitar Gently Weeps." Or consider the high quality and diversity of much of the hit parade music, e.g., "You've Lost That Lovin' Feeling" by the Righteous Brothers, "Mr. Dieingly Sad" by the Critters, "Anyone Who Had a Heart" by Dionne Warwick, or "Love is Blue" by Paul Mauriat. Here we must not overlook the music of Motown and other black artists, e.g., "Village of Love" by Nathaniel Mayer and the Fabulous Twilights, "Lonely Teardrops" by Jackie Wilson, "I Love You" by the Volumes, the Temptations' "You're My Everything" and "My Girl," or "Heat Wave" and "In My Lonely Room" by Martha and the Vandellas. That is a relatively small sampling, but it makes the point.

Sometimes, when I am driving through the city streets of Grand Haven, I hear a song on the radio from the Sixties such as "Standing on the Crossroads of Love," "Love is Here and Now You're Gone," or "Come See About Me" by the Supremes, or Mary Wells' "You Beat Me to the Punch" and "Two Lovers," and the music transports me back through the years as effectively as a time machine. Music—like an old letter—is a window into the past. Long forgotten people are thought of once again; ancient feelings bubble up into consciousness. Sometimes I can't even recollect what is being evoked by the music. The memory is enveloped in mist, but the song definitely touches a nerve. For my generation, music stirs up profound feelings, even if the specific events once associated with that music are now buried deep in the psyche.

The music of the Sixties stands on its own merits, but it is also inseparable from the times. Music is another positive legacy from the period, and it becomes even more positive if we compare it to the popular music of the Nineties, which really isn't very good. (It is largely a rehash of an aging genre. Rock and Roll in fact was pretty much exhausted by the end of the Vietnam War.) The best music of the Sixties will be listened to decades from now, and will always be associated with that period. I can't say that about contemporary music, both in its quality and its capacity to mark time.

The best films of the Sixties were another strong plus. They were daring, they were creative, and they grappled with the moral issues of the day. That trend was passed on to many of the movies that followed. Since the Sixties, serious films have generally been of high quality, much better than the music comparatively speaking. The creativity and courage of the movie industry are one more positive legacy from the Sixties.

The idealism of the times is also highly significant. It did collapse, and we have examined why (it had a weak religious foundation, and it was overly dependant psychologically on the pain of Vietnam). But that idealism still has some pull. Today it largely lies dormant, but at some point in the future this idealism may once again spring upon the culture. This will happen only when the right set of circumstances enables the Sixties Generation *to feel* that idealism once again, to relive it. If that happens, our emotions and creative energies—and our quest for social justice —will reemerge. Then watch out!

Don't give up on the Sixties Generation. Many of us have become materialists, but we are discovering that money alone doesn't satisfy the soul, and it can't buy inner peace. As Jesus said, "If any man would come after me, let him deny himself and take up his cross and follow me. For whoever would save his life will lose it; and whoever loses his life for my sake and the gospel's will save it. For what does it profit a man, to gain the whole world and forfeit his life?" (Mark 8:34–36).

A spiritual revival of sorts is coming, I believe, but it will be one that has a pluralist base, and will be powerful *because of that*. Pluralism is thus another important legacy from the Sixties. Below, I will be arguing that a revival of tradition is desperately needed in our culture, but I don't mean the revival of merely one tradition, Christianity let's say. America is not a "Christian nation," as some argue or hope for. America is a nation comprised of many traditions, and varying traditions even within a single tradition (consider the varieties of Christianity, or Judaism). We are enriched by many voices (and saved from domination by any one voice). Yes, Christianity needs to be revitalized, but then so do Islam and Judaism, and Eastern traditions. Moreover, Native Americans are desperately trying to hold onto their own traditions. All traditions must learn that they can live side by side without feeling that they have to "water down" their truths, or merge with each other, or dominate each other. Dialogue—not imperialistic conversion—must be the future of religion. We all can learn from each other—as long as we don't play God and condemn (or kill) each other.

One of the best things that happened in the Sixties was an increasing tolerance in our culture for traditions other than our own, including traditions from the East. The Sixties Generation became deeply interested in the truths of all the great religions, truths which then in turn enriched our own individual traditions. (The Sixties Generation, however, has also learned the dangers of cults and "fringe" religions.) The imperialism of any one tradition over all others won't wash with most members of my generation. Tolerance of one another's traditions is an additional positive legacy from the Sixties, although this tolerance is something we must constantly fight for, and protect, especially during periods like our own when fundamentalism is emerging in all of the major religions, a phenomenon that usually fosters bigotry and contempt for those who stand outside of one's own tradition.

Changes in our diet, our greater awareness of the importance of exercise and the curtailment of smoking and drinking, and our realization of the dangers of pollution and drugs are other positive legacies from the Sixties. Moreover, these things have been incorporated into the classroom on all levels. My own education rarely touched upon such concerns.

During the Sixties our society also more fully realized the horrors of war, a lesson that many have since forgotten, as evidenced by the recent Gulf War. (There is something sick about a culture that glorified an event that ended the lives of tens of thousands of men, women, and children.) But many of those who did oppose the Gulf War were people who had been influenced by the Sixties, and remembered Vietnam's horrors. The lingering influence of the Vietnam War will, I hope, act as a brake on any hasty or prolonged use of American military force. Sadly, many churches and clergy were as silent about the Gulf War as they had been about Vietnam, although in the Episcopal Church both my own diocesan bishop, Edward Lee Jr., and my presiding bishop, Edmond Browning, opposed our 1991 "adventure." They were not in the majority of American Christians, however, just as those against the Vietnam War were not in the majority.

There are many other positive legacies from the Sixties which I could mention. Here I will close with this final observation. Because of the Sixties, we all are more open to our feelings, or at least more aware of their power. How could we not be after Vietnam? (Although the prolonged violence numbed the feelings of many, too.) In the midst of Vietnam, feelings finally had their hearing. We respected their power, something Freud urged during his entire career. We simply felt more back then as a culture, far more than we do today. No doubt traumas had much to do with our depth of emotion. We learned from our own experience that feelings are what enrich life, that deep feelings for others and sensitivity to their needs, in particular, are the most important things in life. When people are nostalgic for the Sixties, in large part they miss that emotional intensity. Many now long to feel that deeply once again in our rather sterile era.

On the other hand, the level of emotional intensity during the war was more than the culture could endure. And the psychological reaction against it has been profound. A massive cultural repression occurred. Maybe no social system—and no individual psyche—can survive for long such pain and turmoil.

All of these positives of the Sixties justify, in my opinion, our current cultural nostalgia for the era. The Vietnam period launched so much that has been good for us and our society. "But what about the negatives?" you may be asking. There were many, and these are better forgotten—except for the fact many of them are still very much with us.

The Negative Aspects of the Sixties

We will start our examination of the dark side of the Sixties by taking up where we just left off, with what happened to us emotionally. Many repressed their feelings, largely due to traumas. People's libidinal currents became jumbled. Men and women had sex without feelings, others had feelings without sex. Emotionality and sensuality split apart. As a character says of this spiritual plight in D. H. Lawrence's great novel, *Lady Chatterley's Lover* (a cult book of the Sixties, not only because of its frank treatment of sexuality, but also due to the fact the book finally became readily available in that less censorious era):

> "You see, Hilda," said Connie after lunch, when they were nearing London, "you have never known either real tenderness or real sensuality: and if you do know them, with the same person, it makes a great difference."
>
> "For mercy's sake, don't brag about your experiences!" said Hilda. "I've never met the man yet who was capable of intimacy with a woman, giving himself up to her. That was what I wanted." [5]

Indeed, the union of spirit and flesh was what many longed for in the Sixties but failed to ever find. The decline of tradition deprived many people of important spiritual resources, resources which might have enabled them to cope with traumas, resources which might have thereby helped them combine—in a healthy way—the affectionate and sensual currents of the libido.

Not only were the libidinal currents going in different directions during the Sixties, but there was also an imbalance between self-love and object-love. Any revival of tradition must address both tasks of integration. Such a revival would mitigate both individual and cultural narcissism.

One widespread effect of the Sixties' narcissism turned out to be materialism, which we have already emphasized. The materialism of the Eighties, and beyond, had its deepest psychological and social roots in the Sixties.

Another negative effect of narcissism has been a neurotic preoccupation with the self. At the outset, let me say that healthy narcissism and the exploration of the inner life were for many people highly positive developments (and remain so). They were a much needed reaction to a repressive Protestantism and Roman Catholicism, which too often fear both the body and the emotions, and in many instances, the mind. Such traditions also propagated a very unhealthy ideal of self-sacrifice; it was unhealthy because it came at the expense of nurturing one's spiritual life. The destructiveness of that form of religion was very apparent in the Sixties, but the rejection of such traditions left a spiritual vacuum for many. In some cases, narcissism filled up the void. As a result, self-preoccupations sometimes led to a constant worrying about the self—one's weight, one's looks, one's age. You name it, and I have seen people worrying about it in the confidence of my office during pastoral counseling. Without faith in God, without a religious community, and without faith in oneself, life indeed is frightening. One becomes highly vulnerable to spiritual assaults, from both without and within. In a secular age, narcissism attaches itself—like a lamprey eel—to crazy anxieties and nit-picking worries. It intensifies them, thereby making them far worse.

Jesus' moral concerns about our preoccupations—even what we eat and drink, or what we wear (Matthew 6:24–34)—are especially pertinent to modern worry warts who exist without a tradition but with a pocketful of worries.

Selfishness within the Sixties Generation is easy to discern, but a person's secret worries are less easy to diagnose, and may be far more destructive to the soul. During the Sixties, we wanted to "get into ourselves"—but, now, many want to know how to get out! (Here religious decline has been catastrophic.)

The increased drug use and promiscuity that sprung upon our society from the Sixties are obvious negatives, and require no further comment. In assessing the positive legacies of the Sixties, we must always balance them with drugs and promiscuity. We need only point to the disease AIDS to fully realize the dangers of rampant drug use and casual sex. Some even "blessed" drugs and sex as the way to reach higher levels of consciousnes—even union with God! That has been as tragic as it was idiotic.

Now let's consider the damage caused by Vietnam, a trauma that certainly contributed to drug abuse and looser sexual morals. But its effects go even deeper—into the very core of the nation's spirit. Indeed, it poisoned that spirit.

The Vietnam War not only cost American society life and

limb, and untold amounts of money, but it also cost American society a sacred trust in its institutions. The Church suffered. The government suffered. Education suffered. And the business world suffered. Disillusionment and bitterness with *all* of society's institutions have been the poisoned fruit of the Sixties, a destructive legacy we have not yet overcome. Moreover, deficit spending became a way of life in our federal government during Vietnam, a high octane addiction that could eventually bankrupt us. (Especially our children, who will inherit this mountain of debt.)

Liberalism—in large part because of its Vietnam War support —suffered severe damage, as I shall discuss later. As a result, we have lost both the will, and the ability, to use governmental power to improve social conditions. Our educational system is crumbling, our bridges and roads are falling apart, our environment is being polluted, homelessness is widespread (in large part because the wards of state mental hospitals have been emptied to save money), many go to bed hungry in the richest country in the world. In short, government no longer works very well. Before the disillusionment brought by the Sixties, we did have faith that our government could improve social conditions (think back once again to the idealism expressed by President Kennedy's Inaugural Address); we had faith that our government could work effectively for social justice. But who has such faith any longer? Conservatives have filled up the power vacuum, but who now stands up for the poor and the disenfranchised?

To sum up and look ahead, the most destructive legacy of the Sixties was the abandonment, neglect, and rejection of tradition, especially our moral and religious traditions and our civil traditions—even the tradition of civility. The bizarreness of the Sixties often took violent forms, or tasteless ones, and tradition often was the brunt of rage. Several quotations from Sixties' activists illustrate what I am driving at (they also show the insanity of the era). First, this "thought" of Mark Rudd's from 1969: "It's a wonderful feeling to hit a pig. It must be a really wonderful feeling to kill a pig or blow up a building." Another Columbia strategist in the New Left offered this tirade: "We're against everything that's 'good and decent' in honky America. We will burn and loot and destroy. We are the incubation of your mother's nightmare." Lastly, Bernardine Dohrn, who had been a student at the University of Chicago, said this in admiration of Charles Manson: "Dig it! First they killed those pigs, then they ate dinner in the same room with them, then they even shoved a fork into the victim's stomach. Wild!" [2] Todd Gitlin reports that at a Flint, Michigan, convention of the New Left in 1969, the favored greeting was "four slightly spread fingers—to symbolize the fork" used by Charles Manson's family to penetrate Sharon Tate's pregnant body.[3]

The weakening of tradition, including its bloody violations, has affected us all. It has led to a moral and spiritual collapse in American society, and has contributed to numerous psychological and social problems (e.g., the breakdown of the family, diseases brought on by promiscuity and drug use, lack of support for public education, abortion as a form of birth control or sex selection, condoms being passed out in schools, voter apathy, the rise of crime, etc.).

To conclude this book, I will now make a plea for the retrieval of our moral and religious traditions (not when those traditions are repressive, but when they heal and enrich the spirit). I will also offer a brief strategy for such a retrieval.

The Restoration and Reformation of Tradition

I will begin with some evidence that shows social recognition of our need to retrieve and revitalize our traditions, especially religious traditions. In an article about religion in the 1990s ("Are There Episcopalians in the Foxholes?", *National Review*, July 29, 1991), the author Richard Brookhiser states that "the Episcopal Church has been unable to hide its unravelment. In 1960, it had more than 3.25 million baptized members, and a contemporary reference book declared that 'the recent pace' of half a million new members per decade 'shows no sign of slowing down.' By 1970, membership still stood at just over 3.25 million. By 1980, it was under 2.8 million. By 1989, the last year for which figures are available, it had sunk below 2.5 million. Today the flacks at

Episcopal headquarters are happy if the pace of decay shows signs of slowing down."

Then, lending support to my overall argument, he adds that the Sixties played a crucial role in the Episcopal Church's decline: "The flakiness of the Sixties hit Episcopalians hard, as it did the rest of the country. Cathedrals like St. John the Divine in New York and Grace Cathedral in San Francisco hosted rallies, happenings, light shows, and Sufi and Shinto services (they still do), while the national church shelled out cash to Puerto Rican nationalists and black-power groups . . . in the late Seventies, the church showed public signs of severe internal crisis."

Brookhiser's emphasis on the importance of the Sixties in religious decline is now a widely accepted view. For example, the Rev. Richard Kew and the Rt. Rev. Roger White, Bishop of Milwaukee, write in *The Living Church* (September 13, 1992) that "the 1960s were watershed years for Episcopalians. Their churches had experienced unprecedented numerical growth without interruption ever since American soldiers had returned to civilian life following World War II. But in the 1960s, different agendas were thrust to the fore. Whether as a result or coincidentally, this accompanied a nationwide decline in religious involvement." Those "different agendas" were alluded to by Brookheiser, and I will touch upon others shortly.

Lastly, let me include some observations from a *Wall Street Journal* editorial (September 24, 1991) entitled "Billy Graham in Central Park." the author connects the spiritual hunger in American society to weaknesses in mainline traditions since the Sixties, and is wondering why over 250,000 people gathered in Central Park in New York to hear Billy Graham; here is some of what the editorial says:

> What precipitated the flight from the mainstream churches is no mystery. Somewhere along the way those churches began to devalue or even dispense with their traditions and their identities as primarily spiritual institutions. Spiritual life was now to be fully integrated with more secular political goals flying under the rubric of "social justice."

The author goes on to add,

An even larger irony is that the churches' religious leaders decided to wander off to other concerns in the very years when many people could have used the most help trying to make sense of the overwhelming pace of change in American culture. These are the people who now flock to hear Billy Graham.

The editorial concludes with this scathing indictment of American society:

> That we somehow live now in a society much more deficient in psychological and moral health than three decades ago has something to do, we suspect, with the loss of religious tradition and authority. The throngs who came to Central Park Sunday, looking for a way back to religion, seem to know it too.

Whereas I disagree with some of the particulars in that editorial (e.g., its dichotomy between spiritual and social concerns), I share, obviously, its overall thesis about the loss of tradition. Religious decline, however, has not afflicted Christianity alone. The inroads of secularization have been much more widespread. Let me tell you a story to illustrate that.

Right after my first outreach trip to the Wind River Indian Reservation in Wyoming (with members of the Church of the Holy Spirit in Lake Forest, Illinois). I began to read about a series of suicides on the reservation. Young Arapahos were killing themselves. This made the "CBS Evening News." *Time* had an article about it. I learned later on that the tribal leaders tried everything to stop this tragedy. Nothing worked. Not Christianity. Not social work. Not psychiatry. Finally, the tribe turned to its own ancient traditions and its medicine men. They rediscovered the spiritual power of those traditions, and then relied upon them. *After the tribe retrieved its own spiritual roots, the suicides ceased.* Here we see very clearly the power of tradition, and its significance for spiritual and social well-being.

In my subsequent trips to the Wind River Reservation I learned even more about Native American traditions. My group participated in pow-wows, which are social gatherings comprised of many tribes. Whites are welcome, and are even occasionally invited to dance, but for the most part each tribe celebrates its own traditions in song and dance, and with its own food and crafts. The Arapaho, for instance, are famous for their bead work, the Zuni for the quality of their silver jewelry, and Navahos for their rugs. The "Indian tacos" the Arapaho serve at these gatherings are wonderful—beans, beef, cheese, lettuce, tomatoes, onions, all on a scrumptious deep-fried circular soft shell. We also witnessed a Sun Dance, a profoundly moving religious rite. The spiritual overtones of this ritual are Christian for some of the Arapaho; for others, the spirituality is exclusively Native American (which all Christians, or anyone, would benefit from if they would take the time to become familiar with it). Many Arapaho and other Indians amalgamate Christianity with their own traditions, which often predate Christianity itself by many centuries.

The Arapaho and other tribes are preserving their language as well. Arapaho was once in danger of being lost. When I was on the reservation, the Arapaho were working hard through various summer programs to pass on their ancient language to the children.

The destruction of Native American traditions by both Christian missionaries and white secular culture has not only been a disaster for the Indians, but a moral crime as well—indeed, a religious one. Thank God that more and more people now realize that, and are becoming increasingly aware of the arrogance of telling Indians that their religion is "wrong" and only the Christian religion is "right." Native American traditions are now being celebrated, restored, preserved, and shared throughout the United States.

A similar restoration of traditions must now take place in American society at large. But how do we restore our traditions? Where do we begin? Here is a point by point strategy. I begin with a celebration of our cultural diversity, something I have alluded to in my discussion of the Arapaho.

Pluralism

The Sixties Generation has been far too influenced by pluralism to ever gather together under any single umbrella of tradition, be it Christian, Jewish, Islamic, or one of the religions from the East. Nor will its members ever gather together under the umbrella of "secular humanism." Some of us will embrace more than one tradition, and all of us, we may hope, can eventually come to celebrate the diversity of traditions in American culture. Perhaps we can share with one another what we personally cherish, be it religious or secular. My chief concern here, however, is reviving our religious and moral traditions (although our political, civil, educational, and legal traditions desperately need revitalization, too).

I believe that God is working through all the great religious traditions of the world, that "truth" with a capital "T" lies in them all. The Cross and Resurrection of Christ, for instance, have implications for all the world religions, just as the Jewish Decalogue, the prophets' cries for social justice, and the Koran's extremely high ethical ideals have a claim on me as a Christian. God speaks to us through all our venerated religions, including Native American traditions. God speaks to us in them *if* we have ears to hear. Moreover, the spiritual traditions from the East offer the Semitic traditions an important emphasis on interiority that, sadly, is often missing in our Americanized versions.

All religions must abandon their imperialism, their bigotry and prejudice. They must stop claiming to be "the only true religion," or even "the best religion" (which is always shown to be a culture-bound statement anyway). In saying this, I am not arguing for a relativist position. I don't think all religions are equally true, or even equal, nor do I think all of their claims and beliefs are literally true, or even symbolically true. Religions, moreover, are not always wise or moral. However, I am asserting that God's revelation is found in all of the great religions of the world, and let me reemphasize that I consider Native American traditions to be among these.

How all the religions fit together in God's overall plan for history is, obviously, known only to God. God's plan is not for us to know, at least in this arena, a conclusion Paul himself reached in Romans, chapters 9–11, when he was trying to sort out God's purposes in working through both Jews and Gentiles. I am thus pleading for toleration—and appreciation—of one religion for another. I am advocating honest dialogue, not conversion in the old-fashioned sense that the Christian missionaries thought of it when, for instance, they helped to conquer America. They degraded Native American religious traditions, at a great spiritual cost for Indians of all tribes. Even today Christians go into India, for instance, in order to convert all the Hindus and Muslims to Christianity, judging them damned without such a conversion. What spiritual arrogance! World religions must host dialogues with one another—not conquer. They must be tolerant, not bigoted. There are many paths leading to God. All religions must acknowledge that.

In a dialogue between religions—now made possible by the mass media and world travel—people do not have to back away from their own truth claims, about the incarnation of Yahweh in Christ, for instance, or that of Vishnu in Krishna. Or from the cries for social justice one encounters in a prophet such as Amos. However, members of the various religious traditions must not make pronouncements about the "eternal destiny" of others, especially those outside their own traditions. People must not judge whether someone is "saved" or not, although they certainly may share the "good news" of God's grace as they themselves have experienced that grace. We must not judge each other using religious categories, especially in retaliation when others don't accept our own religious claims. Members of all the religions must leave in God's hands what only can be in God's hands: judgment, its criteria, and our eternal destiny. "Judge not, that you be not judged" (Matthew 7:1), as Jesus warned. And I think he was referring precisely to the human propensity to "play God" and make pronouncements about the salvation or damnation of others. That is the ultimate sin in the Bible—putting oneself in place of God, even acting like God. That is idolatry at its worst. Moreover, it is a violation of the First Commandment. Human beings are always trying to limit God's grace.

Pluralism is something we should celebrate, be enriched by,

and fight hard to maintain. However, we must not let pluralism water down tradition in general, as if all traditions were equally "untrue" because there is such a diversity of traditions and truth claims. The oriental mind does not think in such "either/or" categories, as does the occidental mind. Here Americans can learn something crucial from the East—that all the great religions of the world are "true" even if their particular truth claims often contradict one another from the standpoint of our Western myopic mind set. Yes, we must be loyal to our own traditions, but at the same time we must be open to learning spiritual truths and wisdom from other traditions. Such an openness and willingness to learn from all traditions has been far too lacking in all religions. We must be ready to share our truths *without* denouncing the beliefs of others. We must converse, debate, and learn—not condemn or ridicule.

One final point: most members of the great world religions are absolutely ignorant of religions other than their own (assuming that they know even that). This is particularly true of Americans, and one needs to look no further than Christian fundamentalists and evangelicals. This ignorance must be rectified, which now leads us into a consideration of education.

Education

Schools must teach religion—not as an ideology, not as a means for attaining salvation, not as absolute and exclusive truth, but as an important part of the history of civilization, or as a chapter in the history of ideas, or as part of the literature of a culture. The separation of church and state has led to a tragic mistake—the absence of religion from the curricula of many schools. If religion has not been completely removed, its role in history and culture has been drastically underemphasized, far more than is justified by its actual role in world history. The study of religion—all religions —must be restored and offered by schools, on all levels.

As an aspect of that effort, we must include an inquiry into Native American religions because they have been neglected more than others. These traditions offer the world a great deal, especially in their understanding of the spiritual life and their reverence for nature (which we all must develop before we completely destroy our environment). In theological terms, Native Americans have emphasized God's immanence in creation, whereas many traditions within Christianity, Islam, and Judaism emphasize God's transcendence from the world, which at times has been a license to rape the environment. Members of religious traditions must also do a better job of education within churches. For instance, Christian education programs should be coordinated from beginning to end, from the youngest children to the oldest adults. We must learn about other traditions, but first we must learn about our own.

Once we do that, we can enrich our understanding of our own tradition by comparing it to others. If churches had such education, it would be both enlightening and spiritually edifying. Religious prejudice would be reduced through mutual understanding. Christians often denounce other religions, but are often completely ignorant of the traditions they are denouncing. In our society I often hear Christians judging others because they have not accepted Christ (condemning others in the name of Christ is the ultimate historical irony, considering his own fate). Such Christians betray the Cross. They are its modern "enemies," to use Paul's term. They limit God's grace and love by putting God in a box. Education in both schools and churches would help to rectify this deplorable ignorance of religious traditions, and would thereby reduce prejudice.

Renewal Movements

Many denominations reacted to the Sixties by instigating various kinds of renewal movements, especially in the realms of liturgy, community life, and church architecture. Men and women flocked to renewal movements such as Cursillo, which is a phenomenon that arose out of the Roman Catholic tradition in Spain. It organizes weekend retreats that are designed to strengthen commitment to Christ and deepen faith. Men in particular were drawn to these because they were "given permission" to be emotional in public, which for many has been a highly liberating and authentic experience.

The Episcopal Church and many other denominations also renewed themselves by approving new books of worship and new hymnals, which incorporated contemporary liturgies and music. The Episcopal Church's 1979 Book of Common Prayer, like similar attempts in other traditions, attempts to combine the best of "the old" with the best of "the new."

As part of the overall renewal of the Church, women are now ordained in many traditions, a very significant step in the life of the Church. However, this battle has not been universally won, such as within the priesthoods of the Roman Catholic and Orthodox traditions.

Renewal movements in general have been attempts to create in churches a feeling of community. Many churches were even redesigned in their interiors to nurture this feeling, which the liturgies fostered. However, sometimes beautiful traditional churches were ruined. And a sense of mystery—a sense of the numinous—was thereby lost.

Some churches ended up looking ridiculous when altars were moved and sanctuaries were redesigned. On the whole, however, renewal movements should be tolerated, if not encouraged (unless they become overly divisive, turn into an escape from problems, or ruin the architectural integrity of church buildings). Change is the life blood of any tradition, but change must not occur at the expense of cherished traditions, or through the elimination of good taste. The Church must always walk very gingerly on that particular tightrope.

To conclude, the changes which have occurred in denominations such as the Episcopal Church have, for the most part, been very positive, and must be pursued *as long as* there remains a sensitivity to tradition. Renewal movements were a positive legacy from the Vietnam era (although many in the Church would take issue with that assessment). If properly understood, renewal movements must be part of a strategy to revitalize a tradition. They enable a tradition to speak to modern culture.

The Bible

An important aspect of any tradition is learning those texts which nourish it. This means that in both schools and in the Church we must study the "classic texts" of Western and Eastern traditions, especially the Bible for those living in the West. In any restoration of Jewish and Christian traditions—historically, the two dominant traditions in American culture—we must learn the Scriptures. We must let the Word sink into our souls. We must taste it and feel its rhythms. (Members of all traditions, however, must study their own sacred scriptures.) But we must not interpret the Bible (or any scriptures) literally. Fundamentalism betrays the Scriptures by imposing an alien point of view upon the authors and their intentions. Nor should we revitalize the Biblical tradition at the expense of other traditions, such as Islam, which has been gaining such a strong foothold in American society. Native American traditions also should not be left in the Bible's wake. Lastly, we must not try to forge a syncretism of all religions. Each tradition must preserve its own integrity. However, within this diversity—which is the rich harvest of pluralism—there is a unifying symbol, that of God. The symbol of God transcends all traditions, yet they all point to that divine reality, that creative force or power we call Allah, Brahma, Yahweh, or God the Father.

For Christians and Jews, my chief concern here, the Bible is the heart of tradition. It pumps the blood; it keeps life going. So we must ask, what exactly is the Bible? It is a book which combines historical fact, wisdom, ethics, literature, story, liturgy, theology, law, prophecy, and myth. Since the Bible is so crucial to my overall strategy for reviving and revitalizing our American religious traditions, I will now offer a discussion of "myth," because unless we understand that very significant concept, the Bible can not be appreciated (or religion for that matter). But myth is a word that is profoundly misunderstood and misused.

Myth

In a true sense I have been presenting myths about American culture throughout this book. I was doing that when I discussed the role of religion in unifying the self, e.g., the role of religion in helping the believer merge the two currents of the libido (Freud even called his libido theory a myth). One could also say that it is a myth that religion creates a sense of community in American society and provides both an identity and a moral gyroscope. In chapter three I offered a myth about Elvis Presley and explained the significance of that myth for the Sixties Generation. But what is a myth? We need to rescue—once and for all—the word "myth" from its popular misconceptions.

Let me illustrate that popular misconception. Some readers might argue that what I have been presenting about the secularization of America is a myth, which it is, but not in the way they probably mean it. What would this statement—"secularization is a myth"—most likely mean to most people? In the way the word "myth" is popularly understood by the culture at large, this would mean that secularization was "untrue," which is precisely how myth is so often misunderstood. Or when we say that "the Bible is full of myths," or that "the great religions of the world are full of myths," does that mean then that the Bible and world religions are untrue? Of course not. But we have to be careful to define the term "myth" before using it because of these popular misconceptions.

Now I will offer the correct meaning of myth. A myth is a story, account, idea, theory, or theology—usually laced with symbols—which interprets or "makes sense" of something. In the Bible, for instance, myths interpret God, nature, and human beings, including their culture and history. A myth is thus an interpretation, which is often ritualized, as in church services. A myth contains truth (although some myths distort or lie, as in Nazism), *regardless of whether a particular myth is rooted in historical fact.* Some myths are based on historical events, and some are not. Most myths, however, are a combination of historical fact (something that actually happened), fantasy, and interpretation. Myths are given life in the crucible of the human imagination, including the "collective imagination."

I will now give some illustrations. Most scholars would argue, for example, that Adam and Eve in the Book of Genesis are not historical people. (Fundamentalists, however, become highly upset with that conclusion because they believe that such a point of view undermines "the truth" of the account, which it doesn't at all if myth is properly understood.) The story of Adam and Eve contains a truth about human nature and the doctrine of sin—a truth that we neglect at our peril—but the historicity of Adam and Eve has no bearing upon the truth of the story. Like most ancient Jews, the authors were primarily interested in the *meaning* of the story. As members of a community, they were concerned about the spiritual edification of the worshiping community. The myth of Adam and Eve gives us—as it did the Jews—a profound insight into our will to power, and our propensity to rebel against authority, especially God's authority. Even if there were not a historical Adam and Eve, the truth of the myth would endure. ("Adam" comes from the Hebrew word for "man," and in the Genesis account means every man, every woman.)

Some myths, however, do have a historical base. Just think of all the mythology surrounding people such as George Washington (he didn't literally chop down that cherry tree, but he was an honest man), George Armstrong Custer, or Crazy Horse. Or consider religious figures such as the Buddha, Moses, or Jesus. Some of the mythology surrounding such people is undoubtedly historical, but much of it is not. But to repeat, that which is not historical in any myth, still may be "true." It is true because it conveys truth about the people involved, or truths about nature and history, or truths about groups of people and their cultures. Events such as the Civil War, Vietnam, or "Custer's Last Stand," may become myths or give rise to myths. In such cases, historical events may puncture myths (as Vietnam punctured such myths as "American will never lose a war," or "America is always right"). Vietnam also did a great deal of damage to our belief in our military invincibility, one of the most powerful of all the myths the Sixties Generation grew up with. Moreover, our loss in Vietnam shattered our shared myth, our common faith, in the superiority of American moral positions over those of our "enemies" (internal "enemies" included, which is how many Americans viewed the Vietnam war protestors). Let me repeat: myths are usually mixtures of fact and fantasy. They are products of the human imagination, an imagination inspired by historical events in many instances, but an imagination also inspired by powerful needs, hopes, dreams, and desires. Take Jesus' resurrection. It is a myth, obviously, but one that does, I believe, have a historical base. Scripture points to that base, however shrouded in mystery. The transformation of Jesus' disciples also points to that base. They changed from a frightened band of fishermen and laborers into the historical force that reshaped the world. Yet the gospel accounts are full of discrepancies about the Resurrection. They show great imagination on the part of the writers and the preservers of tradition. Jesus appears and then disappears. He walks through walls, yet eats fish. He even invites Thomas to examine his wounds physically in John's account.

The gospel writers brought their own hopes, dreams, culture, and theological positions to bear on their respective Biblical accounts. Yet, without some historical basis for the Resurrection —a historical victory over suffering and death—how do we explain the dramatic changes in the disciples? How do we explain them psychologically? How could a band of defeated human beings, as portrayed by Mark especially, have gained so much strength, confidence, and dedication—enough to transform the world. I can't interpret that without taking into consideration the historical aspects of the myth of the Resurrection. The disciples could not have done that merely inspired by a hallucination (as if five hundred people could have hallucinated Jesus' resurrection in the appearance described by Paul in I Corinthians 15:6 —"Then he appeared to more than five hundred brethren at one time, most of whom are still alive"). I don't think the disciples could have been successful missionaries with only a hallucination to motivate them, or a fabrication, or even a delusion created by their own hopes and dreams. We know that a few of the disciples had desires for power (Mark 9:34, Luke 22:24) and were ambitious—but to the extent that they would create a gigantic hoax, a hoax that continues to this day? Highly unlikely! The

Resurrection myth well illustrates the richness and complexity of the term.

Or take the story of the flood in Genesis. This is another myth which most likely has a historical base. Some ancient disaster no doubt occurred which affected areas of the Middle East (possibly at the same time or on the same order as the catastrophe that so abruptly and mysteriously led to the disappearance of the Minoan civilization). Most likely a serious flood did threaten many families, and Noah and his family might very well be historical. Facts concerning the dim recesses of antiquity are extremely difficult to verify. There is no question, however, that the account of the flood in Genesis is less of a factual historical account than a product of the religious imagination over the course of many years. The story of Noah is mostly "fiction," but fiction which conveys truth through its mythical elements. It does this regardless of our uncertainty about the historicity of the account.

The significance of any myth is the truth it contains, although we must be aware when myths propagate lies. Myths that are used to foster racism, for instance, are particularly dangerous because they often accentuate some things which do have a historical base, however slight. Myths can be caricatures, of nationalities for instance. Myths that convey lies—by exaggerating or falsifying minor truths—are pernicious because so many people believe the partial truth to be the whole truth. Moreover, some people may latch onto myths which are not at all historical, but then believe in their factual nature because they want to, or need to, or are driven to by unconscious impulses. As a result, some people believe in myths regardless of whether the messages communicated by those myths convey truth or have a historical base.

There seems to be something peculiar, or strange, about Americans because we so often equate historicity with truth. For some reason, Americans have failed to learn how to think and feel mythologically, symbolically, and thus religiously. Biblical literalists come immediately to mind (here the New England Puritans could have learned something from the Native Americans they sought to destroy, along with their religion). They can't see, or be convinced of, the truth of a Biblical passage if the events narrated did not literally happen just as they are described in the text. Such people are threatened by scholarly studies of the Bible (which out of fear most churches have failed to teach). They think that if even one Biblical myth can be shown not to have a historical base, all Biblical myths may lose that base, which will never happen because that base is secure for many of the myths. Such fears really arise, however, from a misunderstanding of mythology.

Having said all of that, I do admit that *some* myths would lose much of their truth and meaning, and certainly much of their impact, if their historical base were ever completely disproved. Jesus' resurrection falls into that category (although some would take issue with that; they argue that we forever possess the truth of his life, teaching, and his victory over death because they exist in the text itself).

On the other hand, racial myths *should* be diffused by debunking their purported historical base. Such debunking, however, often does not work, which simply shows once again the power of myths, especially when entangled with sick minds. Each myth must be interpreted and examined on its own merits. It must also be put into its historical context, which many Biblical literalists seem unwilling to do.

The importance of a historical base for any given myth will vary; obviously, the myths of Christianity, for example, would lose much of their power for many people if it ever were proven that Jesus never lived. The mythology surrounding Elvis Presley, however—which does have a historical base—is not as dependent upon that base. With Elvis, it is now the myth that is far more significant for American culture than the bare facts of his life. With Jesus, on the other hand, we are much more concerned with uncovering and substantiating the historical base for the myths surrounding him in both the Bible and in our culture. Many people have even been obsessed with discovering "the historical Jesus," as Albert Schweitzer demonstrated in his book *The Quest for the Historical Jesus*. Some of this interest comes from a natural curiosity, and some from a deep religious concern, but much of it is rooted in an almost pathological fear that the "truth" of Jesus would disappear if the historical base for that truth disappeared. As I said, there is some reason for such a concern in the case of Jesus. With the rise of modern Biblical criticism, many have lost their religious faith because they have lost faith in some of the "historical facts" they had previously believed were literally true. As their historical connections to Jesus have weakened, so has their faith.

Let me add this caveat: I think the religious lives of people (Americans in particular) would be immensely enriched if they could ever learn to appreciate myth and symbol for what they are, and appreciate them for the truths they convey—without falling into the trap of literalism. Such an outlook does not require people to abandon their quest for historical facts. However, we must supplement such a quest with a far richer and broader appreciation for mythology and symbolism. Much will be gained, and far less will be lost, *if* previously believed historical facts do indeed turn out to be "myths" in the popular sense.

Culture is indeed comprised of myths, often competing myths. We have a variety of interpretations of God, nature, history, and ourselves. With a proper understanding of myth, we will celebrate this diversity—not be threatened by it. Such a diversity enriches our spiritual lives as well as our church liturgies (when the drama of myth is skillfully incorporated).

Following the Reformation, Protestantism stripped away from religion far too much of its mythology, mystery, ritual, and symbolism. We see this particularly in the barrenness of its liturgies. Many Protestant traditions now realize the seriousness of this mistake; they see the severe spiritual price which has been paid over the centuries for this liturgical sterility. Protestantism simply overreacted to Roman Catholicism; much of it has become overly doctrinal, intellectual, dry, even boring—not to speak of irrelevant.

Today Protestant traditions are trying to recapture symbol and myth by becoming more liturgical. I applaud those efforts. One reason liturgy has become so important to Episcopalians is because the Book of Common Prayer (in its various revisions throughout the centuries) has effectively combined Scripture, tradition, experience, and reason—the four sources of authority of my denomination—into a set of liturgies which are filled to the brim with mystery, myth, and symbol. The Anglican tradition in general has tried to combine the best of pre-Reformation Roman Catholicism with the best theological thought that emerged from Protestantism. Moreover, Episcopalians participate in worship. It is not passive, as in so much of Protestantism. We don't merely listen to a long sermon, with a few prayers and hymns thrown in. We become actors in a drama—not mere passive onlookers.

Our culture is literally starving for myth and symbol; it is also longing for mystery. In the past much of the energy of religion came from the belief that certain historical events literally happened in the way they are described in the Bible. In modernity that is no longer the case, at least for vast numbers of people. For them, secularization and the work of scholars have forever undermined historical certainty about many of the events narrated in the Bible. A religion that solely depends upon such certainty will be eventually doomed. Religious doubt is now too strong to ground faith upon the absolute certainty that Biblical events happened literally in the way they were said to have happened in the Bible. The energy of religion in modernity will come from recapturing the truths contained in myths and symbols, and by understanding the myths and symbols in religious traditions other than our own. *Myth and symbol will then energize religious belief as historical certainty once did in another age.*

Those of us who are upholding religious traditions in our secular society know what the basic problem is in our culture—spiritual barrenness. Religious leaders are seeking to revitalize, as well as preserve, tradition in the effort to rectify that problem. We must maintain and guard the best in our traditions (their myths, symbols, music, liturgies, architecture, scholarship, community life, and good works), while at the same time we take risks to introduce things that are new and creative. Recapturing our myths, in particular, is indispensable for that task. But without a proper understanding of myth, we will neither understand nor appreciate the Bible, or religious traditions in general. Then our liturgies will truly confuse us.

The Clergy

All religious traditions must improve the quality of their clergy. Even though women can now be ordained in many denominations—and, indeed talented women outnumber the talented men at many seminaries—that has not turned the tide of the professional ministry's overall deterioration. Plus, some of these women are just as incompetent and unstable as some of the men. There is yet another factor at work in the weakening of the professional ministry, a much darker one. I am referring to something very evident in our present society, often made even more evident by newspaper stories about the latest lewd "sex scandal" among the clergy: too many psychologically disturbed people have been entering into the ministry in recent years. Many go into the ministry to meet their own deep emotional needs, rather than those of the men, women, and children they are serving. The Sixties were definitely a factor here.

Many seminary students during the Vietnam War were "called" more by a draft deferment (then offered to seminary students) than by God. These clergy, who went to seminary primarily to dodge the draft, have had, collectively, a deleterious effect upon the Church, one that we should not underestimate when evaluating current problems in organized religion. Today, the draft is no longer a factor, obviously, but far too many people go into the ministry who still are more concerned about fulfilling their own needs rather than those of the Church.

Undoubtedly, part of the reason for this state of things is narcissism, pure and simple. Concerns for the self outweigh all other concerns with some seminarians. Such priorities will interfere with effective ministry unless they are dealt with during the clergy's training.

It is also undoubtedly true that overly needy people have always entered into the ministry (and this is a source of strength if those needs can be properly understood, mastered, and then utilized within one's ministry). It has just been more noticeable since the Sixties because not nearly enough psychologically stable people are going into the ministry to dilute the numbers of disturbed ones. Moreover, ministerial preparation has been eroding.

It will be very difficult for the Church to rectify that overall situation in a culture which less and less values religion and its representatives, and proves it by the abysmal compensation many clergy receive. The low pay of clergy repels many from considering seminary, especially if one wants to have a family. In reality, spouses subsidize the Church in most denominations. As a result, the ordained ministry is rapidly becoming a "second class" profession; it is becoming a "supplementary paycheck," much like teaching school was in the 1950s. Without the spouse's paycheck coming into the household, most clergy would be forced to leave the ministry once children come into the picture. The competition for the few existing decently paid positions is fierce, as anyone can attest who has been in the search process recently. Without the spouse's paycheck to supplement a church's salary to its own clergy, many churches would be forced to go without a full-time minister.

The emotional drain of these economic pressures on clerical families is tremendous, but it is not something which denominations and individual parishes are prepared to recognize, and deal with. If traditions are going to be strong and vital, such economic problems must be addressed. Church denominations seem unwilling to solve the conflict inherent in their own moral positions —the conflict between the Church's emphasis on the importance of the traditional family, where one of the parents can afford to be at home with the children, and the impossibility for many clergy to even make that choice. Because of the inadequate compensation, many clergy can't live according to that traditional model of the family—the one they themselves probably grew up with if they are Baby Boomers.

In American society at large, we are raising a generation of emotionally deprived children because both parents are working away from the home. The rage is already showing up in our churches and school systems. Many children of clergy are falling into the same camp because of the necessity of that second paycheck to make ends meet. I would guess that these children one day are going to feel intense rage at the Church, whose hypocrisy in this matter will eventually be fully understood. As an entire society we are breeding serious psychological problems among our children by the removal of both parents from the home before those children begin school. But the Church, unfortunately, is part of the problem, not the solution. To sum up, churches must compensate their clergy far better than they do. That might revolutionize the way the Church spends its money, but in the long run the institution will become much stronger because more competent, psychologically stable people will enter the ranks of the clergy.

Seminary Education

Now let's consider seminary education. In recent years, many schools have been desperate for students to keep their doors open. Consequently they accept far too many psychologically troubled students. These schools know very well what they are doing. One Episcopal seminary professor told me recently, "We simply have to take students we would have rejected in previous years, either on academic or psychological grounds. But our financial picture is such that we need students—any students."

Seminaries, however, do not do nearly enough to help a psychologically troubled person solve or "work through" his or her conflicts, either through the field training offered by the institutions, or through the academic curriculum. The denominational machinery also does very little to help emotionally disturbed seminarians, either through financial support for psychotherapy or programs designed for that purpose. Moreover, ordination screening processes in many instances are notoriously lax, and few denominations have structured programs for the newly ordained to receive supervision during their first few years of professional service.

In addition, most seminarians and candidates for ordination do not seek their own psychotherapy along the way, nor do the seminaries and denominations require or even urge it, and they rarely help pay for it.

In seminaries there are also precious few courses which integrate the social sciences with the various theological disciplines. Courses on such topics as "religion and depth psychology," "theology and the social sciences," "the psychology of religious symbols and rituals," or "the sociology of religion," are rare, if they exist at all. In other words, the entire training process for the ordained ministry does not do nearly enough to help a candidate take the "log" out of his or her own eye before taking the "speck" out of another's, to use Jesus' famous metaphors. In fact, let me quote him in full because his teaching (Matthew 7:3–5) is so relevant for seminary training:

> Why do you see the speck that is in your brother's eye, but do not notice the log that is in your own eye? Or how can you say to your brother, "Let me take the speck out of your eye," when there is the log in your own eye? You hypocrite, first take the log out of your own eye, and then you will see clearly to take the speck out of your brother's eye.

Most seminarians take some clinical training in their program, and it may help to remove that "speck." But this is only one step in the right direction, and it alone cannot strengthen future clergy where they are particularly weak—in their self-knowledge. In addition, in most clinical education programs there is little integration of theory with practice. And back in the seminary classroom there is often little coordination between academic work and field training.

Lay ministry is now revolutionizing the Church. Baptism is now being looked upon by many traditions as one's "ordination into ministry," rather than merely restricting "priesthood" to the professional clergy (Luther's idea of "the priesthood of all believers" has been very influential). This has been a very positive development for the life of the Church. On the other hand, much of the training for lay ministry has been very weak, if there is any training at all in churches. So on a different level, lay ministers suffer from a weakness in preparation similar to the clergy's—which brings up another aspect of theological education.

One of the worst effects of the Sixties was a general erosion of the quality and rigor of theological education, indeed, the undermining of its very integrity. In the Sixties, many seminaries responded to student demands for "relevance" by changing their traditional curricula and academic requirements—so as to tailor them around a student's needs and desires. The "old-fashioned" classical theological education, one which was thorough, academically demanding, and required knowledge of world religions (originally for missionary work), disappeared from many seminaries and theological schools. The intention to be "relevant" was noble, and in many respects positive, but there have been some negative effects, too. Many seminary graduates have not been adequately prepared for parish ministry. As a result, many clergy are ill-equipped to preach and pastor effectively or train lay ministers.

After the Sixties, one could graduate from many schools not only without any knowledge of Greek, the language of the New Testament, but also without much knowledge of the Bible in English either. Many entering seminary students—who probably begin with a scant knowledge of the Bible and their own religious tradition in the first place—do not rectify their weaknesses *in the very area where restoration is most needed and in the very place where you would expect it to occur.* Churchgoers know all of this only too well from listening to sermons without Biblical background and theological depth. Many of the clergy who went into the ministry in the midst of the upheavals of the Sixties continue to address in their sermons the social issues of the day, but often they don't provide the necessary religious undergirding for their arguments. The sermons moralize but fail to convince, or perhaps better put, they fail to inspire, either the heart or concrete action.

Self-sacrifice, the Work Ethic, and Meaning in Life

The work ethic and the ideal of self-sacrifice must be restored to our society. Here tradition can help, e.g., Jesus' teaching that one must bear his or her cross in service to others. Any revitalization of tradition should include the ethics of hard work and a greater concern for the fulfillment of others' needs than self-fulfillment.

The work ethic, in large part, emerged from the Reformation; it is rooted in the idea that each Christian has a calling in life, a task given to him or her by God. We need to reestablish that profound spiritual insight. I believe that God has given each one of us — regardless of our religion or lack thereof—a purpose in life to carry out, and if we don't discover that purpose, we may very well become just as neurotic as when deprived of love and pleasure, which invites us to consider "meaning in life."

One of the great attributes of the Sixties was the search for meaning. Many have since abandoned the search, or have become disillusioned in the midst of it, but it is urgent that we once again ask the deep questions about the meaning in life. We must seek to find God's purpose in history. This challenge requires us to interpret history as the arena where God's will is being fulfilled, fulfilled *through us* as the Bible teaches. Jesus says, "Seek and you will find, knock and the door shall be opened."

It is imperative that Christians and Jews recognize that God works in religions other than their own, something *all* religious people should be open to. In my view, God is carrying out his purposes in *world* history, not simply through any one religion or any single nation. The mass media and modern communications make that recognition possible for us, unlike ancient peoples. The idea that all of history may be a source of God's revelation should be a teaching in every religion. Participants in all religions must sharpen their skills in interpretation, thereby discovering what it is God wants us to do.

If religion does not help us ask the "big questions" about life, such as its meaning and purpose, then who will?

Recapturing What "Liberalism" Once Meant

One of the most lasting effects of the Sixties has been the collapse of liberalism in the political arena. Many of the Church's clergy were deeply influenced by liberalism in the Sixties, and still uphold the best of its ideals, such as social justice for all and the quest for the common good. This still sometimes puts them at odds with their congregations, who in many instances see social activism as a nightmare they are trying to forget (and in the 1980s they nearly did). We must wake up and restore the high ideals of the 1960s' liberalism. We must put such things as health care, hunger, homelessness, mental health, education, child care, AIDS, and economic opportunity, on the front burner of the political and social agenda.

Why did liberalism become politically bankrupt? Part of the reason was President Johnson's "guns and butter" approach to both the war and his Great Society programs. The failure of that policy doomed liberalism in the Baby Boomers' eyes. Many have found it difficult to trust liberals ever since. The liberals, in large part, got us into Vietnam, and through their policies kept us there (but without the will to win). However, the collapse of liberalism has not only created a political crisis, but also a spiritual one. Who are the political allies of the poor, the mentally ill, the homeless, and the hungry? Who now preaches, "We must get involved!" Who tells us, "Serve rather than take!" We need to somehow combine those traditional concerns of the Democratic Party with the economic opportunities advocated by the Republican Party. If a candidate from either party ever does so, he or she will have great appeal to the Sixties Generation.

Let me now share a few of my own observations about the Left as I saw it operate in Ann Arbor during the 1960s. These observations are relevant for understanding liberalism's demise. SDS had historical roots at the University of Michigan. What I witnessed there was that organization's deliberate disruption of the educational process. Supposedly, this was in the name of protesting the war. But the Left had an ulterior motive: the destruction of the university itself, and the entire capitalist society.

I went to many anti-war rallies where students from the Left spoke out. They tried to manipulate us—using our general discontent—to accomplish their purposes. Outwardly, they seemed to be enlisting us into the noble cause of war protest, but their true goal was much broader than simply ending the war. It was ending capitalism itself, and all relics of the social structure which led to Vietnam.

During my days in Ann Arbor, before and after the fury of the Democratic Convention in Chicago, I always left war protests feeling empty. At that time, I was taking courses in Southeast Asian history in order to learn the background of the war. In class we were assigned such readings as Robert Shaplen's *The Lost Revolution*, the writings of Bernard Fall, and Joseph Buttinger's *Vietnam: A Political History*, among other things. And I could not understand how boycotting such classes could further the anti-war movement (with which otherwise I was in full sympathy). I thought student strikes against classes were more of an excuse to stay at home than a heart-felt sacrifice or a real contribution to the antiwar effort.

Moreover, it disappointed me that more of my fellow students —especially those who spoke at the antiwar rallies—were not taking such "relevant" courses as my history classes. Once again my generation — even in their protest against the war—did not seem committed to reading primary sources. Few students seem interested in learning the history of Vietnam or the background of our military involvement. The war protests seemed to be more of a projection of personal pain and fear than a well-thought-out argument against American intervention. The antiwar movement's leaders had a knowledge of Vietnam that seemed as shallow as that of those standing in the crowds. I would argue that was even true of their knowledge of the writings of Karl Marx (many of the antiwar leaders were self-proclaimed Marxists). Once again, we have an illustration of my generation's ideals being grounded upon a very shaky foundation. Some might argue that Marx's philosophy is itself a shaky foundation, but many from the Left did not know Marx well enough to even realize that.

As with most of the idealism of the Sixties, the ideals of the New Left could not withstand the social changes brought by the war's conclusion. Self-interest and ideological self-righteousness characterized the Left, which is precisely what it accused others of. Such hypocrisy discredited its attempt to disrupt education. The only people in the world now upholding Marxism—outside of some diehards in China and in a few other places—are ideological academics who are nostalgic for the campus disruptions and radicalism of the 1960s. Once again, they are misunderstanding Americans' tenacity in holding on to what they have, which is why most of the Baby Boomers did not enlist in their cause in the first place. They would only go as far as protesting the war when their own self-interest was at stake, and their idealism was still strong. Once the war was over, the New Left lost the one thing—a significant body of supporters—that could activate protest and mobilize opposition to the status quo. Liberalism in general was discredited because many of the Baby Boomers associated it with both Johnson (and thus the war effort) and the New Left. Consequently the Left in general lost much of its support. Even the word "liberal" has been discredited. It now has a bad connotation. Few dare to embrace it in public life. With the collapse of liberalism, however, has come the collapse of concern for the poor and powerless in the political arena, and our concerns about racism have weakened drastically. It is those aspects of liberalism which must be recaptured.

The Church could definitely be of help here if it would only emphasize Jesus' teaching in the twenty-fifth chapter of Matthew and elsewhere. Religious tradition must once again become the vehicle for our service to others and our involvement in healing society's ills. The Church must articulate the Biblical rationale for that kind of ministry.

Stabilizing the Family

The importance of the traditional family for the stability of social structure needs little further comment. We are in the midst of an epidemic of family breakdown. The restoration of our moral and religious traditions would help to stabilize the family, although we must recognize that the definition of "family" has greatly changed and become broadened in recent years.

When I give Holy Communion to an entire family—all kneeling together at the altar—I am convinced that the power of that sacrament helps to keep families whole and healthy. If families were stabilized and protected by tradition, this would have an immense effect on America's mental as well as spiritual health (the breakdown of the family, as Freud discovered, has devastating effects upon the psyche).

The stabilization of the family would break the following vicious circle: family breakdown leading to psychological problems, which in turn contribute to cultural and social breakdown; the fracturing of our society then further undermines the family. That vicious circle must end. The revitalization of our religious and moral traditions can help to accomplish that. Here people from all faiths must unite in a common cause to work together to solve a common problem.

A Return to Sublimation

For religious traditions to be revitalized, and restored, they must face the pressing moral issues of the day. Whenever possible, they must offer moral guidelines. Just as children look for firm, clear, loving guidelines from their parents as they develop, all of God's children need the same thing. Nowhere is this more difficult than in the area of sexuality.

The Church must teach that giving into the sexual impulse outside of marriage does far more damage than does frustration, damage such as guilt, the pain given to others as well as to oneself, and disease. The Church should be honest and acknowledge the difficulties that young people face when they feel passion at so tender an age. In a word, the Church should explain, and then argue for, abstinence and sublimation. Religious tradition can be of immense psychological and spiritual help in that task.

Our sacred traditions help us to balance the sensual and affectionate currents of the libido, as well as to balance self-love with object love. In his essay "The Psychology of Love," Freud argues that a civilization that constantly caves into sexual impulses will eventually exhaust itself (as America now seems to be doing):

> The very incapacity of the sexual instinct to yield complete satisfaction as soon as it submits to the first demands of civilization *becomes the source, however, of the noblest cultural achievements which are brought into being by ever more extensive sublimation of its instinctual components.* For what motive would men have for putting sexual instinctual forces to other uses if, by any distribution of those forces, they could obtain fully satisfying pleasure? They would never abandon

that pleasure and they would never make any further progress (my italics).[4]

If we accept Freud's premise—and attempt to promote sublimation as a benefit to society—we might very well restore some sanity to our culture. Who knows, perhaps even romantic music would become popular once again.

Religion must Be less Narcissistic

One of the ironies of recent years is the fact that churches which foster or blatantly promote narcissism are, it seems, the most "successful." At least in recruiting new members. In my view, this is not a strength of institutional religion, but rather a weakness, even a betrayal, of the Cross of Christ (which for me symbolizes God's involvement with our suffering—not to remove that suffering but to help us bear it, and eventually become victorious over it). Such churches exploit narcissism for their own financial gain.

To illustrate the sort of religious narcissism I am driving at, I will quote some excerpts from a *Wall Street Journal* article (May 13, 1991) entitled "Megachurches Strive to be All Things to All Parishioners (Second Baptist in Houston Uses Billboards, Basketball to Woo the Unchurched)":

> In current religious lingo, Second Baptist is a "megachurch," the hottest thing in Protestantism, religious experts say. Megachurches are huge, drawing average crowds of 2,000 or more on Sundays. They offer as much in the way of activities and entertainment as they do religion. The Christianity they do serve up is mostly conservative and to-the-point, stripped of most of the old hymns, liturgy and denominational dogma that tend to bore the video generation. . . . Second Baptist does as much marketing as proselytizing. Like most megachurches, it is primarily designed for a generation unversed in theology, essentially nonsectarian and unsentimental about the old neighborhood church. As churchgoers, they are pragmatic and pressed for time, and they care passionately about ameni-

ties and services—spotless nurseries, convenient parking, dazzling entertainment. They want sermons that are relevant. "If ever there was a church designed for the Baby-Boomer, its the megachurch," says Elmer Towns, vice president of Liberty University in Lynchburg, Virginia. . . . While most Protestant denominations are in slow but steady decline, megachurches are springing up from Montgomery, Alabama, to Chicago. And some say they are hastening the demise of traditional churches. . . . As megachurches go, Second Baptist— led by the Rev. H. Edwin Young— is considered state-of-the-art. Lying a couple of miles west of Houston's tony Galleria Mall, the church looks little like a traditional house of worship. That's a trademark characteristic of megachurches: *they shun crosses and steeples that might scare people off* (my italics).

Megachurches fit perfectly into my overall thesis about narcissism. They reflect both the decline of loyalty to a specific tradition and ignorance of tradition in general. This form of religion does not curb narcissism, or help people integrate it into their personality structures. Such religion goes far beyond fostering healthy narcissism. Moreover, many of these churches are fundamentalist, and teach that "salvation" is found only within their own belief systems—which is about as narcissistic as institutional religion can get!

The mainline churches today are perhaps showing their "dirty laundry" in public. They are now encouraging open debate about such topics as ordaining homosexuals; they are questioning traditional sexual morality, or at least they are discussing it. And so on. In short, the mainline churches are struggling, honestly, with the moral issues of the day in the context of a pluralist society. In times of cultural upheaval, such as the Sixties, people often seek authoritarianism, as I pointed out some time ago. Ultimately, however, authoritarianism fails because it suppresses reason. It does not build bridges, it withdraws into itself. Jesus said, "where you heart is, there your treasure will be." Megachurches don't seem to be expressive of a religion of the heart, (at least in terms of social ethics) but rather a religion of rigid belief, emotionalism, and self-fulfillment. Their belief system is largely undergirded by narcissism. A truly revitalized religious tradition will teach us to reach out to others—as Jesus did—and not turn within.

Conclusion

The word "tradition" literally means "that which is handed down." In America, we have failed in doing that. We have not been effective in handing down through the generations our religious and moral traditions. Moreover, we have neglected many of our national traditions, such as societal concern for the poor. This is a failure of responsibility.

The various religions must realize that they are united by a mutual problem—the decline of tradition—much more than they are divided by a rivalry in their truth claims, for instance (which are at many points surprisingly similar anyway, e.g., in the field of ethics). All religious traditions are in the same boat—one that is sinking fast vis-à-vis the wider secular society. Revitalized traditions must work together—not in conflict—to solve the world's pressing problems, such as our social and spiritual ills.

The other day I was jogging around the indoor track at our local YMCA. I noticed that a radio station was playing such numbers over the PA as Del Shannon's "Little Town Flirt," "Hound Dog" by Elvis, "Wouldn't It Be Nice" by the Beach Boys, "Ask the Lonely" by the Four Tops and "My Girl" by the Temptations, and Dylan's "Blowin' in the Wind," among other hits from the Fifties and Sixties. Such songs once grabbed my generation with their emotional power and drive, and the ideas they conveyed (however silly or profound). Such songs were our anthems. They were the songs we danced to, or rode around in convertibles to, or "made out" to, or heard blaring from portable radios on Lake Michigan beaches on a hot summer day while the waves crashed on the shore. Now here they were providing the background music for a bunch of overweight Baby Boomers as we worked out in a YMCA weight room and ran around its track.

After exercising, I went to McDonald's and on their sound system they were also playing songs from the Fifties and Sixties, but in the 101 Strings' versions. Now, even our music—like our traditions—has become "routinized." Like our traditions, our music has lost its "life," its power to motivate or move us, at least in the way it once did. The Sixties Generation, it seems, has been reduced to being the subject of historical studies.

Is that what the Sixties Generation has become: a cultural relic, only good for books and classes about the turbulent past? What has happened to us? What has happened to all of that energy that was once harnessed into working for civil rights, or protesting an unjust war, or helping the poor, or even just having a memorable party where people danced to the music of the Temptations and Four Tops? Where has our energy gone?

I will close with this observation from a letter I received from a friend, Andrea Anderson, in 1965:

> Think of all the different paths our friends will take and are taking at present. Seems unbelievable. It's really going to be interesting to see what some of our really good friends will be like in twenty-five years. Will they be complacent, upper middle-class citizens enjoying their lives from day to day, or vital, exuberant searching souls? It'll be extremely interesting. Wonder what you and I will be doing?

Are you proud of where you are today? Are you proud in relation to what you had hoped for during the Sixties? I think materialism is my generation's Achilles' heel. Materialism is my generation's greatest failure, our chief betrayal of once cherished ideals. I pray that it is not written on our collective tombstone: "They came of age as idealists, but they died as hypocrites." There is still time left to change the world. After all, we have changed it once already.

Notes

1. D. H. Lawrence, *Lady Chatterley's Lover* (New York: Greenwich House, 1983), p. 304.

2. Gitlin, *The Sixties*, p. 400.

3. *Ibid.*

4. Freud, "The Psychology of Love,"in *The Standard Edition*, 11:190.

Bibliography

Argyle, Michael, and Beit-Hallahmi, Benjamin. *The Social Psychology of Religion*. London: Routledge & Kegan Paul, 1958.

Bellah, Robert N. *Habits of the Heart*. New York, Harper & Row, Publishers, 1985.

Berger, Peter. *The Sacred Canopy*. Garden City, N.Y.: Doubleday & Co., Inc., 1969

Berger, Peter, Berger, Brigette, and Kellner, Hansfried. *The Homeless Mind*. New York: Vintage Books, 1973.

Bloom, Allan. *The Closing of the American Mind*. New York: Simon and Schuster, 1987.

Caplow, Theodore, Bahr, Howard M., and Chadwick, Bruce A. *All Faithful People*. Minneapolis: University of Minnesota Press, 1983.

D'Souza, Dinesh. *Illiberal Education (The Politics of Race and Sex on Campus)*. New York: The Free Press, 1991

Ellwood, Robert S., *The Sixties Spiritual Awakening (American Religion Moving From Modern to Postmodern)*. New Brunswick, New Jersey: Rutgers University Press, 1994.

Freud, Sigmund. *The Standard Edition*. Edited by James Strachey. 24 vols. London, Hogarth Press, 1961.

Gitlin, Todd. *The Sixties. (Years of Hope, Days of Rage)*. New York: Bantam Books, 1987.

Guralnick, Peter. *Last Train to Memphis (The Rise of Elvis Presley)*. New York: Little, Brown and Company, 1994.

Idema, Henry. *Freud, Religion, and the Roaring Twenties (A Psychoanalytic Theory of Secularization in Three Novelists: Anderson , Hemingway, and Fitzgerald*. Savage, Maryland: Rowman & Littlefield Publishers, Inc., 1990.

Kaiser, Charles. *1968 in America*. New York: Weidenfeld & Nicolson, 1988.

Kohut, Heinz. *The Analysis of the Self*. New York: International Universities Press, Inc., 1971.

Lasch, Christopher. *The Culture of Narcissism*. New York: Warner Books, 1979.

Martin, David. *A General Theory of Secularization*. New York: Harper & Row, 1978.

May, Rollo. *The Cry for Myth*. New York: W.W. Norton & Company, 1991.

Roof, Wade Clark. *A Generation of Seekers (The Spiritual Journeys of the Baby Boom Generation)*. San Francisco: HarperSanFrancisco, 1993.

Turner, James. *Without God, Without Creed*. Baltimore: Johns Hopkins University Press, 1985.

Weber, Max. *The Protestant Ethic and the Spirit of Capitalism*. New York: Charles Scribner's Sons, 1958

Weinstein, Fred, and Platt, Gerald. *Psychoanalytic Sociology*. Baltimore: The Johns Hopkins University Press, 1973.

_____. *The Wish to Be Free.* Berkley: University of California Press, 1969.

Index

About the Author

Henry Idema III is a graduate of East Grand rapids High School (1965), the University of Michigan (B.A. in history, 1969, M.A. in English literature, 1980), the Episcopal Divinity School (M. Div., 1975), and the University of Chicago (Ph.D. in Religion and Psychological Studies, 1987). He is an ordained Episcopal clergyman and has served in parishes in Michigan and Illinois. He is currently the rector St. John's Episcopal Church in Grand Haven, Michigan. He is also the author of *Freud, Religion, and the Roaring Twenties*, (Rowman & Littlefield, 1990).